CONTENTS

GW00838386

COLOUR PLATES

BLACK & WHITE PLATES

The general arrangement of the black and white illustrations follows the text, showing:

ACKNOWLEDGEMENTS

The preparation of this book would not have been possible were it not for the ready assistance willingly given to me by Mr W. E. Brain, the Director of Messrs Coalport China Ltd, and Mr F. E. Ridgway, the Coalport sales manager. Their extreme generosity in allowing me to examine, at my leisure, the original Coalport pattern-books has enabled me to identify much unmarked Coalport porcelain of the 1820–50 period and the work of individual artists.

The identification of the early 1799–1814 Coalport porcelain made by John Rose at the Caughley factory could not have been made so conclusively without the excavations at the Caughley site (see Chapter II and Plates 12 and 14). For the opportunity to study these excavations at first hand I am indebted to Lord Forester for his kind permission to work on the site, and to the staff of Coalmoor Refractories (Horsehay) Ltd, who are engaged in opencast clay mining at the Caughley site. My gratitude is also due to the three firms occupying the old Coalport china factory—Messrs Chillcotts Ltd, Coalport Metalware Ltd, and the Nuway Manufacturing Co Ltd, for the ready co-operation afforded to me by the managements.

Further assistance has been given by: W. A. Billington, Esq. (Curator, Messrs Wedgwoods Works Museum); R. J. Charleston, Esq. (Keeper, Department of Ceramics, Victoria and Albert Museum); Reverend J. Glover (Rector of Broseley); Alan Green, Esq.; Miss Mary C. Hill (Shropshire County Archivist); D. Holgate, Esq.; Dr Houghton; R. James, Esq. (Shrewsbury Museum); the late Alfred Langford; Reverend A. Lord (Rector of Madeley); M. F. Messenger, Esq., F.L.A. (Shrewsbury Borough Librarian); R. Miles, Esq.; R. Minton, Esq.; Reverend L. F. Peltor (Rector of Willey); the Registrar-General, D. B. Roberts, Esq.; C. Shingler, Esq. (former Curator, Worcester Works Museum); Hugh Tait, Esq. (British Museum); and Dr Bernard Watney.

Other valuable information has been provided by the British Museum Newspaper Library, the Guildhall Library, the Patent Office, and the Public Record Office, and acknowledgement is made to their most co-operative staffs. My thanks must also be accorded to Mr T. A. Sprague for his pioneer researches on Shropshire porcelain, for, while I disagree with some of his attributions and dating, the main part of his findings have proved extremely sound.

The many fine illustrations have been supplied by the undermentioned persons, firms or museums and the source of each illustration is acknowledged in the caption.

Her Majesty the Queen
Messrs Christie Manson & Woods

Messrs Coalport China, Ltd
Messrs Godden of Worthing, Ltd
Grand Lodge Museum, Freemasons Hall
David Holgate, Esq.
R. A. F. Johnston, Esq.
Alfred Langford, Esq.
Messrs Lories, Ltd
Los Angeles County Museum of Art
Messrs Minton, Ltd
Messrs D. Newbon, London
Mrs and Mrs Pilkington
Paul Riley, Esq.
Denis Roberts, Esq.
D. Rogers, Esq.
Royal Scottish Museum, Edinburgh
Royal Ontario Museum, University of Toronto
Messrs Jean Sewell, London
Shrewsbury Museum
Shropshire County Record Office
Messrs Sotheby & Co
City Museum and Art Gallery, Stoke-on-Trent
Messrs Trevor Antiques, Brighton and London
F. Turner, Esq.
Messrs J. & E. D. Vandekar, London
Victoria and Albert Museum
M. A. Wilson, Esq.

The uncredited illustrations from my own collection and the numerous ones from the stock of Messrs Godden of Worthing Ltd have been posed and taken by Mr Derek Gardiner, A.I.B.P., of Messrs Walter Gardiner, The Arcade, Worthing; illustrations of distinguishing knobs, etc, have been drawn by Mr Donald F. Abbott, F.R.S.A., heraldic artist.

PREFACE

This book breaks new ground in two ways. In the first place, while others have dealt with the Coalport factory in conjunction with the one near by at Caughley and several general ceramic reference books have sections or chapters giving a résumé of the history of the Coalport works and its later products, this is the first to be devoted entirely to Coalport porcelain. Secondly, with very few exceptions the porcelain made in the first twenty-five years of the factory's existence has not been identified or illustrated in ceramic literature and the present book remedies this, some ninety plates (with supporting text) being devoted to the early unmarked porcelain that for so long has been attributed to other factories, mainly those situated at Worcester. Examples illustrated are unmarked unless otherwise stated in the captions. Apart from the identification of the early John Rose Coalport ware, the closely related porcelain made by the rival Coalport firm of Anstice, Horton & Thomas Rose (see Chapter IV) has been discovered and the key shapes illustrated on the opposite page to the John Rose examples so that the slight differences in form may be apparent.

Much new information, gleaned from the factory pattern-books, the official census returns and a hitherto undiscovered wage list, has been found relating to the Coalport workmen (see Chapter VII and Appendix II)—in particular, the artists responsible for the fine-quality decoration. Detailed information is given on the Coalport marks, on the dating of the porcelain and on patterns that can be attributed to individual artists. Chapter VIII seeks to correct some erroneous traditional attributions of non-Coalport porcelain to the Coalport factory. It is strange that, while true Coalport porcelain has not hitherto been attributed to its rightful birthplace, the reputation of the factory has to some degree been gained by porcelain now shown to have been made in Staffordshire, not Shropshire!

Nevertheless, the porcelain made on the banks of the River Severn at Coalport is amongst the most interesting and decorative of all English ceramics. The vast amount of porcelain produced at Coalport is difficult to imagine, for it has been in existence for over one hundred and seventy years.

The preparation of this book has given my wife and me much pleasure and excitement, especially when fresh facts have been discovered after much patient searching, and we hope that the results of this research will give equal pleasure to both established and new collectors.

GEOFFREY A. GODDEN

INTRODUCTION TO THE 1981 EDITION

Since the first edition of this book was published in 1970 the Coalport porcelains have gained a new respectability and the prices have risen considerably, particularly for the showy later pieces which can be of superb quality with paintings signed by the leading artists of the period such as E. Ball (Plate 207), John Plant (Colour Plate X) or Percy Simpson (Plates 208 and 213).

The more restrained porcelains of the 1820-50 period have also come into their own as their overall quality has become apparent and now we can, with the help of this book, identify and put a name to these unmarked Coalport porcelains.

However, for the student the most interesting period is undoubtedly the first and here we are still largely exploring the unknown.

For example we do not know exactly when the Coalport porcelain factory was established. My first new illustration (Plate A), shows that tantalising entry from the Chamberlain record of letters sent or received, where under the dated June 13th 1791 entry we find: "Do (letter). Mr. Rose manufactory, Salop".

A. An extract from the Chamberlain factory letter book, headed 'Letters & to who wrote'. The entry under June 13th 1791 relates to a Mr. Rose. *Worcester Royal Porcelain Co. Ltd.*

Was the 'manufactory' that owned by Thomas Turner at Caughley, and if so what important position did he hold to have a letter addressed to him there? We must also remember that, if we assume John Rose (the eldest son of the local farmer) to be the person concerned, he was only nineteen at this time but was born and lived at Swinney Farm not a mile from the Caughley factory.

As related on pages 1 and 2 Rose was in partnership with an Edward Blakeway, and by at least February 1793 Blakeway or the firm of Blakeways were mentioned in correspondence when they were apparently in competition with Turner: "...the cream ewers I had off Turner are cheaper than Blakeways".

Excavations on the Caughley factory site — as related and featured in the companion book on the Caughley porcelains — have shown well the type of porcelains produced there under Thomas Turner up to the sale towards the end of 1799. Likewise the present book features the post-1799 shapes and designs produced on the Caughley site after the factory's purchase by the Coalport partnership which then consisted of Edward Blakeway, John Rose and Richard Rose.

The great and important gap is to discover what this Coalport partnership was producing from its establishment in the early 1790s up to the take-over of the Caughley factory in October 1799.

That the early years were successful is self evident. The Coalport partners wished to continue and greatly enlarge their enterprise and apparently they had the means (or backing) to buy out their main rival Thomas Turner.

It is I think reasonable to assume that at least in their early days the Coalport partners would have concentrated on useful wares, tea services and the like. These were most probably reasonably close in style to the well tried Caughley porcelains mostly decorated with blue-printed designs of Oriental inspiration. They would not have blazed a new trail of startling fresh shapes or styles. At least at the commencement of their rival factory it is to be expected that the porcelain body would have been very much the same as Turner's under whom John Rose was trained. John Rose and his younger brother Richard would have had knowledge of the source of the raw materials and the management of the mixture. It is unlikely that they commenced with new untried ingredients.

Our difficulties are therefore great — the same body, similar shapes and patterns as the Caughley porcelains.

There is an additional difficulty for the early ceramic writers were of the opinion that the so-called Coalport partners — Blakeway and John Rose — first worked a manufactory on the west side of the River Severn, at or near Jackfield. Later moving across the river to the site where the present museum is situated — on the land side of the narrow canal that divides (or originally divided) the land. On the thin strip between the canal and the river John Rose's younger brother Thomas with other partners established a rival factory in or about 1800 (see Chapter III).

It is still not known when John Rose and Edward Blakeway moved their works and established the true Coalport factory. There is a reference in the Wedgwood archives to John Rose Esq., of the Calcut China Manufactory in December 1794 and Calcut is on the west bank on the opposite side to Coalport. But certainly they were at Coalport by August 1796 when The Prince and Princess of Orange visited the district and visited the factory "where His Highness bought some pieces of Mr. Rose..." (page 4).

We can in fact take back this date by two months for we have the interesting diary of Charles Hatchett. On Saturday May 28th 1796 this learned writer noted that he visited the "Porcelain manufactory belonging to Messrs Flight & Barr". He then continued:

> I have observed that the Steatites of Cornwall is used as an ingredient ... when the steatite is reduced to powder in a mill at Worcester it is sent to some place about ten miles distance to be mixed and washed.

He was here obviously referring to the Cornish soap-rock, the vital ingredient in the Worcester and the Caughley porcelain body. Interestingly on the following Wednesday (June 1st 1796) Charles Hatchett was in Shropshire in the Severn Valley near Coalbrookdale. After viewing the famous Petroleum Tunnel he visited the nearby Coalport "Porcelain manufactory lately established" and observed further that "the ware is like that of Worcester and the materials are the same". On his observations the Coalport body at this period should include soap-rock and perhaps by stating that "the ware is like that of Worcester" we may deduce that the forms and patterns were similar.

These new Coalport porcelains particularly the teawares may be expected to include the then fashionable spiral-fluted (or 'shankered') shapes and the teapots, covered sugar boxes and the milk jugs would have shown a basic oval (rather than a circular) plan by at least 1793.

One spiral-fluted jug has turned up in recent years and is potentially very important. This blue-printed example is shown here in the two views in Plate B. In its basic form it matches that shown in Plate 11, the example in the Shrewsbury Museum which is linked with the controversial 1796 local election. The interesting aspect of the new jug is that it is of a more standard nature bearing rather naïvely engraved Chinese-styled landscape designs. While both sides of this jug show the same main print, the secondary prints each side of the neck are different giving us a total of three printed designs which almost certainly were used on early Coalport porcelains of the mid-1790s but as yet no such teawares or other items bearing these prints have been observed.

The blue-prints found on the two jugs shown in Plates 100 and 101 are likewise of great interest and importance especially as one is dated 1798, the year before the Coalport partners took over Turner's Caughley factory.

The jugs themselves are very heavy and thickly potted in a compact body which we have recently termed hybrid hard-paste. The copper-plate design

B. Two views of a blue-printed Coalport jug, which in shape relates to the 1796 Shrewsbury Election jug shown in Plate 11. *c.* 1796-8. 8¼ ins. high. *Godden Reference Collection.*

is rather wooden in its engraving and the main design is rather abruptly ended in a circular manner as if the copper-plates were made for saucers or plates. The arrangement for these prints on the jugs can be very cramped (Plate 101) and not as workmanlike as one would expect from the Caughley factory.

You will observe that two different versions can occur on the same piece; one has no figure in the 'boat-house' which is built out into the river or lake, and the uninhabited version has two trees growing on its right. In fact several different copper-plates produced slightly different versions but in all no figure appears on the bridge in the foreground.

I consider that this design is a Coalport one, not found on Turner's pre-1800 Caughley porcelain. In addition to the jugs shown in Plates 100 and 101 I now show a plain coffee pot (Plate C), a selection from a fluted tea service (Plate D) and a spiral-fluted jug of a rather later c.1800 form (Plate E).

C. An early Coalport coffee pot bearing early blue prints which link with the jugs shown in Plates 100 and 101. *c.* 1796-1800. 9¼ ins. high. *Clive House Museum, Shrewsbury.*

D. Representative pieces of an early Coalport fluted teaset, bearing prints relating to the jugs shown in Plates 100 and 101. *c.* 1796-1800. Teapot 6½ ins. high. *Godden Reference Collection.*

E. A Coalport spiral-fluted jug bearing the early prints relating to the examples shown in Plates 100 and 101. *c.* 1800. 7¼ ins. high. *Godden of Worthing Ltd.*

It is noteworthy that none of these pieces or any other examples of this print known to me bear the 'S' or 'C' initial marks which are to be found on many Caughley blue-printed specimens. On the other hand some of these thickly potted hybrid hard-paste pieces bear a small blue cross-mark.

The blue-printed jug shown in Plate 101 has in addition to the Chinese-styled landscape prints an engraving of a vase of flowers. This same print occurs on the faceted saucers shown in my new Plate F. As yet no other matching teaware shapes — such as a teapot, covered sugar or creamer have been reported. Such pieces must have been made and the discovery of the knob and handle shapes will be of the utmost interest.

The saucer shown in Plate G, matches in form and body that just discussed and is I believe another Coalport example of the 1795-1800 period. While versions of this Oriental type elephant print are to be found on various earthenwares mostly of Staffordshire origin, this version is the

F. A rare sixteen-sided Coalport saucer, the vase of flowers print appearing on the front of some early Coalport jugs (Plate 101). *c.* 1798-1800. Diameter 5⅛ ins. *Godden Reference Collection.*

G. A blue-printed saucer of the form shown in Plate F. The print matches that on a dated 1795 mug. *c.* 1795-8. Diameter 5⅛ ins. *Godden Reference Collection.*

only one known to me on porcelain and it represents a new early Coalport print to watch out for. It also occurs on a small cylindrical mug in the collection of the Reverend Maurice H. Wright, an example which also bears the gilt initials W.L. and the date 1795. It is noteworthy that if my attribution is correct this is the earliest known noted piece of Coalport porcelain.

My next two additional illustrations (Plates H and I) depict types of porcelain which I think the Coalport management would have been producing in the 1795-9 period, as the Caughley factory was declining. The simple enamelled motifs on 'shankered' or spiral-fluted shapes are of the type that was being produced by the contemporary firms down the River Severn at Worcester — the Flight management at the original factory and by the new Chamberlain concern.

Within a very few years of the amalgamation of the Caughley and the Coalport factories and the enlargement of the workforce (see page 9) some very ambitious forms were being produced probably in an effort to compete with the elaborate and richly decorated Barr, Flight & Barr (1807-13) and the Chamberlain pieces plus, of course, the Staffordshire bone china wares as produced by Spode or Minton.

H. A spiral-fluted coffee cup and saucer, enamelled with a simple floral design similar to that on the contemporary Worcester porcelains. *c.* 1795-1800. Cup 2¼ ins. high. *Godden Reference Collection.*

I. An oval Coalport covered sugar box decorated in the Flight-Worcester style. *c.* 1800. 4⅞ ins. high. *Godden of Worthing Ltd.*

I now show some of these magnificent Coalport pieces of the 1805-15 period — examples that will surely surprise many readers used only to the more mundane pieces. Firstly, I show two views of a large punch bowl which by its decoration and inscription reminds us of the troubled times of the early 1800s when we were at war with France and were expecting to be

J *above* and K *opposite*. The Wenlock Royal Volunteers punch bowl. The front shows military trophies, etc., with the Royal Arms. The reverse shows Lord Forrister's home and church. *c.* 1800. Diameter 12¼ ins. *Godden Reference Collection.*

invaded. Hence this special piece which was no doubt made for the Officers mess of the local 'Wenlock-volunteers'.

Within a few years however the French porcelains were in high fashion, at least in London, and Paris style porcelains were being produced by our manufacturers including John Rose at Coalport. The delightful little fancy inkwell and pen stand shown in Plate L is such a French-style piece.

L. An attractive Coalport inkpot and pen holder in the French style. *c.* 1810. 5¼ ins. long. *Godden of Worthing Ltd.*

Of course, most of our porcelain manufacturers produced French-style vases of the type seen in Plate M. The gilt handles and the mask-heads and ornamentation down the sides of these Coalport vases are noteworthy. Also in the French style we have the smaller urn-shaped vase with its white flowers applied in relief (Plate N).

Perhaps the most startling and important ornament to be made at Coalport in the 1800-20 period is the centrepiece shown in Plate O. The body serves as a bowl whilst, when the little flame-like finials are removed, the head and shell handles become candle-holders. Another of these fine ornaments is in the Godden collection and is painted with flowers on a gold ground.

One noteworthy decorative feature of these early Coalport porcelains is

M *left.* A superb quality Coalport vase (one of a set of three) with rich gilding and well-modelled handles, again in the French style. *c.* 1810. 12 ins. high. *Godden of Worthing Ltd.*

N *right.* A Coalport urn-shaped vase with unglazed applied flowers in the French taste. *c.* 1815-20. 6½ ins. high. *Godden of Worthing Ltd.*

O *left.* A superb Coalport covered centrepiece with candle-holders, with rich gilding. *c.* 1805-10. 13½ ins. high. *Mrs. Shortt Collection.*

P *right.* An elegant figure candlestick, originally one of a pair, the figure coloured to emulate bronze, the base lustred perhaps in imitation of silver. The candle-holder is a later replacement. *c.* 1805-10. 11 ins. high. *Godden of Worthing Ltd.*

the use of a particular pinkish silver-lustre which was usually used in wide washes, as on the base of the porcelain figure-supported candlestick illustrated in Plate P. The white porcelain body of the figure was in this case painted to emulate bronze. This smokey silver effect is also seen on the columns of the flat-backed classical chimney ornament seen in Plate Q. Apart from its real decorative value this piece is hollow and is a flower container. The silver lustre is here used in conjunction with conventional gilding and with the enamelled figures and emblems.

A more conventional form of flower container, jardinière or cache-pot is here shown in Plate R. This model was made in at least three different sizes

Q. An imposing chimney ornament to hold flowers decorated with brown, gold and silver lustre of a pink tone. *c.*1805-10. 11½ ins. long. *Godden of Worthing Ltd.*

and many examples were sold in the undecorated state to the Baxters in London. Their studio there is depicted in Plate 42; see also page 43. While discussing this form I can conveniently remind readers to compare shapes very closely when they are seeking to identify pieces by comparison with illustrations in this or in any other book, for very similar two-piece jardinières were made at the Spode factory, by Chamberlains of Worcester and at the Herculaneum factory at Liverpool.

The well-moulded intricate shapes into which the compact early Coalport porcelain body could be formed is evidenced by the magnificent cabinet cup and saucer in the Continental-taste which I now show in Plate S. The sharply moulded handle could not be bettered at any English factory.

Lest the reader may think that all the newly discovered pieces are of an ornamental nature, I include two tureen shapes which I believe have not previously been illustrated. The pair of small tureens (Plate T) are decorated with a typical so-called Japan pattern with its areas of deep underglaze blue. But here the relief-moulded and gilt handles are the noteworthy feature and one which should serve as a means of attribution.

Many readers will prefer the much more restrained decoration on the large soup tureen shown in Plate U. Here again one sees the sharp moulding and the general high level of workmanship and even design. Like all the pre-1820 Coalport porcelains just featured, these tureens do not bear a factory mark.

Now many fine examples of Coalport porcelains of all periods are

R. A Coalport jardinière on loose base, of the type that was made in at least three sizes. The general shape was also made at other factories. *c.* 1805-10. 8¼ ins. high. *Godden of Worthing Ltd.*

S: A green ground large size Coalport cabinet cup and saucer in the Continental style and of superb quality. *c.* 1810-15. Cup 5 ins. high. *Godden of Worthing Ltd.*

displayed in a dramatic setting in one of the original kilns on the factory site on the east bank of the River Severn at Coalport, two miles or so downstream from the famous Ironbridge. Happily, the documentary printed creamware mug shown in Plate 8 is back home, as are some other pieces featured in this book; for example one of the magnificent vases shown in Colour Plate IX.

Since the publication of this book in 1970 many past employees of the company and their relations have written to me, giving further information or corrections, and I here take the opportunity of clarifying the dating system which is to be found impressed into the underside of so many

T. A pair of Coalport dinner service tureens decorated in the popular 'Japan' style but with unusual handles. *c.* 1810-15. 8½ ins. long. *Godden of Worthing Ltd.*

U. A well-moulded soup tureen and cover from a Coalport dinner service of the 1815-20 period. 13¾ ins. long. *Godden of Worthing Ltd.*

present century plates, dishes or saucers. The first of the impressed numerals is the personal number of the potter concerned, the middle letter denotes the month A — January, B — February and so on, with the exception of I which was not used. The last numeral relates to the year of manufacture. At a later period, from about 1930 onwards, these date marks often took a simple fractional form — 8/32 for August 1932 and so on.

On page 90 Mr. Brocksidge was mentioned, this should have been Mr. Blocksidge. Ted Ball (see page 102) was employed at the Coalport factory in the present century, not from late in the nineteenth: this talented painter died in February 1951, aged 67. I originally misread the sex of Aquila Evans (page 109) who was male and a painter and gilder.

I have also been given helpful information on the artist Tom Keeling (page 115) who originally worked at the Copeland factory at Stoke. He left the Coalport company in about 1909 to open a china shop at Kidderminster but later went into insurance. Thomas Keeling was born on August 8th 1863 and died on Christmas Day 1938. Another leading artist Arthur Perry (page 120) has died since this book was first published; he died in January 1974, aged 102. Richard Spendlove (page 126) was born in 1804 and died at Madeley in August 1873.

I would, of course, be very pleased to receive any further information on any aspect of Coalport porcelains and of the workforce, as I hope in the future to publish a new greatly revised edition of this book.

This work will underline the great importance of the Coalport factories particularly in the early years of the nineteenth century when John Rose managed his own original factory and also Thomas Turner's nearby Caughley factory, where according to Thomas Telford (page 5) "...the most china is manufactured of any works of that sort in Great Britain..." and where according to this authority about two hundred and fifty persons were employed.

Apart from the John Rose empire there was also the rival factory just across the narrow canal established in 1800 by Messrs. Reynold, Horton & Rose, the last named being John Rose's youngest brother Thomas. On William Reynold's death, the new partners were Anstice, Horton & Rose who traded from c.1803 to 1814 when their factory was put up for sale and was acquired by the John Rose partners who were thus able to combine the two factories and concentrate all their activities at Coalport, closing the Caughley factory. The basic details concerning this rival factory are set out in Chapter IV but much research still remains to be carried out on this aspect of Coalport porcelains; undoubtedly some fine pieces were produced (the vase shown in Plate M may well be an Anstice example) and at least 1419 patterns were produced, in tea, dessert and dinner services.

Yes, the Coalport porcelains hold great promise, not only for their decorative merit but for the many problems they still pose for the inquiring collector.

17 Crescent Road   Geoffrey Godden
Worthing, Sussex, England

CHAPTER I

GENERAL HISTORY PRIOR TO 1850 WITH RÉSUMÉ OF FACTORY MARKS

It is generally believed by many collectors that the Coalport works superseded those at near-by Caughley,[1] but this is not so. The Coalport works were established independently some three or more years before Thomas Turner, the proprietor of the Caughley factory, entered into an agreement in 1799 to lease the Caughley china works, including all fixtures and unglazed stock, to 'Edward Blakeway, John Rose and Richard Rose, of Coalport . . . porcelain manufacturers'. It should be noted that at the time of this agreement (October 12th, 1799) the Coalport proprietors were already described as 'porcelain manufacturers'. The remains of the Coalport factory can still be seen, situated on the banks of the River Severn at Coalport, but these works were originally divided by a canal (Plate 6) and were two separate factories run by different proprietors until 1814 (see Chapter IV).

The early history of Coalport porcelain is still obscure. Llewellynn Jewitt, the nineteenth-century historian, in an article published in the March 1862 issue of the *Art Journal* (based on material gathered on a visit to Coalport in January 1862) wrote of the Jackfield Pottery, formerly run by Maurice Thursfield on the west side of the River Severn:

> In these works, Mr. Rose, in conjunction with a Mr. Blakeway, soon after the death of Maurice Thursfield, began making china. The works were not, however, carried on long, but were removed to Coalport, on the opposite

---

[1] The history of the Caughley factory and an account of its varied products are the subject of a separate book, *Caughley and Worcester Porcelains, 1775–1800* (1969).

General history prior
to 1850, with résumé
of factory marks

side of the Severn, where they began in some buildings what had formerly been a pottery, I believe belonging to a Mr. Young, a mercer, of Shrewsbury . . .

The earliest mention of 'Mr Rose' is contained in the Chamberlain records, where a letter is recorded as being sent to (or received from) 'Mr Rose, Manufactory, Salop' on June 13th, 1791; but this does not constitute *definite* evidence that Rose was then established at Coalport, for the manufactory could have been Thomas Turner's Caughley factory, where John Rose was apprenticed before leaving to manufacture porcelain with Edward Blakeway at near-by Coalport.

There are several references to Blakeway in letters exchanged between Joseph Lygo (the manager of the Derby factory's London showroom) and Richard Egan, the Bath retailer, in 1793. It is probable that the following references relate to Blakeway soon after he and John Rose had taken over Thursfield's Jackfield Pottery. Lygo certainly supplied Egan with Coalport china in 1797, as is shown by the accounts printed on Page 5. The 1793 references are:

February 16th, 1793.
. . . I could not get any oval trifle dishes at the price you mention, nor any round ones from Blakeways . . . the cream ewers I had off Turner are cheaper than Blakeways . . .

May 7th, 1793.
. . . Blakeways will not give me a list of Prices you sent—if you give them an order they will do them on the most reasonable terms . . .

December 7th, 1793.
I am afraid Blakeways have lost the pattern for the sugar bason . . .

The earliest example so far discovered of *marked* Coalport passed almost unnoticed in Sotheby's in January 1965, when it was sold in a mixed lot with three other unrelated pieces from the collection of the late Ernest Allman. This documentary example was a cream-coloured *earthenware* mug, lacking its handle and in a very chipped state. This piece was decorated with printed panels, one of the side panels depicting a stone or tablet bearing the inscription 'Manufactured at Coalport 1797' (see Plate 8). As this printed mug is not otherwise inscribed with initials or a name, it is unlikely to have been made for a wedding, birth or other special occasion, but was probably made to commemorate the establishment of a new factory in the locality. This pottery belonged to Walter Bradley & Co, a hitherto unrecorded firm. The only reference to this firm by name that I have been able to trace appeared in the *Salopian Journal* of May 3rd, 1797:

WHOLESALE
EARTHEN-WARE WAREHOUSE
WALTER BRADLEY & Co.

Respectfully inform their friends and the public that they have opened a Warehouse at the Canal Wharf in the Castle Foregate, Shrewsbury, where

Dealers and others may be supplied with Earthen Ware (for ready money) on the lowest Terms. Attendance every Wednesday and Saturday from ten-oclock till four . . .

COALPORT POTTERY.   April 26th, 1797.

This important advertisement was repeated in the next issue of the *Salopian Journal* of May 10th, 1797, but I have been unable to trace any further direct mention of Messrs Bradley & Co of the Coalport pottery.

The famous canal builder and engineer, Thomas Telford, mentions an earthenware factory at Coalport in a notice on Shropshire canals contributed to the *General View of the Agriculture of Shropshire*, 1803, by Joseph Plymley. Telford's contribution is dated November 13th, 1800, and reads:

> . . . houses to the number of thirty have been built there (at Coalport) and more are still wanted to accommodate the people employed at a large china manufactory, a considerable earthenware manufactory, another for making ropes . . .

In the 'Manufacturers' section of Joseph Plymley's book there are further references to the Coalport earthenware factory, but it is not known when the author obtained his notes on the subject or wrote this section; his Preface is dated May 25th, 1801, but some footnotes refer to 1802, so it was obviously before the date of publication in 1803.

> . . . more immediately at Coal-port . . . is a manufacture of earthenware, in imitation of that made at Etruria and called the Queen's or Wedgwood's ware. In the lordship of Cardington, in this county, a quartz and clay may be gotten for compounding this ware, the former superior, as I am well informed, to that imported out of Carnarvonshire to the Staffordshire potteries . . .

Certain black basalt teapots (see Plate 9) bearing the impressed mark BRADLEY & Co / Coalport. or BRADLEY / Coalport must now be attributed to this firm of manufacturers, not to the London retailers of the same name, as has hitherto been thought. Apart from the basalt ware, Messrs Bradley also made cream-coloured earthenware, which is evidenced by the 'Manufactured at Coalport, 1797' tankard.

Marked examples of Bradley's creamware are extremely rare, but an unusual pair of candlesticks with two nun-like faces below the candle-holders are illustrated in the *Connoisseur* magazine of June 1909. These specimens are 11 inches high and the body of each is attractively decorated with enamel colour. One stick bears the impressed mark BRADLEY & Co / Coalport.

It would seem that Bradley's pottery was of brief duration and was perhaps taken over and enlarged by John Rose or by Messrs Anstice, Horton & Rose

General history prior
to 1850, with résumé
of factory marks

(see Chapter IV). Apart from Bradley's ware, no pottery was made at Coalport, all John Rose's products being in translucent porcelain. Some few, probably experimental, pieces of pottery were, however, made at the Caughley factory during John Rose's management about 1805–10 (see Page 41 and Plate 89).

Now to concentrate on Coalport translucent porcelain as opposed to opaque pottery. The earliest firm evidence relating to John Rose and the Coalport porcelain factory has so far been the reference to 'Edward Blakeway, John Rose and Richard Rose of Coalport (a partnership often shortened to "Rose & Co") . . . porcelain manufacturers' in the October 1799, agreement to take over Thomas Turner's near-by factory at Caughley. I have, however, been able to trace references relating to the Coalport china works in August 1796, when the Prince and Princess of Orange visited Shropshire. The local paper, the *Shropshire Journal*, in its issue of August 24th, 1796, reported:

> Their Highnesses the Prince and Princess of Orange . . . visited the (Coalbrook) Dale Company's ironworks . . . went by water to see Mr. Brodie's Cannon foundry . . . and thence proceeded to the china factory at Coalpark, where his Highness bought some pieces of Mr. Rose: and viewing the Tar Spring, the inclined Plane etc returned to the Tontine Inn.

This hitherto unrecorded account is of vital importance because of its early date. It must be understood that the term 'china factory' does not *necessarily* mean that porcelain was being produced in 1796, as the expression was a loose one at that period and often included earthenware. But here it was probably correctly used, and the products were apparently worthy of the attention of Royalty; and as 'Mr Rose' is mentioned, there can be no confusion with Messrs Bradley & Co's pottery. The place-name 'Coalpark' was almost certainly an error for Coalport, the papers of the period containing many such minor typographical errors. The 'inclined plane' joined the Shropshire Canal some two hundred yards north of the Coalport factory; the 'Tontine Inn' was the leading hotel of the district and is still situated opposite the Ironbridge, just upstream from Coalport. Apart from the fact that the Prince purchased china 'of Mr Rose' in August 1796, this newspaper report is of great interest, showing as it does that the works had by this date moved from the Jackfield or west side of the River Severn to Coalport on the east side.

The blue and white election jugs shown in Plates 10 and 11 are dated 1796 and, although unmarked, are almost certainly of Coalport manufacture on the evidence of the body and potting characteristics. They record the election of John Hill as Member of Parliament for Shrewsbury in 1796 (see Page 44).

Further evidence on early Coalport porcelain is incorporated in documents relating to the Derby factory and, in particular, the letters sent by Joseph Lygo (the manager of the Derby factory's London showrooms) to Duesbury at Derby and to his brother-in-law, Richard Egan, a retailer at Bath, which include two references to Rose & Co. The documents suggest that Rose & Co were supplying goods in December 1796, and certainly in August 1797:

Mr. Egan.   *Dr. to Rose & Co.*   15th Augt. 1797.

1796 Decr. 17th	To Goods	£8 : 10 : 6
	Box	2 : 6
1797 Augt.	To Goods, part of this sent	
	to the Derby warehouse.	6 : 0 : 6
	Box	1 : 6
		£14 : 15 : 0

Sirs,

By above we hand you our acct. with the late Mr. Egan agreeable to your request.

We are very Respectfully

Your mo. obt. servts.

Rose Blakeway & Rose.

A further account dated August 9th, 1797, is of the utmost interest, being the earliest discovered detailed account for Coalport wares:

Mr. Egan.   *Bot. of Rose & Co.*

18 cups (&) saucers, Bute (shape) gold edge, band & sprigs.	£1 : 19 : 0
7¼ Pint Basins & stands.	1 : 1 : 0
12 Coffee Cups.	17 : 0
1 large ovall [*sic*] milk.	3 : 6
9 Bute (shape) saucers.	9 : 0
1 B & B plate 1st (size).	3 : 0
1 ,, ,, ,, 2nd (size).	4 : 0
	£4 : 16 : 6

Writing of the benefit that canal navigation had afforded, Thomas Telford noted in November 1800:

Formerly the place (Coalport) consisted of a very rugged uncultivated bank, which scarcely produced even grass, but owing to the judicious regulations and encouragement of Mr. (William) Reynolds joined to the benefit arising from the canal and the river, houses to the number of thirty have been built there, and more are still wanted, to accommodate the people employed at a large china manufactory, a considerable earthenware manufactory, another for making ropes, one for bag-making and one for chairs . . .

In the china manufactory, not established more than five years, and in which perhaps the last, and including its dependencies,[1] the most china is

[1] The reference to dependencies may well relate to the near-by Caughley porcelain works taken over by the Coalport partners in October 1799, and run concurrently with the Coalport works until 1814.

General history prior
to 1850, with résumé
of factory marks

manufactured of any works of that sort in Great Britain, there are employed about 250 persons . . .

The above extract, dated November 1800, is contained in Joseph Plymley's *General View of the Agriculture of Shropshire* published in 1803. The author gives, in the section on 'Manufacturers', further information on Coalport porcelain; and as he notes that the Caughley factory had been taken over by the Coalport management, the period of writing must be subsequent to October 1799. Plymley noted:

> At Caughley is a china manufacture of great excellence. The blue & white and the blue, white and gold china there, is, in many instances, more like that from the East than any other I have seen. These works have been purchased by the proprietors of a later establishment, the Coal-port china works and are confined to the ware specified above. At Coalport coloured china of all sorts and of exquisite taste and beauty is made . . .

This contemporary account would seem to indicate that at this period—some time between October 1799 and 1803—the Caughley factory was producing only blue and white porcelain, as opposed to the more colourful Coalport ware. This may perhaps be explained by Jewitt's theory that the undecorated porcelain made at Caughley was transported to Coalport for the decoration to be added. However, 'finds' on the site do not wholly substantiate this view.

The Chamberlain accounts contain an intriguing reference to one of the Coalport partners at an early date. Under the date February 16th, 1797, there is a long list of white porcelain to be supplied to William Hewson of London, with the margin note 'To be sent at Rose's prices'—which suggests that Rose was at that date a competitor of Chamberlain, who sought to keep his prices to the level of his new competitor, John Rose of Coalport.

Further, on July 10th, 1797, Mr Phillips, the auctioneer, sold:

> An elegant and beautiful coffee and tea equipage of Shropshire porcelain, 41 pieces. (Sold for £2/7/-)
> An elegant dessert set of ditto, 46 pieces. (Sold for £7/17/6)

It is possible that these lots were of Caughley manufacture, but this ware was normally catalogued as 'Salopian' and it is likely that this teaset and dessert set were of early Coalport make. Other early references to sales of Coalport porcelain are given in Appendix I.

In 1797 the Coalport partners entered into an agreement to take over further property at Coalport under the following Indenture which, if nothing else, shows the full names of the three partners at this period:

> 24th October 1797. Indre. of this date made betn. Chas. Lumley, Samuel Smith & Wm. Smith, John Pritchard, Hy Major, John Griffith & Robt Griffiths . . . of the one part and Edward Blakeway, John Rose and Richard Rose of the other part being Lease of certain property at Coalport in the Parish of Madeley in the Co. of Salop.

The Wedgwood archives contain two very important early letters from Messrs Rose, Blakeway & Co, of Coalport, which show that by February 1798 clay was required and indicate that earlier inquiries had been made:

Coalport, 13th. Febry '98

Gentm,

Some time ago we were informed from your house that you expected a fresh supply of clay in shortly and would spare us part of it, we should therefore be obliged to favour us with a line to say when you expect the next to arrive and what you can spare us of it, we shall want a greater quantity and wish you to prepare us 10, 15 or 20 Tons, ensuing summer (? word indistinct) and if agreeable to you should be glad to take the same quantity annually, the favour of an answer will much oblige. Gentm.

Your most hble Servts,
Rose Blakeway & Co.

It is regrettable that no clue is given as to the period meant by the phrase 'some time ago' in the first line. A letter written to Wedgwoods four days later is of vital importance, as it shows that experiments had been carried out for the manufacture of porcelain at Coalport:

Coalport 17th Feb. 1798

Gentm,

We have received your favour of (the) 15th and shall be obliged if you will forward us the 20 Casks of Clay to York & Co. Stourport.

At the time you mentioned respecting the clay, we were at the greatest uncertainty in succeeding in the manufacturing of porcelain owing to the various changes and alterations amongst ourselves—as soon as you can learn about the quantity of clay you shall have to dispose of we shall be obliged to you for a line.

Rose, Blakeway & Co.

Unfortunately, Wedgwoods' reply to the first letter has not been preserved; but it is perhaps reasonable to speculate that Wedgwoods stated, in effect, 'we did, in fact, notify you that the clay was on hand but were not favoured with your order'. The Coalport firm then (on February 17th, 1798) defended their earlier lack of interest by stating that previously their experiments in porcelain manufacture were not completed, and they were awaiting the successful outcome of these before ordering clay in bulk. In any event, these two letters, written in February 1798, show that Messrs Rose, Blakeway & Co were then seeking supplies of china clay and by the past-tense wording of the paragraph 'at the time you mention . . . we were at the greatest uncertainty in succeeding in the manufacture of porcelain . . .' the obstacles had then been overcome—a fact underlined by the account of August 1797, printed on Page 5. It would appear from a letter quoted on Page 8 that earlier supplies of clay had been obtained from Messrs Warrick & Dickins (Clay Merchants), but that this proved too costly.

General history prior
to 1850, with résumé
of factory marks

Subsequent letters show that by May 1798 Messrs Wedgwoods had supplied the Coalport firm with two consignments of clay, at a cost of £39 18s, and that then Rose, Blakeway & Co were writing for a further 10 tons and inquiring 'if it will be in your power to help us to any further quantity this summer'. In June 1798 Messrs Rose wrote to say that they were in urgent want of clay 'and shall be obliged if (you) will forward some immediately . . .' Porcelain was therefore being manufactured, probably on a large scale, by Messrs Rose, Blakeway & Co of Coalport by at least the first part of 1798. Further letters from them to Messrs Wedgwoods for the supply of clay have been preserved, bearing dates up to April 1801, and all are signed for 'Rose, Blakeway & Co' or, in one instance, for 'Blakeway, Rose & Co'.

Further information on Messrs Rose, Blakeway & Co's search for supplies of clay has been discovered by Mrs R. M. Barton during her researches for her excellent and interesting book *A History of the Cornish China-Clay Industry* (D. Bradford Barton Ltd, Truro, 1966). A letter dated 'London. March 12th, 1799' from William Ludlam to Charles Cowper, agents for Lord Camelford, concerns the supply of clay from Carloggas Moor, Cornwall, and reads in part:

> I came home and found Rose, Blakeway & Co. (Coalbrook-Dale). They came to Town . . . on purpose to deliver in these proposals which are for the liberty of taking up—
>
> | | | |
> |---|---|---|
> | 300 ton clay at | 33/- per ton. | £495 |
> | 1200 ton stone | 2/- „ „ | £120 |
>
> I had a good deal of conversation with them and told them 39/- and 5/- had been offered. They wanted an answer by Thursday for their Government in another offer. I have got them to promise to mend their offer . . . for the privilege of taking-up 300 ton clay and 1200 stone, and no more, provided so much is in the mine. Annually to pay rent half yearly . . .
>
> If they come up to 40/- and 5/- it would be £900. I think they will be short of that—but between that and this present offer (of 33/- and 2/-) . . .
>
> This is the most shapable thing we have had offered. They say they have had clay of Wedgwood at £4 and can have it now, they even insist that it is as good and comes from only the other side of the Ridge, but this I don't believe. They say they have given £5/-/- to Warrick (Messrs. Warrick & Dickins, Clay Merchants) but left off on account of high price.

Messrs Rose, Blakeway's offer was not accepted, but this letter gives an indication of the price of Cornish china clay, of the price the Coalport management paid to Wedgwood's for their clay, and of the fact that they had also purchased supplies from Messrs Warrick & Dickins, probably at a date prior to the 1798 correspondence with Wedgwoods (see Page 7).

The porcelain body produced from this clay is remarkably heavy and compact, and with its thick potting it is unlike any other porcelain of the period; except, that is, the porcelain produced by the rival Coalport firm of Anstice, Horton & Rose (see Chapter IV). Early in my researches on Coalport ware and on the fragments from the Caughley factory I was struck by the similarity of the body to hard-paste porcelain (as made by the Eastern potters, most Continental firms, and the Plymouth, Bristol, and New Hall porcelain companies in this country). This visual diagnosis has been confirmed by the researches of Mr David Holgate and the point is enlarged upon on Page 28. It may also be significant that Wedgwoods had access to the Cornish raw materials formerly used by Richard Champion to make his hard-paste Bristol porcelain. Was the later John Rose porcelain formed from the same clay as the Bristol porcelain?

In October 1799 the Coalport works had expanded to such an extent that the following advertisement was inserted in the *Shropshire Journal* on October 2nd and 9th, 1799:

COALPORT CHINA MANUFACTORY

Workmen wanted in the gilding, enamelling and blue painting lines: twelve good hands of each work will meet with constant employ.

Unfortunately, a calamity befell some of the Coalport employees within the month—some of the hands concerned possibly having been among those who had answered the above advertisement. The events are here told in the words of Rose, who wrote to the editor of the *Shropshire Journal* giving a first-hand account:

Coalport, October 26th. 1799.

Sir,

As there will be many erroneous accounts circulated respecting the unfortunate and shocking accident that happened here on Wednesday evening (October 23rd) at 9 o'clock, I beg leave to state as near the particulars I have yet been able to learn.

As the people from the Coalport Manufactory, to the number of 43 were leaving there at 9 o'clock at night, to go home over the usual passage boat, owing to the inattention of the man whom the boatman had entrusted to steer over, the boat unfortunately went down with all on board, when only 15 out of the whole could save themselves, the remaining 28 were unfortunately lost. In consequence of the great fog and the darkness of the night, no one was able to give the least assistance. Ten have since been taken out of the water and the coroner's inquest is to be held over them this day . . .

There follows a list of the persons drowned, under the headings Men, Women and Girls, and Pottery (Potters). This letter shows that at least forty-three people were employed at the Coalport works in 1799, the number probably being much greater—for a later account of the accident mentions 'several persons who used to go over at that hour (9 o'clock) but by some unseen Providence had left work at six o'clock'. There is the further point that not all the workmen would have lived on the opposite bank of the river and would consequently not have been involved. In the 1803 sale notice twelve dwelling-houses were described as adjoining the factory (see Page 13). The list of the lost hands shows that women and girls were also employed, and these would have been engaged in burnishing the gilding, applying printed patterns and perhaps overpainting printed outlines or painting simple sprig-type designs.

The 1797 partnership of Edward Blakeway, John and Richard Rose quickly prospered—or at least the partners enjoyed ample financial backing, for in the same month of October 1799 they entered into agreement to take over the near-by Caughley factory where John Rose had been apprenticed. This was a large and expensive venture, the yearly rents for the Caughley concern (porcelain factory, colliery and mills) amounting to £526, with subsequent leases increasing the annual rents to £624.

The fact that the Coalport works were continued and the Caughley factory purchased suggests that the partners envisaged a good and growing demand for their ware. They had the largest, and probably the most expensive, porcelain-producing estate in Great Britain during the early years of the nineteenth century. The large total Coalport/Caughley yearly rental of £748 16s 2d was partly offset by the fact that the estate was self-supporting in regard to the coals for firing the ware. The clay on the estate was also suitable for the manufacture of saggars, in which the porcelain was fired, and the estate contained a separate saggar-making works and mills for grinding the raw materials. A further consideration was that the John Rose Company also took over the markets and retail outlets built up by Thomas Turner of Caughley over many years.

The fact that the Coalport partners purchased the Caughley works in 1799 and ran it concurrently with the Coalport factory has enabled a large range of early Blakeway, Rose & Co porcelain to be identified, for the Caughley site has remained untouched for over a hundred and fifty years and has recently yielded a vast array of factory wasters (see Chapter II).

The early Coalport porcelain was unmarked and has for years been attributed to the Chamberlain factory at Worcester and to several other early nineteenth-century factories. The attribution to Coalport of porcelain illustrated in Plates 12–62, 78, 81, and 83 is based on matching, often unglazed, fragments found at the site of the Caughley factory, where most of John Rose's porcelain was manufactured from 1799 until c. 1814, when the Caughley works were dismantled and the materials used to enlarge the original Coalport factory.

A most interesting reference to Coalport porcelain early in 1801 is contained in the advertisement of a Shrewsbury china dealer—Thomas Brockas—in the *Salopian Journal* of Wednesday, March 11th, 1801, and repeated in the following issue:

COALPORT CHINA WAREHOUSE
RAVEN STREET, SHREWSBURY.
THOMAS BROCKAS.

Thankful for the many favours received from the Families in and about Shrewsbury, especially for the great encouragement he has met with since his entering on this present warehouse, takes this opportunity of acquainting Ladies and Gentlemen and the Public in general, that he has this day received a very elegant assortment of goods from Coalport, consisting of Table (Dinner) services at from 25 to 200 Guineas the Service, Dessert services from 12 to 35 Guineas the service, Tea and Breakfast services of the newest Patterns and shapes at from £2/12/6 to 20 Guineas the set, Garden pots (jardinières or bulb pots?), Cabinet cups &c. of the most curious and rich kinds. He begs leave to add it is now generally allowed the Coalport china stands hot water best and the gilding is the purest of any china got up in Europe . . .

Shrewsbury, March 10th, 1801.

While it is not surprising that this Coalport porcelain mainly consisted of tableware, the price range of the dinner service 'to 200 Guineas' causes considerable surprise when one considers that the present-day monetary equivalent would be in the region of £2,000.

The earliest recorded use of the alternative name 'Coalbrook Dale' appears in the *Salopian Journal* of November 11th, 1801:

> Three very elegant services of Coalbrook Dale china, finished in a most superb style, with rich burnished gold, have been completed for the Marquis Cornwallis . . .

The name also occurs in Messrs Christie's catalogues from 1802, and is used on retailers' trade cards and advertisements. It also constitutes the earliest factory mark, although such examples are extremely rare (see Colour Plate I; Plates 32 and 104). To later collectors the term 'Coalbrook Dale' signifies a class of rich floral-encrusted Coalport porcelain of the 1820–40 period, which does, in fact, often bear the name 'Coalbrook Dale', or the abbreviations 'C. Dale' or 'C.D.'

A year after Thomas Brockas's 1801 advertisement quoted earlier a further one was published in the *Salopian Journal*. This 1802 advertisement is of the greatest importance, heralding the introduction of BRITISH NANKEEN ware in imitation of the Chinese blue and white Nankin porcelain and the Coalport services with moulded basketwork borders (see Plates 16 and 84). Mention is also made of the fact that Coalport porcelain had been finely gilded and enamelled for 'four years past' and that 'new and very fine articles in ornaments' were being prepared:

COALPORT CHINA WAREHOUSE.
CASTLE STREET, SHREWSBURY
THOMAS BROCKAS.

Sensible to the many Favours conferred upon him by the Shropshire Families, and by the Public in general, since his commencement in business, especially since his opening the above warehouse, takes this opportunity of returning his most sincere and hearty thanks. He has the satisfaction to inform them he has just received from Coalport Table services of an entire new article called BRITISH NANKEEN, so exactly like the foreign, both as to shapes, colour &c., that few can distinguish it from Foreign

11

General history prior
to 1850, with résumé
of factory marks

Blue & White china: and if there is any difference, it will be found the
BRITISH NANKEEN excels both as to beauty and strength: he has
two kinds of it, one an exact imitation of India Blue & White china, of a
pale colour, which he offers at 18 guineas the Table (Dinner) service,
Manufacturer's price; the other exactly like the old fine dark Blue Stone
Ware, or Nankeen, at 25 guineas. When it is considered the above Ware will
be equally durable with the Foreign, more beautiful, and comes at less than
half the price of Foreign, he flatters himself it will be found an object
worthy the consideration of those Families who, since the Establishment
of Coalport Manufactory, have been pleased to countenance and encourage ingenuity and honest Industry at Home rather than send their
money abroad for an inferior article, which for ages was the case before
the commencement of the late War.

He has also by him full Table services of White China with basketwork
on the edges, blue sprigs, chantillia &c. at 20 guineas the service, such as
was sold before the War, in French china at 35 guineas. That preference
given their gilding and enamelled china for Four Years past, and which is
still given in London, and that increasing demand for it in different parts
of the world, leaves it unnecessary for him to say anything in its Favour.
He continues to sell Dessert services of this at from 12 to 50 guineas: Table
services at from 40 to 170 guineas; Tea services from 3 to 14 Guineas:
Breakfast services from 5 to 25 Guineas.

He has also the Pleasure to inform the Public they are now getting up a
new and very fine article in ornaments, and tea and dessert services, equally
white and transparent as the French. This is certainly the most delicate
article of china ever manufactured in England . . .

Many fragments of porcelain which appear to match ware described in these
advertisements were found on the Caughley site, which the Coalport partners
worked from 1799—both of 'British Nankin' (see Plate 12) and 'Table services
of white china with basket-work on the edges, blue sprigs . . .' (see Plate 84).
These Brockas advertisements, as well as other contemporary records, show
clearly that the porcelain made at Caughley after 1799 was sold as 'Coalport',
after the parent factory. I believe this description to be correct and all porcelains
made under the management of John Rose and his partners are termed COAL-
PORT in this book, although some objects were undoubtedly formed at the
branch factory at Caughley.

In August 1803 the proprietors of the Coalport factory—then Edward Blakeway, John Rose and Robert Winter—were surprisingly declared bankrupt, perhaps owing to their banking interests (in the Coalport Bank) rather than the
failure in the ceramic field.

BLAKEWAY, ROSE AND WINTER'S BANKRUPTCY.

Notice is hereby given that all Persons who stand indebted to the estate
and effects of Blakeway, Rose & Winter, late of Coalport in the County of

Salop, Porcelaine Manufacturers and Bankers are requested to pay their respective Debts to Mr. Pritchard of Broseley, Solicitor to the assignees . . . Broseley. 15th August, 1803.

(Notice published in the *Salopian Journal* on Wednesday, August 24th, and August 31st, 1803).

This bankruptcy has proved fortunate to present-day ceramic historians, for as a result both the Caughley and the Coalport factories were offered for sale and details of the premises and leases published in the local *Salopian Journal* on September 21st and 28th, 1803. Details of the Coalport works were:

All that capital CHINA FACTORY, situate at Coalport, in the County of Salop, with the Warehouses, Counting Houses, Kilns, Stove Houses and all other building necessary for carrying on the PORCELAIN MANU-FACTORY to a very great extent. Also all the machinery, implements, utensils and tools thereto belonging: together with a large stock of china, materials, ingredients and other articles necessary for carrying on the said works and also 12 Dwelling Houses adjoining thereto. The said factory and hovels, part of the above building, are held by Indenture of Lease for the residue of a Term of twenty one years, 14 of which were unexpired at Lady Day Past, under the yearly rent of £61/14/2.

The dwelling houses, other part of the said Buildings are held for a like Term, under the yearly Rent of £43/8/- and the warehouses, stove houses and slip kiln are held by an Indenture of Lease for the residue of a Term of 88 years, 82 of which were unexpired at Lady Day Past, under the yearly rent of £19/14/-.

. . . The works at Coalport are upon the Banks of the Shropshire Canal which brings the Coals down thereto and adjoins the River Severn . . .

The repute of these works (at Caughley as well as Coalport) and the superior excellence of the china made thereat are so well known as to render any comment upon them unnecessary . . '

. . . Mr. John Rose of Broseley aforesaid, will show the whole of the Premises, and further particulars may be had by applying to Mr. Bird, Solicitor, Birmingham, Mr. Timothy Yate [Yates?] of Madeley, Mr. C. Guest, the younger or Mr. Prestwich of Broseley (the assignees of the Estate and affects of the said Bankrupts) or to Mr. Pritchard, Attorney, in Broseley aforesaid.

This 1803 sale notice therefore shows that Indentures of Lease for the Coalport works and related buildings were entered into in 1797 and 1798. The total rent due was £124 16*s* 2*d* a year; and on a tithe map of the 1840s the landowner is shown as Joseph Reynolds. The references to 'kilns' and 'slip kilns' are also interesting, as they show that porcelain was then being manufactured at Coalport as well as at Caughley. Some nineteenth-century writers had suggested that the porcelain was made at Caughley and transported to Coalport for the decoration

General history prior
to 1850, with résumé
of factory marks

to be added—a theory that fails to take into account the fact that the Coalport works were producing porcelain before the partners took over the lease of the Caughley factory in 1799.

Having established that the leases for the Coalport factory date back at least to 1797, it must be stated that at that period John Rose was a relatively young man, having been born on February 8th, 1772, the son of a local farmer. John's apprenticeship to Thomas Turner at the Caughley works probably lasted until 1793, when John Rose was twenty-one, which means that his reputed connection with a pottery at Jackfield (see Page 1) could not have been longer than some four years and may have been less. His brother Richard was even younger, as he was born in September 1774.

John Rose's youthfulness when the Coalport factory leases were drawn up in 1797–98 suggests that Edward Blakeway was the senior partner or the financial backer. I have been unable to discover information relating to Richard Rose (John's brother), apart from the fact that he was born in September 1774, his name not being mentioned in the 1803 bankruptcy notices or sale announcements.

After the 1803 bankruptcy, the assignees sold the works to Cuthbert Johnson and William Clarke, who apparently had capital, but no practical experience of potting, and they consequently arranged for John Rose to continue the Caughley/Coalport manufactories. There were subsequently other changes in the partnership, but John Rose's name continued to be prominently featured and the title 'John Rose & Co' remained the official designation of the Coalport porcelain factory throughout the nineteenth century.

In 1820 Rose & Co were awarded the Society of Arts Gold Medal for a leadless felspathic glaze to replace the earlier lead glaze so injurious to the potters. This award brought Rose and his Coalport porcelain great publicity, and large self-explanatory printed marks (see Page 19) were placed on fine porcelain from June 1820, advertising the fact that the medal had been won.

The porcelain bearing this mark from 1820 is very different, both in form and in the new softer body and glaze, from that made during the Caughley/Coalport period before 1815. The shapes became less severe, showing some rococo influence. Moulded edge plates and dishes, close copies of Swansea and Nantgarw forms (see Colour Plate III; Plates 121–3, 133, and 134), are an important feature. It must, however, be remembered that other factories, notably Derby and Davenport, produced similar ware with these Swansea-type moulded edges. It is also possible that this attractive form of modelling often associated with the Welsh factories was, in fact, introduced by John Rose, for an unglazed fragment has been found on the Caughley site worked by Rose before 1815.

In appearance, the 1820 Society of Arts marked pieces, now of soft-paste, are whiter than the rather grey hard-bodied Caughley/Coalport plates, and the later pieces show much better translucency than many of the early ones. On the 1820 plates, which are often thickly potted and therefore heavy, the glaze is generously applied so that it gathers in the angle of the footrim, rounding the angle and giving it a moulded appearance, quite different from that of the pre-

1815 plates, where the glaze is normally partly wiped from the more sharply angled footrim, which thus has the appearance of being turned.

Apart from plates and their accompanying dinner and dessert services, other fine ware such as tea services, as well as the rarer ornamental articles, bear this Society of Arts mark. Typical marked examples are illustrated in Colour Plate III and Plates 133, 135, and 140, where the quality of the painting, particularly the flower studies, is extremely fine.

From about 1820 much fine Coalport porcelain was enriched with encrusted flowers. This style is termed 'Coalbrookdale' and is discussed in Chapter V, as also are the many rococo-style vases produced at the Coalport factory.

After about ten years—that is, in about 1830—the Society of Arts mark, with its variations (see Page 19), was discontinued, although on some printed pieces it was used later, as the mark occurred on the engraved copper plate. From about 1830 the porcelain was thin in the potting and consequently lighter in weight.

The Coalport porcelain of the 1825–50 period is very refined and well potted. Examples are normally unmarked and bear only a pattern number expressed in fractional form 2/123, 2/124, or 3/123, 3/124 etc (see Page 56). Although this ware is seldom attributed to Coalport, the survival of many of the original factory pattern-books enables us to compare the pattern-numbered ware with the relevant design in the original books, so proving their Coalport origin. Porcelain illustrated in Plates 65, 69, 73–5, 142, 143, 144, 147, and 160 has been checked in this way, and from these checked key pieces other examples of identical form can be identified with confidence.

Other unmarked Coalport porcelain of the 1830s and 1840s can be identified by comparison with the fragments illustrated in Plate 150—relief-moulded factory wasters acquired by wading in the River Severn in front of the Coalport factory! It would appear that barrow-loads of defective porcelain were simply dumped by the river, gradually heightening the banks of the Severn by the factory in the process so that now they appear to be composed almost entirely of china fragments. Naturally, the earlier pieces are lower down the banks, with the later, less interesting, pieces piled on top; and parts of the china-imbedded bank have been washed into the river by the combined action of the stream and the weather, so that now its bed appears to be lined with broken china.

The washed fragments shown in Plate 150 represent only a small proportion of the pieces gathered in a mere twenty minutes. Unfortunately, it is not possible to discover what interesting fragments are buried at the base of the banks under tons of later factory wasters, for one can pick up only the pieces washed down and exposed by the elements.

A further selection of Coalport porcelain issued without a factory mark can be identified by means of the diamond-shaped device which shows that a design or shape had been registered at the Patent Office in London. Between January 1845 and December 1850 John Rose of the Coalport Company registered thirteen designs, some of which are illustrated in Plates 128, 129, 147, and 149. Other pieces of these forms will also be of Coalport manufacture.

The period from *c.* 1797 to 1850 was one of great activity for the Coalport

General history prior
to 1850, with résumé
of factory marks

Porcelain Company, marred only by the bankruptcy in 1803. From very small beginnings at Coalport in the 1790s John Rose acquired, in 1799, Thomas Turner's large factory at Caughley, the rival Coalport works of Anstice, Horton and Rose in 1814 (see Chapter IV), and the Swansea and Nantgarw factory moulds and receipts in 1820.

The leading London retailers, Messrs Mortlocks of Oxford Street, sold Coalport porcelain to the nobility, and their advertisements and billheads proclaimed the fact that they were 'Manufacturers of Colebrook Dale porcelain to Her Majesty and the Royal Family', which must have added greatly to the prestige of the Coalport Company. This was even further enhanced when the Company won the Society of Arts Gold Medal for a leadless glaze in May 1820.

The early Coalport porcelain of the 1815–20 period is probably today the most misunderstood and neglected of all early nineteenth-century English porcelain, even though it is among the most beautiful—especially in regard to the flower painting.

The area around Coalport, within about a five-mile radius, was of extreme importance ceramically, the small potteries at Jackfield (and its neighbourhood) on the opposite side of the river being of some antiquity, probably dating back to Roman times, while the ground at Jackfield, Broseley, Madeley, and other near-by townships yielded both the vital clays and the coal for the kilns. Much of Messrs Chamberlains' raw materials was shipped downriver to Worcester from Coalport, Broseley, Ironbridge, and Madeley, as is proved by numerous references in the Chamberlain account-books:

May 19th, 1794.　　Bot. of William Yates, Broseley.
　　Bill delivered for Coals, Clays & Bricks　　　£13/-/-
Feb. 28th, 1815.　　John Burton, Ironbridge.
　　For 27 Tons,　4 cwts, 3 quarts Sagger clay @ 16/-　　£21/15/9
　　　,,　　4　,,　18　,,　1　,,　Fine clay @ 19/-　　£4/12/5

to quote but two examples. In one instance, when other, more expensive, clay was offered to Chamberlains, they replied '. . . The Shropshire (clay) for saggar making possesses every quality wished for that purpose at about 13/- a Ton carriage included.'

The Chamberlain records contain one further entry which may suggest that there was a small decorating establishment at Madeley, some two miles to the north of Coalport, in the 1790s, for under the date February 21st, 1794, there is recorded the sale of undecorated white porcelain—four tea services, thirty-eight ewers, twelve teapot-stands, four oval sugar-boxes, ten pieces handled chocolate-cups, and several other items—to a Mr Yates of Madeley. Also sold were '2 old Burnt Cast Iron Muffs' or muffle kilns, used to fire the added enamel decoration on porcelain. It will be seen above that a William Yates supplied Chamberlains with coals and clays, and he may also have tried to decorate porcelain.

Chapters II–V deal in more detail with various aspects of pre-1850 Coalport china, while Chapter VI gives the history of the Coalport Company from 1850 to the present day; but first, it will prove helpful to give a résumé of the marks that can be expected on Coalport porcelain.

Factory Marks and Pattern Numbers

The earliest Coalport porcelain is unmarked and often does not even bear a pattern number, but during the 1805–10 period some very rare painted marks occur which comprise the names 'Coalbrookdale' or 'Coal-port' clearly painted in red enamel (see below). Examples with these marks are a blue-bordered lobed plate painted with a basket of flowers, in the Victoria and Albert Museum, another is shown in Plate 32; two 'Japan'-pattern plates, in the Godden collection (Colour Plate I); and a gilt jug (Plate 104) of the same form as one in the Victoria and Albert Museum which is dated January 1806. I have seen a covered cup, finely painted with flowers on a gold ground, bearing one of these early painted marks, and other examples will no doubt be discovered.

From about 1810 many Coalport plates from fine dessert and dinner services bear an impressed numeral—a rather top-heavy figure '2' (see below); and small plates may bear the impressed numeral '1'. This form of impressed mark was used for many years, examples having been found on the pre-1815 Caughley site, and sometimes on specimens bearing the Royal Society of Arts printed mark, proving a date after May 1820.

The fine oval, or shaped-edged, dishes or platters found in Coalport dinner services of the 1805–20 period have various numerals impressed near the centre of the underside, according to the size. The *approximate* sizes of platters are given below, with the relevant size numeral:

10 in. × 7¾ in.		'1'
11½ in. × 8½ in.		'2'
13½ in. × 10 in.		'3'
15 in. × 11½ in.		'4'
17 in. × 12¼ in.		'5'
18½ in. × 14 in.		'6'
19½ in. × 15¾ in.		'7'
21½ in. × 16½ in.		'8'

Teapots and sugar-basins very rarely bear impressed numbers, but factory wasters with these marks were discovered on the Caughley site. These marks are more in the category of workmen's signs or, in the case of dishes and plates, size marks than factory trade marks; but their existence does enable a large range of 1810–25 Coalport to be identified.

An impressed fouled-anchor mark has formerly been attributed to the Davenport factory in Staffordshire (which certainly used the anchor device incorporated in their marks). This mark, however, occurs on a plate in the Godden collection with the impressed numeral '2' also. Furthermore, the plate bears the pattern $\frac{2}{103}$ which matches that in the Coalport pattern-book of the early 1820s.

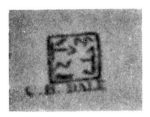

An impressed mark made up of the word 'COALBROOKDALE' in circular form occurs on some very rare porcelain plaques which were not all necessarily decorated at the factory, as one is signed E. Doe—the name of a talented independent decorator. Another plaque bears the incised mark 'J. Rose & Co. Coalport', the painting being by the former Derby artist William Corden, and is dated 1822.

Some blue-printed ware of the 1810–15 period bear a printed mark basically showing a Chinese-style square with 'C. B. Dale' below. This is very rare, but occurs on pieces bearing a willow-pattern-type design. The mark $\frac{\text{C.B.}}{100}$, or similar pattern numbers expressed under the initials C.B., relate to the porcelain made in Staffordshire by Charles Bourne during the 1810–30 period, not to 'Coalbrook Dale' or 'Coalport' ware.

From June 1820 some large circular printed marks occur, denoting the fact that on May 30th, 1820, the Society of Arts awarded John Rose & Co the Gold Medal for a glaze free of the poisoning agent, lead. The name 'J. Rose & Co' (or 'Rose & Co') and the place-name 'Coalport' are incorporated in these marks. At least five variations of this mark occur (see opposite). The first is extremely rare and is probably the earliest of these Society of Arts marks. The second and third are also rare; the fourth is the variation most often found; the fifth has the additional word 'Improved' before the description 'Felspar Porcelain'—and it is therefore probably of slightly later date than the previous four. One or other of these printed marks is normally found on porcelain of the 1820s, but at least one example has been recorded where one appears on a mug bearing a print of the 1851 Exhibition. As a general rule, however, the circular Society of Arts mark was not used after 1830.

On most examples of these 1820-plus Society of Arts marks, the name 'I Rose & Co' or 'J Rose & Co' appears below the main mark; but it may occur above.

Some fine-quality Coalport porcelains of the 1820–30 period, including superb floral-encrusted 'Coalbrookdale'-type porcelain (see Plates 177–95 and

19

Pages 74–77) bear name or initial marks—'Coalport'; 'Coalbrookdale'; 'C Dale'; 'CD'; or the crossed-swords mark of Dresden painted in underglaze blue. The latter also occurs on other English porcelain, notably that of Derby and Minton. The reader should be warned that the name or initial marks have, in recent years, been added to later porcelain in an effort to enhance its interest. These added marks are in overglaze enamel which can be felt with a fingernail to be on top of the glaze—not below it, as is the case with the originals. Some floral-encrusted Coalport porcelain bears the initials 'W.T.', but some Minton marks also incorporate these initials.

Coalport.   *Dale*   *D*

From *c.* 1822, when he purchased the moulds of the Swansea works and of the Nantgarw factory, John Rose may occasionally have used their standard marks, comprising the words S W A N S E A and N A N T G A R W, on his own porcelain made at Coalport, as both these Welsh factories enjoyed a wide reputation for the quality of their porcelain.

In the 1820s and 1830s several printed marks were used—although only occasionally, as most Coalport porcelain of the period is unmarked. These rare printed marks incorporate the words 'Coalport' or 'Coalbrookdale' and 'John Rose & Co', or the initials 'J' (or 'I') 'R. & Co'. The last mark reproduced occurs with the initials 'J R & Co' or 'I R & Co' in the ribbon below.

However, some specimens bear the name and address of the retailer through whom the ware was supplied. The six examples following appear in the Coalport rag-book (which includes pulls from engraved copper plates once used by the factory and is in the nature of a record file of Coalport engraved crests and marks). The first mark reproduced is unusual in that the name of the manufacturer is given with that of the retailer. The marks incorporating the place-names 'Windsor Castle', 'St James's Palace' are examples only: the same basic marks were engraved with the names of other Royal palaces (see Plate 174) or residences, but, of course, these porcelains seldom appear on the market.

During the 1830s and 1840s the majority of Coalport porcelain was unmarked, as is proved by pieces bearing the diamond-shaped registration mark (Page 71), but no factory mark, and I have been unable to trace any factory marks on the many shapes depicted in the Coalport traveller's design-book (see Page 74 and Plates 220–8). Otherwise, the identification of Coalport porcelain of this period   21

General history prior
to 1850, with résumé
of factory marks

largely depends on known shapes (identified as Coalport by reference to the Patent Office records, see Plates 128, 129, 147, and 149). Other specimens, and often other forms, can be correctly attributed by comparing the pattern number and the design with the original Coalport pattern-books, many of which have been preserved (see Pages 79–80). Some useful ware of the 1840s, 1850s and 1860s bear impressed workmen's marks such as stars or letters (often impressed twice on the same object); but as similar signs appear on the products of other factories, they are not very helpful to present-day students or collectors.

The Victoria and Albert Museum has two very fine-quality plates, presented to them in 1850 by John Rose. These are inscribed 'John Rose. Colebrook Dale. 1850', showing that the name Colebrookdale was still used at the period. A parian figure of Wellington, of the same period, is marked 'Made at Coalbrook Dale': note here the alternative spelling of Coalbrook Dale. The name also occurs as one word, but at the time was more often written as two. The impressed mark 'John Rose & Co' is found on some mid-nineteenth-century Coalport porcelain, but is rare.

Many decorative copies of Chelsea or Sèvres porcelain bear imitations of the original marks. Joseph Marryat in his *A History of Pottery and Porcelain Medieval and Modern* of 1850 had cause to note; 'We regret to have observed upon some recent specimens of this (Coalport) manufacture marks of double L and anchor, in imitation of Sèvres and Chelsea.' Sometimes these copied marks have the initial 'c' added, but this is not always present. In general, the anchor mark on Coalport porcelain is larger than that on genuine Chelsea porcelain, where it does not exceed a quarter of an inch in height.

The useful ware—tea, dessert, and dinner services of the 1850–70 period—like the earlier ware is seldom marked. But the fine quality decorative cabinet pieces, centrepieces and vases of the 1851–61 period often bear a monogram of the initials C.B.D. (see below) which on the finest pieces is generally in gold.

From *c*. 1861 to 1875 the painted or gilt ampersand-shaped mark incorporating the initials C.S.N. (for Caughley or Coalport, Swansea and Nantgarw, factories taken over by John Rose) appears on good-quality porcelain, and occasionally the name 'Coalport' or 'English Porcelain, Coalport' is found with this basic ampersand-shaped mark. Several other printed marks were also used at this period, some of which incorporate the ampersand-like device and the names 'Coalport' or 'Salopian'. An example is reproduced below.

In about 1875 the printed or painted two-line mark 'Coalport. A.D. 1750' was used. This was superseded in 1881 by the printed mark of the crown over the word 'Coalport', with 'A.D. 1750' (the claimed, but incorrect, date of establishment of the Caughley works purchased by John Rose in 1799). This standard mark was used on all Coalport porcelain after 1881, with its later variations comprising the addition of the word 'England' in 1891, superseded by 'Made in England' from about 1920.

With the advent of the crown mark, impressed potting-date marks were employed, taking the form '14 J 8', '20 A 23', for example, indicating the month and year that the piece was potted. The decoration may well be of *slightly* later date. Printed postwar marks include the following. Some slight variations occur, mainly in the addition of the names of special patterns.

The old floral-encrusted Coalbrookdale type ware was reintroduced in the 1960s, bearing the written mark 'Coalbrookdale by Coalport. Made in England'. Copies of old porcelain cottage pastille-burners were introduced in January 1963. These, when sent from the factory, bear modern marks. The first early

23

General history prior
to 1850, with résumé
of factory marks

examples made in 1963 had the standard Coalport printed mark, but this was soon amended to a script mark reading:

The Umbrella House (or other title according to the model)
   by Coalport
   Fine Bone China.
   Made in England.

In some cases these printed marks have been erased and the modern cottages offered in auction sales and some shops, presumably as antique examples. In order to stop this despicable practice, the year of manufacture has recently been incised into the porcelain base during manufacture. It is worth noting that the underside of the base of all such cottages is fully glazed and should be equally glossy; any matt patch should be regarded with suspicion, as in erasing the printed mark the glaze is often damaged, destroying the original surface gloss.

CHAPTER II

EXCAVATIONS ON THE CAUGHLEY SITE AND THE IDENTIFICATION OF EARLY COALPORT PORCELAIN

The Caughley factory was situated on high ground across the River Severn, slightly downstream from John Rose's Coalport factory and some two miles away. In October 1799 John Rose and his partners, Edward Blakeway and Richard Rose, 'porcelain manufacturers', purchased the leases relating to the Caughley porcelain works with the colliery and grinding mills from Thomas Turner, so that from 1799 John Rose had two porcelain factories—one at Coalport and one at Caughley. The map reproduced as Plate 1 shows the relative position of the two factories.

Nineteenth-century writers stated that from 1799 the John Rose porcelain was made and fired at Caughley and was then transported to Coalport to be decorated. Factory wasters found on the Caughley site prove, however, that the underglaze-blue portions of patterns demanding this colour were added at Caughley and that most, if not all, examples were glazed at Caughley. Some factory wasters found at Caughley were fully decorated with overglaze enamel colours and gilding, but admittedly these finished pieces were rather rare and seem confined to the 1799–1805 period. This fact underlines the point made by the ceramics historian Llewellynn Jewitt, in 1862, that the Caughley workmen were gradually moved to Coalport; and it would seem that at first some post-1799 John Rose porcelain was completely decorated at Caughley, but that after about 1805 the *overglaze* decoration was carried out at Coalport.

The same Llewellynn Jewitt (who went to great pains to visit ceramic centres and interview, where possible, former workmen to get first-hand information on

Excavations on the
Caughley site and the
identification of early
Coalport porcelain

the manufactories about which he wrote) in an article published in the *Art Journal* of March 1862 (that is, within the lifetime of some former employees) recorded:

> The coal at Caughley beginning to work out, and the cost of carrying the unfinished ware from thence down the hill and across the water to Coalport was so great,—the unfinished ware being carried on women's heads the whole distance,—that Mr. Rose determined to remove the works to Coalport, which he did at different times, gradually drafting off the workmen, until about 1814 or 1815 when they were finally removed, the kilns and rooms taken down, and the materials used for the enlargement of the works at Coalport . . .

The assertion that production at the Caughley site ceased in 1814 or 1815 has been repeated by subsequent writers and has apparently never been questioned. It would appear to be confirmed by the fact that in 1814 John Rose purchased the rival factory run by his brother, Thomas Rose, with Robert Anstice and Robert Horton (see Chapter IV), which was separated from his own only by a narrow canal, so that its acquisition saved the carriage of breakable porcelain from the very inconvenient Caughley site. It is, then, reasonable to assume that, on acquiring the neighbouring factory, he would have closed the Caughley factory, if this had not already been done.

It would therefore appear that for some fifteen years, from 1799, some of John Rose's porcelain was made at the Caughley factory formerly run by Thomas Turner. This fact, although previously known, has hitherto seemed of little importance; but it is now of vital importance, for opencast clay mining is being carried on and this has exposed many of the dumped factory wasters— unglazed as well as glazed fragments, some of large size, and partly decorated specimens which, for one reason or another, were rejected as being unsuitable to complete or transport to Coalport. Selections of these fragments which, in general, were found less than 18 inches below the surface, and many of which, owing to the removal of much of the topsoil by the clay-mining company, were lying on the surface, are reproduced in Plates 78–89. Many plaster-of-Paris moulds were also discovered (see Plate 77) and from these much porcelain of the period was moulded.

These fragments, representing John Rose's porcelain of the 1799–1814 period, are especially important, as Coalport porcelain of this period is generally unmarked and, being unlike the later marked ware, the early pieces have been classified as Chamberlain-Worcester, and other factories, in error. In them, therefore, we have the key to the true identification of early Coalport porcelain—the range of which will surprise many collectors.

Before dealing with the fragments in detail, one complication must be stated. This is that, generally, pre-1799 Caughley porcelain fragments were found with post-1799 Coalport period porcelain, there being no clear-cut line or other division on the site between the two. This may have been due to the fact that the factories' mode of management was the same, and that the same Caughley hands

26

dumped the Coalport wasters in the same places that they used for the earlier Caughley ware. The site may also have been disturbed over the years from 1814. Part of it was certainly greatly disturbed by bulldozers when I first visited the site during the early summer of 1965. It is, of course, in most cases possible to distinguish between the pre-1799 Caughley and the later Coalport porcelain by the shape, style of decoration, body of the porcelain, and its translucency; but some few transitional fragments offer difficulties of attribution.

The majority of fragments can be clearly recognized either as Caughley or post-1799 Coalport ware. The post-1799 John Rose fragments, for instance, do not show the characteristic Caughley orange colour by transmitted light; the body is thicker in the potting; and the glaze is glassy and thickly applied. Other shapes can be dated to the early 1800s by comparison with surviving dated pieces, but nevertheless a great many fragments are difficult to date and to ascribe definitely to Thomas Turner's Caughley period or the post-1799 period when Messrs Rose, Blakeway & Co of Coalport managed the former Caughley factory. With the help of Dr Bernard Watney and his ultra-violet lamp, however, it has proved possible to differentiate between marked, obviously Caughley, porcelain and fragments which can be proved to be of nineteenth-century date and therefore made by Messrs Rose, Blakeway & Co. This is possible, as the unglazed Rose, Blakeway & Co fragments show under ultra-violet light a purple colour far deeper than that shown by the Caughley fragments.

The differences between the two bodies lies in the basic ingredient. The standard Thomas Turner pre-1799 Caughley porcelain is of the type known as a soapstone body because it contains a relatively high percentage of magnesia (about 11 per cent),[1] whereas the post-1799 John Rose porcelain, made on the same Caughley site, is of a totally different composition containing little more than a trace of magnesia. Sample fragments of typical 1800–10 period John Rose lobed-edge plates (as depicted in Colour Plate I; Plates 13, 24, 26, 28, 30–3, etc.) found on the Caughley site were tested for me at the Ceramic Testing Laboratory of the North Staffordshire College of Technology at Stoke-on-Trent and gave the following analyses:

	%
Silica	75·94
Alumina	18·95
Potash	2·12
Soda	1·21
Lime	0·78
Ferric oxide	0·34
Magnesia	0·17
Titanic oxide	0·02
Loss, calcines at 950°C	0·33
	99·86

[1] See my *Caughley and Worcester Porcelains 1775–1800* (1969), page 118.

Excavations on the
Caughley site and the
identification of early
Coalport porcelain

The post-1799 porcelain is of an extremely heavy, compact body which, when broken, shows an almost conchoidal fracture like that found in true hard-paste porcelain—quite unlike the granular fracture found in the normal soft-paste body. The characteristic of hard-paste porcelain is that the second firing, after glazing, is at a higher temperature than the first, or bisque, firing—which is not the case with the manufacture of the normal soft-paste body; and it is noticeable that the glazed site-fragments display the hard-paste characteristics to a far greater extent than the unglazed once-fired fragments.

The difficulty is to decide when the change was made from the normal Thomas Turner Caughley soapstone body to the new, compact, hard-paste composition. Did Thomas Turner continue his old Worcester/Caughley soapstone-type body up to the 1799 sale of the leases to John Rose, who could then have introduced his own new body? or did Thomas Turner himself introduce a new, harder body in the 1790s?

Mr David Holgate has suggested to me that it is significant that the patent giving the New Hall partners sole rights to the hard-paste materials for the manufacture of porcelain (but not earthenware) became ineffective in 1796, permitting any manufacturer to use the key Cornish clay if he so wished. As the New Hall Company had prospered and made its name by this period, it seems likely that some potters would have experimented and adopted the newly released material and made a type of hard-paste porcelain for themselves.

On the evidence of the 1798 jug, illustrated in Plate 100, John Rose at Coalport was using a heavy, compact, hard-paste porcelain by this date; but we cannot at the moment be sure if this new type of body was also in use at Thomas Turner's near-by Caughley factory, or if it was introduced there when John Rose and his partners took over in 1799. It is to be hoped that a key dated example of Caughley porcelain will be discovered to prove what type was being produced by Thomas Turner at Coalport between 1796 and 1799. As the 1798 John Rose jug shown in Plate 100 was made from the new paste, I have found it convenient to regard all pieces of this new, heavy, compact paste as being made by John Rose. Hence, the hard-paste fragments (and the related whole articles) found on the Caughley site have been regarded as post-1799 John Rose porcelain, rather than Thomas Turner's Caughley porcelain. Further evidence may come to light proving that this demarcation is incorrect and that the hard-paste porcelains were made at Caughley a few years prior to 1799; but until it does, the basic differences between the two bodies offer a clear-cut and convenient division between the pre-1799 Caughley porcelain and the post-1799 porcelain made at Caughley under the Coalport management. This post-1799 porcelain is henceforth termed 'Coalport' in this book, rather than 'Caughley' (a term favoured by previous writers), for it was made under the Coalport management, some pieces being decorated at the parent Coalport factory and the finished ware most certainly sold as 'Coalport' or 'Coalbrook Dale', even though it may have been formed at Caughley. In my opinion, Caughley should be regarded as purely an eighteenth-century factory, having ceased when the leases were sold to the Coalport partners in 1799.

28

The Coalport fragments fall into three main divisions: (*a*) Dinner- and dessert-ware; (*b*) Teaware; and (*c*) Ornamental objects. The range of fragments and their matching finished objects will be discussed in this order. Patterns found on the site will be discussed last.

Dinner Services (Plates 12–21)

The first, so far, identified type of John Rose dinner service is represented by the sauce-tureen and cover shown in Plate 12. The shape is a very close copy of the standard Chinese 'Nankin' export-market tureen so popular from about 1780 into the nineteenth century. The underglaze-blue scenic design and border motif are also strongly reminiscent of these Chinese Nankin dinner services.

This type of blue and white dinner service surely links with the 'Coalport China Warehouse' advertisement of 1802, quoted in full on Page 11:

> Coalport Table services . . . called British Nankeen so exactly like the foreign, both as to shape, colour, etc. . . . exactly like the old fine dark blue stone-ware, or Nankeen, at 25 guineas . . .'

These Chinese Nankin-styled Coalport dinner services would appear to be very rare—far rarer than the services with oval tureens (see Plates 13–16), the shape of which seem far better suited to the European styles of decoration.

The basic Coalport dinner service forms of the 1800–10 period are shown in Plates 13–16. Unglazed portions of oval soup-tureens and the smaller sauce-tureens were found. Interesting characteristics of these soup-tureens are the lop-sided side handles—presumably intentional, as all examples are the same—and the fact that the knobs on the covers are slightly turned to one side (see Plate 14). Several fragments of matching salad-bowls—both oval and of lobed square form—were found, as were many pieces of the oval lobed-edged platters or meat-dishes. These platters, made in various sizes, often have impressed numbers underneath, the numbers indicating the size of the dish. Unglazed, as well as glazed, fragments so marked were found on the site.

The plates found with the standard Coalport services of the 1800–10 period have six indentations around the edge, so that they are slightly lobed. The Caughley site is littered with fragments of these, unglazed as well as glazed and partly decorated, and all are of the John Rose hard-paste body. They are found with dinner and dessert sets, and were also decorated to serve as purely ornamental cabinet plates.

Many of them were sold in the white undecorated state to independent decorators, one example in Earl Spencer's collection being signed by Thomas Baxter and bearing the early date 1801. Later examples by this talented London decorator are dated 1808 and 1809 and are illustrated in Plate 92. Similar lobed-edged plates bear the signature marks of Thomas Pardoe, the Bristol decorator. Several are inscribed John Taylor, while others bear the name mark of Donovan, the Dublin retailer and decorator. Other outside-decorated Coalport plates of this type are displayed in the Victoria and Albert Museum.

Excavations on the
Caughley site and the
identification of early
Coalport porcelain

A wide variety of styles of decoration can be found on these lobed-edged Coalport plates of the 1800–10 period, some of which are illustrated in Colour Plate I and Plates 32, 33, 90, 92, 96, and 98, including the standard printed Coalport designs like, for instance, the dragon patterns (see Plates 24, 84, and 87). These plates are nearly always classed as Worcester, though no marked Worcester examples have been recorded and two of those illustrated in this book bear early Coalport marks and, furthermore, link with the very many fragments found on the factory site, and as I have stated, all examples are of the typical John Rose hard-paste body.

Most early Coalport dinner services of the 1800–10 period are of the type shown in Plates 13–16, with oval tureens and platters, though a version with moulded basketwork edging was used and may date from 1802 (see Page 12). However, another basic dinner-service design was used, having rather tall oblong tureens with the top knob in the form of a basket of fruit, and with platters also of curved oblong form (see Plate 20). Some fine dinner- and soup-plates, as well as dishes and related dinnerware, bear an attractive raised design (see Plate 22), a mould for which, with some fragments of the pattern, was found on the Caughley site.

Dessert Services (Plates 23–33)

The earliest type of Coalport dessert services closely match the dinner services, with their oval soup-tureens and dishes, and their sauce-tureens, which are scaled-down versions of those in the dinner services with different handles at the ends. Many unglazed fragments of these—including knobs and handles—were found on the site, together with fragments of the oval centrepieces and unglazed and glazed pieces of the various side dishes seen in early Coalport dessert services. These dishes exist for the most part in three shapes—square, shaped oval, and heart-shaped—all of which can be seen in Plate 24. The dessert-plates are of the same slightly lobed, circular form as the dinner-plates, but smaller, having an average diameter of 8¼ inches instead of 9½ inches. Again, the approximate date, *c.* 1800–10, of these dessert services can be gauged from dated examples of the lobed plates which were sold in the white and painted by independent decorators.

A rare form of pre-1814 Coalport dessert service is shown in Plate 31, a service in the Royal Collection at Buckingham Palace. Apart from the lobed-edged plates, numerous fragments of which litter the Caughley site, two sections of such sauce tureens were found on the site, matching in form the tureens of the Royal service with their moulded bottom border and unusual handle form.

Several unglazed, as well as glazed, fragments of fruit-coolers (or ice-pails) were also found. These objects, made in three parts—the main body, the liner and the cover—were originally part of large, expensive dessert services (see Page 12), but were also supplied in pairs on their own: '2 pair of rich pattern Colebrook Dale Ice pails £4' (Christie's sale, July 12th, 1815, see Page 145). The ice-pail shape shown in Plates 25 and 31 also occurs in Caughley porcelain of the 1790–9 period.

Excavations on the
Caughley site and the
identification of early
Coalport porcelain

Tea Services (Plates 34–75)

The Caughley site has yielded fragments of at least six *basic* forms of tea service of the Coalport period, as well as some fragments of which only teapots have as yet been found to match. There were, of course, also many fragments of pre-1799 Caughley teaware.

The first type of teaset (termed Class A) to be attributed to the John Rose period is rather problematical, since many collectors will perhaps regard them as late Caughley rather than post-1799 Coalport made under the John Rose management. The basic shape of the teapot and covered sugar-basin is oval in plan—of 'bell' shape, to use the contemporary term—but it was issued with various moulded flutings. The shapes are shown in Plates 34–7.

My reasons for attributing this teaware to the post-1799 Coalport period are:

(*a*) All examples known to me, and the site fragments, are of the new hard-paste body, not of Thomas Turner's soapstone body.

(*b*) No examples appear to have been decorated with Caughley underglaze-blue printed designs or bear pre-1799 Caughley marks.

(*c*) Examples do not show the normal Caughley footrim with the inner angle wiped clear of glaze. The footrim is, on the other hand, similar to obviously post-1800 John Rose porcelain.

It could well be argued that the oval 'bell' shape of teapot was in use at Worcester by at least 1796 (a 1796-dated Chamberlain-Worcester oval teapot of this *general* type is shown in my *Illustrated Encyclopaedia of British Pottery and Porcelain*, Plate 104), but it is equally true that the Chamberlain firm continued selling this type of oval teapot into the 1800s, as is proved by their accounts.

As a general rule, the porcelain manufacturers did not *suddenly* drop an old shape, although from time to time new basic forms were introduced. The previous shape or shapes were still available and the customer could choose which form he preferred. It is possible to tell, in some instances, when a new form was in use, but it is dangerous to state when it ceased to be made. The oval 'bell' type of Class A teapot was probably made up to at least 1805, although by then Classes B and C (see Page 32) were also being made; and the same added decoration can be found on the different basic shapes. It can also happen that a service contains odd pieces of an earlier form.

Class A Teaware (Plates 34–7)

As stated above, these teapot forms are oval in plan with a 'bell'-shaped body, the basic forms being found in the plain unembellished state, with wide straight fluting, with straight convex ribbing, or with spiral fluting.

The characteristic John Rose shapes can be discovered by comparing the finished articles with the very numerous unglazed and glazed fragments found on the Caughley site. The comparison with these key fragments is most

Excavations on the
Caughley site and the
identification of early
Coalport porcelain

important, for very similar shapes were made by other manufacturers of the period.[1]

The characteristic features of the John Rose teapots are illustrated in Plate 37, with the knob, as drawn below, oval with twelve straight ribs (not curved as in Chamberlain examples) forming twelve recessed panels, the ribs carried over to the underside of the umbrella-shaped knob. These knobs are quite characteristic and serve also to identify the matching covered sugar basins. But the John Rose spout offers another useful guide to distinguish between these teapots and similar forms made by other manufacturers. The lower part of the spout has ten raised ribs separating ten flutes, and the looped line separating these ornamental features from the plain top section of the spout is at an angle of about forty-five degrees from the vertical (see Plate 37). The characteristic handle is plainly seen in Plate 34 and in the comparative illustrations.

In the oval covered sugar-basins found with these early John Rose teasets, shown in Plate 34, the knob, seen above, is the main tell-tale feature. The cream-jugs are of two types: one tall, of elegant 'bell' shape with an 'S' handle, the later variety oval with straight sides and angular handle (see Plates 33 and 34). Both handle-less tea-bowls and handled cups may be found in these early teasets, but the small spoon-tray and covered tea-canister found with the earlier Thomas Turner Caughley porcelain teasets are not found with the John Rose services.

As with subsequent John Rose tea-service shapes, these oval 'bell'-shaped teapots and related ware would appear to have been closely copied by the rival Coalport firm of Anstice, Horton & (Thomas) Rose (see Chapter IV, Page 57, and Plates 36–7).

Class B Teaware (Plate 38)

For a short period from about 1800 a straight-sided form of teapot, sucrier and creamer was employed. The teapot is of general New Hall type, with a circular raised 'turret' forming the filling aperture, and the cover has a neat, oval, bud-like knob. The covered sugar-basin has a simple oval plan with upright sides—relieved by a moulded border near the base—with moulded mock ring handles at each end, and a cover which has the same bud-like knob as the teapot.

The creamer is also oval, with a simple handle with flat top, and is very similar to that employed at Mintons in about 1800—although the Coalport example is of

[1] The reader should be warned that the teapot illustrated in Plate 201 of the *Transactions of the English Ceramic Circle*, Vol. 6, part 3, does *not* as is claimed, match fragments found on the Caughley site. This teapot is quite different in spout, handle, and knob from the normal Coalport examples, and I cannot agree that the E.C.C. illustration depicts a Caughley teapot decorated by the Chamberlain firm.

harder porcelain. The teasets of this rare type have handled teacups and straight-sided coffee-cans.

The shapes found with this form of early Coalport teaset are illustrated in Plate 38. As yet I have not discovered or identified any pieces of this form which might have been made by the rival firm of Anstice, Horton & (Thomas) Rose; but this is not to say that examples were not made.

This basic B form was soon superseded by Class C, but some services comprise a mixture of the two forms, e.g. a Class B sucrier with a Class C teapot.

Class C Teaware (Plates 40–1)

From about 1803 a new type of teaware design was introduced having oval *straight*-sided teapots (without the Class B turret) and sugar-basins. The basic type of creamer is retained from the earlier oval teasets of Classes A and B, as is the teacup and the straight-sided coffee-can form with slight variations in the handles. The most noticeable feature of these teasets is the graceful curved handle and the neat, narrow, oval knob to the teapot and sucrier covers (see Plates 40–1).

Straight-sided oval teapots and covered sugars were also featured in tea services made by the Spode and Minton factories during the period *c.* 1798–1805, but these can be easily distinguished by their thinner potting and light weight from the thicker, heavy Coalport examples with their hard body. The Minton teapots do not have the double-curved handle with a kick (or return) at the bottom, which is a characteristic of the Spode and Coalport pots. In shape the Spode and Coalport oval teapots are very similar, although other pieces in the service vary considerably. Noticeably, the Spode creamer and cup handles have the same double-curved handles as the teapot, whereas the Coalport pieces have simple curved handles.

There is abundant proof, in the form of factory wasters, that these straight-sided oval teapots, with their companion pieces, were made at the Caughley site. Numerous fragments from matching covered sugars, creamers, and cups were also found, as was—most interesting of all—half a mould from which the teapot handles were formed.

John Rose's practice of selling white porcelain to other decorators (which may well have been a natural continuation of Turner's policy of selling his white Caughley porcelain to Chamberlains and other decorators) had apparently already been established at this period, *c.* 1804, for a straight-sided oval sugar-bowl base, apparently of Coalport make, is marked 'Billingsley Mansfield N.54'. William Billingsley, formerly a Derby ceramic artist, established several small porcelain works or decorating establishments after leaving Derby—one of them being at Mansfield, which he apparently left in or before 1804. The existence of this marked 'Billingsley Mansfield' Coalport-type sugar in the Lincoln Museum indicates that this basic form of Coalport teaset was in production in or before 1804. I have an initialled Caughley/Coalport covered sugar of similar type which is dated 1806.

This type of teaware was very closely copied by John Rose's rival firm of Anstice, Horton & Rose (see Chapter IV and Plate 41).

33

Excavations on the
Caughley site and the
identification of early
Coalport porcelain

Class D Teaware (Plates 42–7)

The fourth type of Coalport teaware was introduced by 1807, for dated examples are known (see Plate 44). It was still in favour in 1810 and was apparently the standard Coalport form of the period, for it is featured in Thomas Baxter's drawing of his father's London decorating-studio in 1810, reproduced in Plate 42, the original of which is in the Victoria and Albert Museum. The notice pinned to the wall is headed 'New Price List. Coalport White China', emphasizing the trade in undecorated Coalport porcelain, which was sold to numerous decorators and some small factories. Unfortunately, it was on such a small scale that Baxter did not attempt to copy the list in detail, though there are sixty lines of articles arranged in three columns, but represented only by lines of pigment. Teaware of Class D can be seen on the workbench, but, while the arrangement of similarly shaped objects has been reproduced in Plate 43, it has not been possible to match the patterns or undecorated blanks depicted in the original drawing.

The main features of Class D teaware can be readily seen. The oval boat-shaped teapots have a spout coming directly from the lines of the body without a break, rather in the form of the prow of a boat. The form of handle, with an inward step, is repeated on the cream-jug. The handle of the oval-covered sugar, which takes the form of a relief-moulded animal (or demon's) face with a half ring falling from the mouth, is distinctive and would seem unique to the Coalport factories. It is totally fixed to the body of the basin and is therefore a decorative feature rather than a useful handle.

As can be seen from Thomas Baxter's 1810 drawing and the reconstructed group of teaware (Plates 42 and 43), this basic shape was used in plain form, in simple broad fluting (middle distance), and in spiral fluted (rear teapot) variations.

A variation of this standard D form of teaset, with a prow spout to the teapot and moulded animal-head handles to the oval sucrier, has teapots and creamers with a different handle form which joins the body at two points at the lower end. Several unglazed handles of this type were found on the Caughley site (see Plate 52).

A further variation occurs (Plates 55 and 57) in which the main differences are that the spout no longer appears to arise naturally from the flowing lines of the body but is applied as a separate unit; there is a moulded ornamental bridge joining the spout to the shoulder of the pot; and the handle is of a simple, graceful curve (with thumb grip at the top) instead of the instepped handle shown in the 1810 drawing. The basic shapes of the other pieces—such as covered sugars, creamers, bowls and cups—are the same as those included in teasets with the 1810 simple boat-shaped teapot.

Another slight variation of the boat-shaped teapot has a moulded ring handle of twig form, an unglazed teapot cover of this type having been found on the site, as was a mould for the twig knob. Similar oval sucriers of the same general shape as the animal-headed variety have handles of different forms (see Plate 56), but these variations are very rarely found.

The numerous fragments of Class D teaware found on the Caughley site included both forms of fluting—spiral and straight—as well as the plain basic shape. Pieces of covered sugar basins with the animal-head handles were found, both unglazed and decorated, and many fragments of teapots, all of which help to differentiate between John Rose's teasets and the very similar examples made by the rival works of Anstice, Horton & Rose (see Chapter IV and Plates 45, 46, and 47).

Class E Teaware (Plates 61 and 62)

The next form of Coalport teaware would appear to be restricted to the Coalport and Minton[1] factories. The shapes are difficult to describe and the reader should refer to Plate 61, where the basic forms are clearly illustrated. The ornamental bridge motif has been carried over from the Class D teapot (Plate 57), although here there is no airspace under the bridge. The knob is in the form of an ornamental finial or bud. The handle has mock screw-, rivet-, or bolt-heads at the top and bottom, as if the handle was fixed by these means. These mock bolt-heads occur on several other pieces of Coalport porcelain of the 1810–15 period.

The cup forms in teasets of Class E are basically different from the simple curved teacups and straight-sided coffee-cans found in teaware of Classes A, B, C, and D. The E-shaped cups have turned, stepped profiles with upswept handles —a characteristic repeated in the waste bowls, which previously had been of simple outline. These new cup forms, which can be seen in Plates 61, 65, 69, 72, and 73, also occur on teasets made at Coalport after 1815, when the Caughley works were closed. Some unglazed fragments of this form of cup were found with sharp, high, narrow ribbing; but as yet no matching finished examples have been reported.

As with all other teasets previously discussed, matching fragments of them were found on the pre-1815 Caughley site; and also the shapes were closely copied at Messrs Anstice, Horton & Rose's factory at Coalport (see Chapter IV).

Class F Teaware (Plates 63–7)

The last type of Coalport tea service to link with factory wasters found on the pre-1815 Caughley site is that illustrated in Plates 63–7. The teapot handle, spout, and knob are well modelled, but this moulded modelling is often blunted by the added glaze and gilding. The teaset shown in Plate 64 bears the painted pattern number '315', which matches this design in the factory pattern-book and indicates that this pattern number had been reached before the Caughley works (where matching unglazed fragments of these shapes were found) closure in 1814.

A slight variation of this basic shape occurs with a shaped top edge to the teapot and sucrier, and with a long leaf-like moulded design on the top of the spout. Such a service, of pattern 385, is shown in Plate 65 against the design drawn in the factory pattern-book. A similar set, with a different form of creamer and earlier cup shapes, is shown in Plate 66. Other amendments of this basic shape have various flutings, or a moulded ribbed body to the teapot and matching pieces. A marked teapot of this ribbed form is shown in Plate 67.

A further variation occurs with an ornate, raised, moulded, floral design with

[1] See G. Godden's *Minton Pottery and Porcelain of the First Period, 1793–1850* (1968), Plate 16.

Excavations on the
Caughley site and the
identification of early
Coalport porcelain

reserve panels. A mould for such a pattern was found on the Caughley site, as well as some glazed fragments. This basic moulded design is also found on plates and dishes (see Plate 22).

Although this teaware is the last to link with fragments found on the pre-1815 factory site, there is a further shape of Coalport teaware which must have been introduced before this period because the forms were also made by the rival Anstice, Horton & Thomas Rose partnership, which was dissolved in February, 1814 (see Page 53).

This new form (Class G) pre-1814 Coalport teaware is illustrated in Plate 74, with Anstice examples shown in Plate 75. It is not certain why fragments were not found on the factory site, but it seems probable that Jewitt was correct in stating (see Page 26) that the workpeople were gradually moved from Caughley to the Coalport works and that production declined before the final closure and demolition of the Caughley buildings, so that this pre-1814 Class G teaware was formed at Coalport rather than at Caughley. A rather similar form of tea service was made at the Welsh Nantgarw factory (see E. Morton Nance's *The Pottery and Porcelain of Swansea and Nantgarw*, Plate CLXI).

Later, post-1815, teaware from the Coalport factory is discussed in Chapter V and is illustrated in Plates 151–65.

The teaware listed on the previous pages is of the general, standard forms most commonly found. It would appear, however, that some other rare shapes were produced. Quite recently I found the charming small teapot shown in Plate 49, which is a scaled-down version of the Class D teapots with prow-like spout but having several important differences, such as a ring twig-like handle to the cover, while the main handle incorporates a lug to hold the cover in place when the teapot is tipped up for pouring. There is also a strange hump in the body, under the handle aperture. An unglazed cover showing part of the twig handle and a fragment showing the slight hump in the body were found on the Caughley site, where the pre-1815 Coalport porcelain was produced, and two moulds for the twig-like ring handle were also found. I have discovered only the teapot of this type and, as yet, no matching creamer, covered sugar or other piece to indicate if such teapots were made as individual articles or as part of a service.

The teapot shown in Plate 59, against the design in the Coalport pattern-book, constitutes a further rare form of Coalport teapot of the 1810 period. The new form of knob should be noted, for which matching covered sugar-basins or other teaware have not as yet been reported.

At least one further class of pre-1815 Coalport teapot should exist, having a finely modelled twig handle to the cover, and borders of moulded ribbing, incorporating four slightly larger plain flutes. A plaster mould for such a teapot or sugar-bowl cover was found on the site, but no matching finished piece has yet been discovered.

In addition to tea- and coffee-cups, many unglazed fragments of large-sized breakfast cups were found, showing that breakfast services as well as tea sets were made. Such items as covered muffin- or toast-dishes, jam-pots, and egg-cups and egg-cup stands were included in such sets.

Excavations on the
Caughley site and the
identification of early
Coalport porcelain

The *vast* majority of fragments found on the Caughley site were of useful ware—pieces of dinner, dessert, or tea services. Many were of very small size and of little interest, apart from underlining the point that the main output of the Caughley factory during the Rose period, as at the earlier Turner period, was devoted to useful ware. Nevertheless, some ornamental objects were made prior to 1815, and fragments were found which identify some of this rare and un-marked ornamental ware. Many other objects were undoubtedly made, but factory wasters relating to them have not as yet been discovered.

Ornamental Ware

For the purpose of this section, ornamental ware has been taken to include all objects not normally found in dinner, dessert, or tea services, although their use may be utilitarian as well as ornamental.

Several pieces of early John Rose ware very closely copy the earlier Thomas Turner Caughley porcelain, both in form and in the added blue-printed designs, some of which seem to have been taken from the original engraved copper plates used at Caughley.

The small cream boats (called 'Chelsea ewers' at Caughley) are cases in point (see Plate 78). In shape, they are simplified versions of the Caughley—the foot being straight and not arched into small feet as on the Caughley examples, the handle also being simplified and no longer showing the snake(?)-head at the bottom juncture. Unglazed fragments of both versions were found on the Caughley site and are shown with the complete creamers in Plate 78.

The underglaze blue is lighter and brighter on the John Rose examples than on the Caughley ones, the potting is thicker and the glaze has not contracted or been wiped away from inside the footrim, as happened with the pre-1799 Caughley examples; and, of course, the porcelain body is of the later hard-paste type.

The deep oblong dish, $11\frac{1}{2}$ inches $\times$ 8 inches, illustrated in Plate 79, is decorated with an all-over underglaze-blue print of formal flower-and-branch pattern. Fragments of other articles bearing this design were found on the Caughley site, as were fragments of similar dishes. This object, and similar deep dishes, may have been a part of a dinner service, as it bears the same printed pattern as dinner-plate and dish fragments, but I have not as yet discovered one still in such a service. At least two different forms of these oblong dishes were made.

The flower-pots (or jardinières) and stands illustrated in Plate 80 are of a type normally attributed to Chamberlain's factory at Worcester. The unglazed and glazed fragments found on the Caughley site, however, clearly show that they were made by John Rose of Coalport. Similar flower-pots were made by most early nineteenth-century porcelain manufacturers. The salient features of Coal-port examples, as proved by the factory wasters, are slightly raised bands near the top and bottom of the main body (which can be seen on the unglazed frag-ment affixed to the side of the silhouette decorated pot illustrated). The bottom of the main body is chamfered to fit inside the rim of the base (as can be seen in

Excavations on the
Caughley site and the
identification of early
Coalport porcelain

the two unglazed fragments in front of the finished articles). The stepped outline of the separate base can be seen on the glazed fragment in the foreground, with an unglazed waster behind it. The approximate date of these pots is *c.* 1805–10. The silhouette portrait of George III is like that appearing on similar pieces made to commemorate the Jubilee of October 1809. Silhouette subjects were featured on other Coalport-type ware of this period (see Plates 96–9). These Coalport flower-pots were decorated in a wide variety of styles, many of which are surprisingly rich in effect. The smaller one illustrated has a yellow ground, with reserve panels of landscape subjects, delicately painted in monochrome with finely gilt borders. It shows the high standard reached by this neglected factory before 1815.

The two flower-pots shown in Plate 80 illustrate two further points: (*a*) that these objects, as well as most other basic forms of vases, etc, were made in several sizes; and (*b*) the coverage of high-class Coalport porcelain, this silhouette example being decorated especially for sale in a fashionable watering-place. The Coalport factory undoubtedly enjoyed a large sale in West Country towns, as well as its London trade, fostered by Messrs Mortlock, the leading retailer of the day, and by the leading London decorating establishment of Thomas Baxter's. Flower-pots or jardinières of this type, decorated and signed by Thomas Baxter, are illustrated in Plate 91. Another flower-pot form is discussed on Page 48.

Pieces of paint-trays were found at Caughley, both glazed and unglazed (Plate 81). These had three or four circular depressions, with a long groove for brushes at the front. It is not known if they were made for resale or if they were used only by the painters employed at Caughley or Coalport. They may have been saleable objects, for Chamberlain of Worcester was selling white 'paint-stands' at 2*d* each in 1794. Other small single paint- or patch-stands (or perhaps rouge-pots) were found, mostly in an unglazed state, although one piece was finished in yellow.

Although fragments of some pre-1815 John Rose jugs were found on the Caughley site, the range of jug shapes is discussed in the following chapter as no fragments have as yet been discovered to match *some* obvious early Coalport jugs. The full range of jugs is therefore discussed together, in chronological order.

BASIC PATTERNS FOUND AT THE PRE-1815 CAUGHLEY SITE

Moulded Designs

Apart from the normal reeded or fluted variations of basic plain teaware shapes, the most numerous type of moulded design on Coalport fragments found on the pre-1815 site comprised basketwork-edged plates, dishes and other dinner-service objects, which in other respects match the standard dinner-service form of the 1800–10 period with oval tureens. A selection of these fragments is shown in

Plate 84. It is interesting to note that the 1802 advertisement quoted on Page 11 mentions dinner services 'with basket-work on the edges . . .'

A more ambitious moulded pattern found on the Caughley site is a relief design of complex form with scroll-bordered panels and floral motifs. Plates, dishes, teaware, and other objects such as handled trays occur with this pattern (see Plates 22 and 150). The early examples are of the compact, hard, greyish body with sharp moulding. The pattern was used over many years, fragments of later dates having been discovered on the Coalport factory site or in the River Severn by the factory—although the later, post-1815, pieces are not as sharp in the moulding as examples of the pre-1815 period which were made at Caughley rather than at Coalport.

A further moulded design was found on the Caughley site—one normally associated with the Swansea and Nantgarw factories and with Coalport at a date after the closure of the Caughley works (see Plate 150). It would therefore seem possible that John Rose originated this decorative design before 1815, rather than acquired the moulds for it from the Swansea and Nantgarw factories on their closure.

Japan Patterns

Very many fragments of bold Japan patterns, with their underglaze blue and overglaze red, green and gold, so popular in the first twenty years of the nineteenth century, were found at the Caughley site. In most cases the fragments had received only the underglaze blue, but in some instances the pattern had been completed with the addition of overglaze enamels and gilding.

Several of these Japan-pattern fragments, a selection of which are shown in Plates 82, 83, and 85, matched services already attributed in the author's mind to Coalport of the 1800–10 period. Plate 83 shows a reconstructed plate painted with the underglaze-blue parts of the vase pattern, seen in its completed form in Plate 48. It some cases Japan-pattern fragments were found in their bisque—unglazed—state, with unfired blue. It is here presumed that the painter made some mistake which necessitated the pieces being destroyed before the glazing.

These colourful Japan patterns were made in great variety, and would seem to have composed almost one-half of the total output of the post-1799 Caughley and Coalport factories. Some of them were included in the 'Household furniture . . . of a Gentleman' sold by Mr Christie in London in February 1808. 'A beautiful dessert service of the Colebrook-Dale, in imitation of the old colored Japan, comprising 1 centre dish, 12 comports (or side dishes), 2 sugar and cream terrines, covers and stands, 24 plates and 2 ice pails, covers and linners. £16.16.0.' Such ware would be similar to that shown in Plates 20, 21, 28, and 29. In 1809 Mr Christie sold a 'Tea and coffee set of Colebrook Dale china to imitate Japan. £8.8.0.' (see Plates 40, 48, and 55).

Blue-painted Patterns

Some fragments, mainly of dinnerware, were painted with simple floral designs—sprig, cornflower, and carnation motifs in underglaze blue. These were both

Excavations on the
Caughley site and the
identification of early
Coalport porcelain

unglazed and glazed, and examples have moulded basketwork edges (see Plate 84).

Blue-painted Patterns

Several fragments of willow-pattern-type Chinese landscape designs were found, mainly on teaware. The blue is noticeably much paler than that on similar pre-1799 Caughley porcelain, but it is also brighter. Other blue-printed patterns included that of the Dragon and the Royal Lily, as well as some formal floral ones, some of which would appear to have been employed only at Coalport.

Black-printed Outline Patterns

A surprising number of fragments were found bearing a thin black-printed outline, occurring on patterns which were coloured-in by girls or apprentices. Typical fragments are shown in Plates 86 and 87. This outline printed is well known on mid-nineteenth-century porcelain, but it was rather surprising to find it on this pre-1815 site. Some printed-outline floral designs are superbly delicate, with a very fine stippled effect.

Enamelled Patterns

Enamel-painted fragments were rather rare. Some simple floral patterns of New Hall type were found (Plate 88), and also sprig patterns; but in the main the enamel-painted teaware was of Classes A and C of the 1800–7 period.

Other enamelled pieces were of the so-called Bishop Sumner or Dragon pattern, coloured Japan patterns, and porcelain with coloured overprinted patterns.

Other Fragments

The Caughley site contained a wide assortment of fragments. Most were blue-printed, readily identifiable (and sometimes marked) Caughley porcelain (and rare basalt ware) of the 1775–99 Turner period, or post-1799 Coalport ware of the types mentioned earlier in this chapter.

Other fragments included:

(a) Thick slip-decorated pottery, parts of dishes and utilitarian pots.

(b) Unglazed red ware of Elers type.

(c) A large number of fragments of eighteenth-century Chinese porcelain, both blue and white and enamelled pieces. These mainly comprised parts of plates, teacups or saucers; but Chinese teapot and vase fragments were also found.

(d) Parts of a white bisque figure or group of Derby type.

(e) Chocolate-coloured earthenware.

The early slip-decorated pottery may have been wasters from a pottery on or near the Caughley site, before Thomas Turner took over and started the manufacture of porcelain in the 1770s; but there is the other possibility that they were parts of the vessels used by Caughley workmen. The same explanations would hold good for the unglazed red earthenware. A base of a teapot(?) in this material is in the Shrewsbury Museum collection of Caughley fragments.

Excavations on the
Caughley site and the
identification of early
Coalport porcelain

The large number of broken pieces of Chinese porcelain tends to discount the theory that Turner purchased these pieces as patterns to be copied on his own ware. It is, however, true that several Caughley shapes and patterns are close copies of Chinese export porcelain of the period.

A study of the surviving Chamberlain-Worcester account-books shows that Turner of Caughley supplied to Chamberlains (and presumably to other firms and retailers) porcelain other than his own make. References are made to Nankin (Chinese) ware and to Derby porcelain. It would seem that the Caughley factory served also as a wholesale house, supplying a wide assortment of ware, some of which were delivered damaged or became broken whilst at Caughley, so accounting for the different types discovered on the site. The Chinese blue-and-white porcelain could also have been enriched with added English gilt borders, etc, for some of the pieces have gilder's initials inside the footrim—and in this respect they match Caughley pieces of the same general type.

The rare fragments of chocolate-coloured earthenware found on the pre-1815 Caughley site are interesting and seem to represent an experimental class of John Rose earthenware made to the same forms as the Coalport porcelain of the same period. Fragments match the well-known lobed-edged plates, sauce-tureens of the same form as porcelain examples found with Coalport dessert sets of the 1800–10 period (indicating that complete sets were made), and also the standard 1800–5 John Rose jug form (see Plate 89).

A feature of the chocolate-coloured earthenware is that the underside of plates and the inside of jugs and sauce-tureens were washed over with a white slip, probably in an effort to pass the coloured pottery off as having a white porcelain body. As yet, I have discovered only two finished articles to match this class of pottery, one of which is the gilt plate shown in Plate 90 (the other is a Class C oval teapot); but as knowledge of the existence of this class of Coalport earthenware spreads, further finished articles will no doubt be found. This chocolate-coloured pottery would appear to be the only class of *earthenware* made by the John Rose partnership.

CHAPTER III

OTHER EARLY COALPORT PORCELAIN

The previous chapter contained information on early Coalport porcelain identified by means of matching fragments found on the Caughley factory site, from when the factory was managed by John Rose & Co, 1799 to *c.* 1814. The story is, however, by no means complete. Apart from the fact that it gives no account of any ware that might have been made only at the parent Coalport factory, it is not at all certain that the Caughley site has delivered up all its fragments. There are the further points that many fragments were so small as to be unidentifiable and that certain objects may have been produced without loss, so that no factory wasters were produced.

The wasters found on the Caughley site (and discussed in Chapter II) therefore show only *some* types of porcelain produced by John Rose & Co from 1799 to *c.* 1814. In this chapter other forms of early Coalport porcelain will be discussed and the reasons for their attribution given.

Firstly, I should like to expound a theory that will surprise many readers—which is that the porcelains decorated (and signed) by Thomas Baxter, Junior, in London from about 1800 to 1814, when Baxter moved to Worcester, were painted on Coalport porcelain, not on Chamberlain ware. Numerous signed examples of this fine painter's work are known and these have always been attributed to Chamberlain of Worcester without, as far as can be ascertained, the slightest evidence. In fact, there are reasons which strongly suggest that this London-decorated ware is *not* of Worcester origin.

The original Chamberlain sales records have been preserved, and with one exception—a white teaset sold for £1 14*s* 2*d* on May 6th, 1797—there is no record of any porcelain having been sold to the Baxters, although this studio must have required over some seventeen years a very considerable amount of porcelain, its sole concern being the decoration of white or blue-printed porcelain. There is also the point that no porcelain matching in form any of the shapes bearing signed Baxter painting is known to have a Chamberlain mark or even a Chamberlain pattern number. This is highly significant, for well over half the early nineteenth century Chamberlain porcelain bears the name mark or at least pattern number that can be checked against the full Chamberlain factory records. It is inconceivable that, if the Chamberlain firm were supplying Baxter with porcelain, they would have made special shapes for him—shapes not used by their own painters.

Having suggested two reasons why the Baxter-decorated porcelain should not have been attributed to the Chamberlain factory at Worcester, I shall give my grounds for attributing it to the Coalport and Caughley factories operating under the John Rose management.

In 1810 Thomas Baxter, Junior, painted an interior view of his father's decorating studio at No. 1 Goldsmith Street, Gough Square, London (see Plate 42). This interesting drawing was shown at the 1811 Royal Academy Exhibition and is now preserved in the Victoria and Albert Museum. In the present context it is of vital importance, for Baxter included a notice (pinned on the wall of the studio) with the heading:

NEW PRICE LIST. COALPORT WHITE CHINA.

Further, the numerous pieces of oval teaware shown on the work-bench match in their forms unglazed as well as glazed fragments recently discovered on the Caughley site worked by John Rose of Coalport up to 1814. One oval covered sugar-bowl depicted in this drawing, with moulded animal-head handles and a blue-printed willow-pattern-like design, is matched by fragments of a completed sugar found on the site. Such blue-printed porcelain was probably enhanced with gilt borders, added by Baxter at London.

A selection of Baxter signed porcelain is shown in Plates 91–5, including a monumental covered vase (previously attributed to Chamberlains) which actually depicts a named view of the 'COALBROOK DALE CHINA MANUFACTORY' (Frontispiece). The most numerous signed examples of Baxter's ceramic painting are those on lobed-edged plates (see Plate 92). Fragments—unglazed, glazed and partly decorated—litter the Caughley factory site, as this form of lobed-edged plate was the standard Coalport one and is found in the many Coalport dinner and dessert services of the 1800–10 period. It does not appear to have been made at the Worcester factories.

The pair of jardinières shown in Plate 91, which are signed 'T. Baxter, London', are certainly of Coalport manufacture, as numerous unglazed and glazed fragments of such pieces have been found on the site worked by John Rose of Coalport prior to 1815. Some site fragments also seem to match in form the extremely finely decorated cabaret service shown in Plate 94, which is signed and dated 'T. Baxter, 1802—London'.

If the reader accepts the above evidence of a Coalport source for this porcelain decorated by Baxter in London, then it follows that similar shapes with other decoration are also of early Coalport manufacture—for example, the vase form shown in Plate 95, which bears signed Baxter painting.

In addition to these signed Baxter paintings on Coalport blanks, formerly thought to have been made at the Chamberlain factory at Worcester, there is

43

one further class of ceramic decoration which has in the past been attributed to Chamberlains, but which the writer believes to have been made by John Rose of Coalport and Caughley. The class is decorated with silhouette portraits of George III, several pieces commemorating the Jubilee of October 1809 (see Plate 80). This style of decoration does not feature in the preserved Chamberlain factory or retail-shop records. On the other hand, fragments from the pre-1815 Caughley site match in form one jardinière and stand bearing this style of decoration (see Plate 80). A fine Coalport-like vase is illustrated in E. Nevill Jackson's *The History of Silhouettes* (1911), Plate XXXII.

The silhouette-style of figure decoration also occurs on Coalport useful ware (see Plate 96), and on spill vases and other objects (see Plate 97). The writer has handled a Coalport teaset of the straight-sided teapot form (as Plate 40) bearing similar black classical figure decoration. The following 'lots' included in Messrs Mortlock's ('Manufacturer of Coalbrook Dale Porcelain to Her Majesty and all the Royal Family') 1820 Sale could well have been painted in a similar style:

> Six deep fruit dishes, with medallion centres and arabesque gold borders, and 18 Colebrook Dale dessert Plates, with figured centres and black and red Etruscan borders.

A similar attractive form of figure decoration also occurs, with the colours reversed—the figures or other motifs in white, silhouetted against a dark ground which has been painted around the design—treatment which is shown in Plates 98-9. The style would appear to have been restricted to this factory.

Here follows a list of early Coalport objects—with the reasons for their present attribution. It is hoped that with the publicity now given to this neglected factory further forms will be added to this nucleus.

Jugs

As many as six basic shapes of early Coalport jugs can be identified—which is not surprising, for the jug is not only an object required on every dining-table but also an article chosen on many occasions to be inscribed with names, arms, crests, mottoes, poems and, sometimes, dates for presentation.

The fine jug shown in Plate 10 is decorated in underglaze blue and marks the Shrewsbury election of 1796, when John Hill won the seat with a majority of forty-four. It is in the City Museum, Stoke-on-Trent. A further example bearing this inscription, but of slightly different form, has recently been presented to the Shrewsbury Museum (see Plate 11). Apart from these 1796 election jugs, I have not been able to trace further examples of these graceful early forms bearing more orthodox decoration.

It is, of course, possible that these jugs were made at Caughley or another factory rather than Coalport; but the general appearance of the body and glaze, together with details which also occur on slightly later Coalport jugs, suggests strongly that these John Hill election jugs are the earliest dated examples of Coalport porcelain.

The heavily potted jug shown in Plate 100 is inscribed and dated 'James Turner. 1798'. It shows the same ribbing under the spout as is found on the 1796 election jugs. In potting and porcelain it is quite unlike the Caughley porcelains of the same period; but the Chinese-styled blue-printed pattern suggests that the Coalport management were seeking to copy the traditional Caughley designs, which they were to purchase in the following year. The simple but graceful handle form should be noted, as it occurs again on the next three Coalport jug forms, and also on key documentary specimens.

Chronologically, the next Coalport jug form is shown in Plate 102. The fine blue-printed jug shows a view of the iron bridge over the River Severn, upstream from the Coalport factory. The engraved copper-plate from which this subject was printed was, until recent years, preserved by the Coalport management and is recorded in the factory 'rag book' with numerous other Caughley and early Coalport printed designs. The engraved spray of carnations placed under the handle is also found on other early Coalport porcelain. The wide and ornate Chinese-styled border occurs again on the inscribed and dated 'Coalport . . . 1802' footed bowl shown in Plate 113.

Apart from blue-printed designs of Willow-pattern type (some of which also occur on early Coalport teaware), jugs of this same form were decorated with enamelled patterns including, in some rare instances, armorial bearings. There are two variations of this basic shape; the smaller jugs shown in Plate 103 show a slight groove at the peak of each flute, while the top line of the fluted band is slightly scalloped. These two features do not occur on the larger jugs shown on Plate 102. A variation of this basic shape occurs without the band of spiral fluting. Fluting, however, appears under the spout. The approximate period of the jugs shown in Plates 100–3 is c. 1798–1808.

The next distinguishable shape of early Coalport jug form is illustrated in Plate 104. It is a simplified version, squatter than the previous form, and retains the same general handle used on the two earlier shapes. An unglazed handle matching these jugs was found on the Caughley site. It would appear to overlap in period the form discussed above, for identical commemorative decoration marking the election of William Clive and John Robinson as Members of Parliament for Bishop's Castle, Shropshire, from 1806 to 1818, occurs on jugs of the previously discussed form and on the new squat shape.

One of the latter bears the name 'COAL-PORT' painted in red enamel capital letters, of the same type as the rare 'COALBROOKDALE' marks reproduced on Page 17. A finely gilded example in the Victoria and Albert Museum is dated January 1806. The range of designs found on these rather heavy, squat jugs is large, from simple gilt motifs to rich 'Japan' patterns and including armorial election jugs, a feature of which is the slight fluting under the spout, with nine raised ribs. This fluting is often nearly filled with glaze. In several cases, it is entirely painted or gilded over. Nevertheless, the flutes serve to differentiate between Coalport jugs and similar ones from the Chamberlain factory at Worcester. At this point the reader's attention should be drawn to the fact that the rival Coalport firm of Anstice, Horton & Rose made very similar

Other early Coalport porcelain

45

jugs, with seven rather pronounced ribs under the spout (see Page 65). The approximate date of the Coalport jugs would appear to be *c.* 1805–10.

The next definite shape of Coalport jug was certainly made on the pre-1814 Caughley factory site, for both unglazed fragments and a half mould for the characteristic handle were found there. This shape, with the stepped handle, is shown in Plate 106. The handle has mock rivet- or screw-heads at the top and bottom junction and in this respect is similar to the handles found on Class E teapots, etc (see Page 35). Examples are known dated 1810 and 1811, including the most interesting 1810 'Royal Cornwall Topographical Society' jug in the Grand Lodge Museum, London (see Plate 107, and Mrs R. M. Barton's *A History of the Cornish China-Clay Industry*, 1966). The approximate date of these jugs, some of which have covers, would appear to be *c.* 1810–14.

As with the previously discussed early Coalport jug forms, very close copies exist which were in all probability made at the rival Anstice, Horton & Rose factory at Coalport (see Chapter IV and Plate 108). Briefly, the differences are that the Anstice, Horton & Rose examples do not have the mock screw- or rivet-heads and that the bottom of the handle where it joins the body is slightly shaped into a tail, the downward scroll at the top of the handle being more pointed on the Anstice specimens.

The shapes of any other post-1814 Coalport jugs produced before the granting of the Society of Arts Gold Medal in 1820, and the subsequent use of the large circular printed 'Felt Spar' mark, have not as yet been identified with certainty; but the later post-1820 jug forms are discussed in Chapter V.

Mugs or Tankards

These were produced by most late eighteenth- and early nineteenth-century porcelain manufacturers, sometimes being made and decorated to match a jug so that the customer might purchase a jug and two matching mugs. As with jugs, the mugs were a popular present, and specimens might be specially decorated with the recipient's name or initials.

Coalport mugs were undoubtedly made to match the early jugs of the 1796–1808 period, discussed on pages 44–45, but as yet I have been unable to trace a documentary specimen. The handle on mugs made to match jugs would presumably be of the same simple form—thus the specimen shown in Plate 109 is in all probability an early Coalport mug of the 1800–10 period, the handle being very similar to those of the jugs shown in Plates 100–4, of which the potting and porcelain body are of the same nature.

One form of Coalport mug is, however, readily identifiable—an early version, which has previously been attributed to the New Hall factory, shown in Plate 110. The ornate moulded handle is a simplified version of one found on Caughley teapots and teaware of the 1780s. A matching mug handle was found on the site, so confirming the attribution originally made on the evidence of the hard body and thick, heavy potting.

A small example of this mug form recently presented to the Victoria and Albert Museum is dated December 6th, 1809, and is believed to have been decorated by Thomas Baxter, whose initials it bears. A further example in my own collection, with the initials 'M.A.B.' at the front, has the gilt initials 'T.A.'—presumably those of the donor—in the raised heart at the top of the moulded handle. As with the jugs, each basic form of mug was made in several sizes.

A very similar form, with moulded handle, was made at the rival factory of Anstice, Horton & Rose (see Chapter IV); but in these the handle joins directly to the side of the mug and is not raised slightly from it as on the John Rose examples (see Plate 110).

Bulb- or 'Bough'-pots

These decorative and useful chimney-piece or side-table ornaments, with their flat backs and pierced covers (now so often broken or missing) were extremely popular in the early years of the nineteenth century. Fine marked examples were made by Chamberlains and by the Derby firm, as well as by many other establishments.

The rather heavy-looking example (Plate 111) painted with a yellow ground is a rare early Coalport specimen. Apart from the general heavy style of potting and the hard appearance of the paste, its present attribution is based on the discovery of an unglazed fragment of the side, showing the characteristic scroll ornamentation.

A further form of bulb-pot may be attributed to the Coalport management, if one agrees with the writer's contention that signed paintings by the London decorator Thomas Baxter were all on Coalport blanks (see Page 42). The example shown in Plate 91 is signed 'T. Baxter, London' and, in the writer's opinion, constitutes a second basic form of early Coalport bulb-pot. A pair of similar bulb-pots, but without the four feet, are in the Allen collection at the Victoria and Albert Museum, Allen Catalogue No. 203.

A third shape of bulb-pot may be considered to be Coalport on the evidence of the general characteristics of potting and paste. This decorative form, shown in Plate 98, is very large, being 11¼ inches long, and represents, with the related lot shown in Plate 112, the most ornate bulb-pot shape made by any manufacturer.

As with other early Coalport porcelain, these bulb-pots are invariably attributed to the Chamberlain factory at Worcester—but no example would appear to bear a Chamberlain mark or even a Chamberlain pattern number. The following Sotheby sale description of one sold in 1961 proves that some bulb-pots of this form were decorated in the finest style and that such (unmarked) pieces have been attributed to Chamberlains:

> A commemorative Chamberlain Worcester bough pot of bombe shape, painted at the front with Admiral Nelson's glorious victory at the Battle of the Nile, the ships engaged in combat beneath a cloudy sky, the scene contained within an octagonal gilt edged panel, the side trophies of arms also within elaborately gilt panels, the chambered corners with chains pendent from cockle shells, the whole raised on four gilt feet, the cover with four cup-shaped flower holders. 7½ inches high.

The Chamberlain firm did, of course, produce fine bulb-pots, but these are of different form from those here attributed to Coalport; and the Chamberlain examples nearly always bear the name mark, or a pattern number which matches the original Chamberlain pattern records.

Jardinières

Jardinières were also made to contain flowers or bulbs. Normally, a jardinière has a circular plan and therefore differs from the flat-backed bulb-pots discussed previously. In most cases the circular jardinière has a loose base to contain and hold the surplus water which comes through the drainage hole in the top section (see Plate 80).

Jardinières were originally sold in pairs, in some cases with a matching flat-backed bulb-pot and in others with a matching vase (or vases).

One basic form of early Coalport jardinière has already been discussed on Page 37, and numerous matching unglazed fragments were found on the pre-1815 Caughley factory site. Following the theory that signed Baxter paintings are on Coalport blanks, as put forward on Page 42, the attractively simple jardinières shown in Plate 93 represent a further Coalport basic shape of this product.

Footed Bowls

The footed bowl shown in Plate 113 is decorated in a bright underglaze blue with Caughley-period prints of birds in foliage, and with the wide Chinese-styled border which appears on the large jug with the print of the iron bridge (see Plate 102).

The inside of the bowl is inscribed 'Success to Trade. Peace & Plenty. Coalport for ever. Thos. Groome. 1802'. It is therefore a key documentary piece.

Honey-pots

On the evidence of body and styles of decoration, the Coalport management, in keeping with other leading firms, made porcelain honey-pots in the form of bee-hives.

That shown in Plate 114 bears the Worcester-style bright blue scale ground found on much other early Coalport porcelain of the 1800–10 period. The floral painting is also found on Coalport lobed-edged plates (Plate 33) and other objects. The potting is thick, and this honey-pot is therefore much heavier than contemporary examples from other factories.

The smaller example shown in Plate 114 is of the 1810–15 period. In potting and body it appears to be Coalport, differing from contemporary Spode or Worcester examples.

Inkstands

It is highly improbable that the John Rose company did not produce inkstands, pen-trays and similar objects, although no fragments or early marked specimens have as yet been discovered.

The rich 'Japan'-pattern inkstand shown in Plate 115 is, on the evidence of its heavy potting and hard body, of early Coalport manufacture, although its basic form was also made at the Worcester factories. The Worcester examples are thinner in the potting and are nearly twice as light as this Coalport specimen. The marked Chamberlain examples, although similar at first sight, show several differences in the moulded form.

At least one other form of inkstand was produced:

> An inkstand of Colebrook Dale china, fashioned as an Etruscan drinking horn.
>
> (Christie's sale. April, 1810)

but in all probability several other different inkstands were made and await identification.

Early Morning or Tête-à-Tête Teasets

These sets were made by most factories of the period. That shown in Plate 116 is most probably of Coalport manufacture, as witness the lobed-edged plates found so frequently on the site. A fragment of the creamer base was also found, and there is the added point that Baxter signed and dated (1802) a similar teapot (see Page 43 and Plate 94).

Vases

Although as yet the Caughley/Coalport factory site has apparently yielded only one fragment of a vase—a square base with a circular stem rising from it, similar to the bases of vases shown in Plates 95, 97, and 117—it is highly probable that several different vase forms were made by the John Rose Company, either at Coalport or at the former Caughley site. On the evidence of the body, the vases illustrated in Plates 95, 97, and 117–19 seem to be of Coalport manufacture; and it is likely that, as the study of early Coalport porcelain increases, other standard vase forms hitherto classed as Worcester will be discovered.

Contemporary sale catalogues refer to Coalport/Coalbrookdale vases:

> Three vases and 2 match pots, Colebrook Dale £1. (March, 1811)

and, of course, Thomas Baxter signed some examples painted in London on blanks, believed by the author to be of Coalport manufacture (see Page 42). The vase shown in the Frontispiece, with its panel showing the 'Coalbrook Dale China Manufactory', illustrates well the heights that Coalport vases could reach —heights in two senses, for this example is nearly 2 feet tall!

'Supper' or Sandwich Sets

The English porcelain manufacturers, as well as the potters, produced elegant sets of four segment-shaped covered dishes with an oval or circular centre tureen. These originally fitted into an oval or circular wood tray, often with brass carrying handles, and sometimes had plates matching the design on the dishes. For

49

many years they have been called 'supper' sets, but the original term was 'sandwich sets'. They seem an entirely English article, as I have not seen Continental examples.

The sales of Coalbrookdale or Coalport porcelain included such sets:

> A Coalbrook Dale sandwich set, 4 compotiers (segment dishes), centre piece and cover, and 7 plates.
> (October, 1802; sold for £2.3.0),

or at a later date, in 1819:

> A sandwich tray, consisting of a centre bowl of Colebrook Dale china, in imitation of old Japan, in a mahogany tray. £4.4.0.

Some years ago I saw a fine 'Japan'-pattern sandwich service of obviously Coalbrook Dale (or Coalport) make. The knobs to each of the four covered segment dishes were of the off-centre pistol-grip type found on the 1805–10 soup- and sauce-tureens and on the vegetable-dish covers of such dinner services (see Plates 14 and 15 for ware with this type of knob).

Spill-vases or 'Match-pots'

The narrow cylindrical objects some 3 to 5 inches high are often called spill-vases, although the contemporary name was 'match-pots'. Their place was on the mantelpiece or fireside table.

Match-pots were sometimes sold with mantel vases, as in the set shown in Plate 97. Sale catalogues confirm this amalgamation of vases with match-pots or spill-vases:

> Three vases and 2 match pots, Colebrook Dale £1. (March, 1811)

Other match pots were sold in pairs, in sets of three, and even in sets of five or seven.

CHAPTER IV

MESSRS ANSTICE, HORTON & ROSE'S COALPORT PORCELAIN

It is not generally realized that for some years prior to 1814 there were two separate porcelain factories at Coalport, operated by (*a*) Edward Blakeway, John Rose and Richard Rose—the partners in the best-known firm, later to become famous as John Rose & Co—and (*b*) Robert Anstice, William Horton and Thomas Rose. Their two works were separated only by a narrow canal and the site and buildings now known as the Coalport Porcelain Factory were originally the *two* factories separated by the canal—now filled in.

The nineteenth-century tithe map reproduced in Plate 5 indicates the two factories, one on each side of the canal; the old photograph reproduced in Plate 6 shows the canal between the two sets of buildings; and on Plate 7 can be seen the factory at the present time, with the canal filled in. Recent research suggests that the Anstice, Horton & Rose company was not a small factory of little importance but a large concern—in its time perhaps larger and more important than the John Rose Company, which has hitherto monopolized the interests of ceramic writers and collectors.

Nineteenth-century writers recorded the existence of the two factories. In 1862 Llewellynn Jewitt wrote:

> Mr. Rose had not long established himself at Coalport, it appears before he met with opposition, for other works were started on the opposite side of the canal, and only a few yards distant, by his brother, Mr. Thomas Rose and his partners, who commenced business under the style of 'Anstice, Horton and Rose'. These works, however, did not continue long, but passed into the hands of Mr. John Rose and his partners, who, with other additions, formed them into one establishment . . .
>
> (*Art Journal*, March, 1862, subsequently repeated in *Ceramic Art of Great Britain*)

51

The Shropshire historian John Randall, who was an artist at the Coalport factory from *c.* 1835 to 1881, wrote in *The Clay Industries . . . on the Banks of the Severn* (1877):

> The first works at Coalport were we believe founded and carried on by William Reynolds, Thomas Rose, Robert Horton, and Robert Anstice; the former William Reynolds being then Lord of the Manor. The buildings or a good portion occupied by them are still standing.

We therefore have two conflicting statements—one to the effect that Messrs Anstice, Horton & Rose commenced after the John Rose partnership had established their factory, while on the other hand Randall states that the reverse was the case. I have been unable to trace any documentary evidence to settle the point except for the important fact that the 1800 account of the Coalport district mentions only one porcelain factory, which must have been John Rose's. The fact remains that by the time the John Rose Company had issued some three hundred and fifty patterns Messrs Anstice, Horton & Rose had issued at least one thousand four hundred and nineteen designs prior to 1814.

It is advisable to consider the history of the factory backwards from its closure, for the later period is that best documented. The most important evidence is the notice of letting advertised in the *Salopian Journal* of February 16th, February 23rd, and March 2nd, 1814.

SHROPSHIRE
TO PORCELAIN MANUFACTURERS, AND OTHERS
TO BE LET

and may be entered upon immediately

> All that well known capital Porcelain Manufactory situate at Coalport in the County of Salop, the property of Messrs. Anstice, Horton and Rose, adjoining the River Severn on the one side, and the Shropshire Canal Navigation on the other (from which it is supplied with coals) with the extensive warehouses, counting houses, kilns, stove houses, and all other buildings, necessary for carrying on the Porcelain Trade to a very large extent.

> The commodious works are enclosed and are furnished with all proper and needful machinery, utensils, and other implements for carrying on the same, which may be taken to by a respectable Tenant at a fair appraisement.

> Mr. Charles Lumley, of Coalport aforesaid, will shew the Premises, and further Particulars may be known by applying to Mr. Pritchard, Solicitors, Broseley.

This notice describes the factory as 'adjoining the River Severn on the one side, and the Shropshire Canal Navigation on the other'. Reference to the tithe-map detail (see Plate 5) will show that the works between the river and the canal were of far larger extent (with four kilns) than the John Rose factory on the other side of the canal. It is, of course, possible that by the time this tithe map was prepared, *c.* 1840, the two factories had been rebuilt in part; but the fact remains that the riverside site must have been the more advantageous of the two. The 1814 sale notice makes it clear that Messrs Anstice, Horton & Thomas Rose's factory, and not the works of the better-known John Rose Company, was situated on the river bank.

This sale of the factory closely followed the notice of dissolution of partnership. The *Salopian Journal* of Wednesday, February 9th, 1814, contains the following notice (repeated on February 16th):

DISSOLUTION OF PARTNERSHIP

> Notice is hereby given that the Partnership subsisting between the undersigned Robert Anstice, William Horton and Thomas Rose of Coalport, in the County of Salop, Porcelain Manufacturers, was this day dissolved by mutual consent . . .
>
> Witness our Hands this seventh day of February, one thousand eight hundred and fourteen.
>
> Robert Anstice
> William Horton
> Thomas Rose

The dissolution of partnership and subsequent closing of the factory was apparently contemplated some weeks before the official notice was published. An advertisement in *The Times* of February 1st, 1814, and repeated up to February 25th, probably relates to the Anstice, Horton & Rose works at Coalport and an effort to sell the factory by private treaty. The location is not given, as the dissolution of partnership had not been announced and publicity of the intended closure may have been unwelcome.

> Waterside Premises. To Manufacturers, Public Companies, etc. To be Let or Sold, Premises sufficiently extensive for the large manufacturing or other concern: or might, at a small expense (the buildings thereon being well adapted) be converted into Barracks sufficiently large to accommodate from 4 to 5,000 men. A capital steam-engine on the Premises. Letters post paid, addressed to A.B. at Mr. Mist's[1] china warehouse, 82 Fleet Street.

The initials 'A.B.' were freely used in *The Times* and other newspaper advertisements of the period and were unlikely to refer to a person with these initials. They were merely a reference—the equivalent of a box number. An interesting

[1] A few pieces of Coalport-type porcelain do bear the name and address of this London retailer, so linking him with the Coalport factories.

notice relating to the sale in London of an 'Extensive stock of costly china . . . in consequence of a dissolution of Partnership' is contained in *The Times* early in January 1814. The facts strongly suggest that this was the stock of Messrs Anstice, Horton & Rose.

> Extensive Stock of costly china, earthenware and white china—by Mr. Farebrother, at Messrs. Hindlers' Rooms, No. 28, Chancery Lane, on Thursday, January 20th and following days, at 11 on account of the Manufacturers, and in consequence of a dissolution of Partnership.
>
> The genuine and extensive Stock, consisting of several superb and costly dinner and dessert services, in imitation of fine old Dresden, and rich Japan déjeune services and supper sets, cabinet and ornamental vases, cups and cans, tea and coffee equipages, and bowls, pencilled in landscape, birds, fruit, flowers, figures and various designs, and painted in rich colours, and superbly gilt; an assortment of blue and white of every description, and a profusion of white china . . .

However, the sale was postponed:

> Mr Farebrother has the honour respectfully to inform the Nobility and Public that the sale of costly china, advertised to take place Tomorrow, and following day at Mr. Hindles' Rooms in Chancery Lane is postponed in consequence of the inclemency of the weather, which prevents the removal, with safety from the manufacturer's warehouse and the manufactory, of the most valuable articles of this splendid stock . . .
> (*The Times*, January 19th, 1814)

As the sale of this stock 'in consequence of a dissolution of Partnership' does not seem to have been re-advertised in *The Times*, the partners may well have found other means of disposing of it—perhaps at reduced prices to their former customers, or in sales nearer to Coalport. There are, however, various advertisements in *The Times* of the period for the sale by auction of stocks of china; but the details do not include the key wording 'on account of the manufacturers' or 'in consequence of a dissolution of Partnership', and white (undecorated) china is not included in the other routine sale notices. I have been unable to trace any other dissolution of a pottery manufacturer's partnership of this period which could have had available for sale 'several superb and costly dinner and dessert services . . . rich Japan (pattern) déjeune services and supper sets . . .'—items made only by the larger porcelain manufacturers.

As we have seen, the closing days of the Anstice, Horton & Rose partnership are well documented in the notices of dissolution of partnership and subsequent sale notices of the factory. Unfortunately, the date of establishment and early history does not seem to have been recorded. I have been able to trace only one definite reference to the company—a letter written to Wedgwood in 1808, requesting a supply of clay.

Gent^m.

We shall be obliged by your informing us as soon as you can conveniently, whether it would be agreeable to you to supply us regularly with china clay & unground stone, and if it would, on what terms, either delivered here or in Cornwall.

If it should suit you to supply us & your terms are such as we approve, we should have no objection to contract with you for the whole we consume. An early answer will oblige.

Your obed^t. servants,

Anstice, Horton & Co.

Coalport, 4th April, 1808.

near Shiffnal, Salop.

It is debatable whether Anstice, Horton & Co were writing for their first supply of raw materials or were only seeking a new supplier, having previously traded with another firm. It may be relevant that no references were offered, the writer perhaps having presumed that the firm and its ware would be well known to Wedgwood. It is also interesting to see that 'unground stone' was required—a fact that suggests that the firm had mills to grind the raw material—and that Thomas Rose's name was not included in the signature to this 1808 letter, although he may, of course, have been included in the all-embracing term '& Co'. Having been born in 1780, he was probably the junior partner for several years. Regarding the other partners, a Robert Anstice was born on December 9th, 1757, and died on April 30th, 1845.[1] William Horton 'of Coalport in the County of Salop, Gentleman' was apparently an important person, for he was one of two umpires chosen in 1804 to adjudicate on a disagreement between Thomas Turner and the John Rose Coalport Company concerning the lease of the Caughley porcelain factory. It must, however, be stated that both Anstice and Horton are names which appear many times in the eighteenth- and nineteenth-century records of the Coalport district.

Following the notice that the Anstice, Horton & Rose factory was available, in February and March 1814 (see Pages 52–53), it is clear that the John Rose Company, situated on the opposite bank of the Shropshire Canal, took over the rival concern. This was an obvious step, as the lease of the Caughley factory was due to run out in 1816. And in any case, the purchase of the ready-made factory—the width of a canal from its own—at one stroke stopped a rival firm taking the premises and obviated the costly and troublesome necessity of transporting ware from the Caughley site to Coalport.

The first available pattern-book of the John Rose Company contains patterns from 235 to 603 (with several designs missing). Against some patterns there are written notes drawing attention to the fact that the same design, with a different number, was used at Mr Thomas Rose's Works (Thomas Rose being one of the partners in the Anstice, Horton & Rose Company). The list of such duplicated patterns is as follows:

[1] Barrow Church Registers.

Messrs Anstice, Horton & Rose's Coalport porcelain	Thomas Rose's Pattern No.	John Rose & Co's Pattern No.
	165	317
	303	336
	499	318
	500	297
	501	299
	502	300
	503	298
	505	296
	561	302
	696	319
	819	316
	835	303
	1019	305
	1032	335
	1130	346
	1149	337
	1213	320
	1290	301
	1300	308
	1417	333
	1419	338

Several of these designs, reproduced from the pattern books, are shown in Plate 76.

A most significant fact, that his numbers exceeded 1000 and reached at least 1419, arises from these contemporary notes of Thomas Rose's pattern numbers. At a later date, after the 1814 termination of the Anstice, Horton & Rose partnership, the John Rose Company designs in turn exceeded 1000; but when this occurred they started their numbering afresh at 1, expressed in fractional form under the numeral 2 to denote the second series. Thus, the John Rose numbers ran 998, 999, 1000, 2/1, 2/2, 2/3 and so on. In due course a third, fourth, fifth, sixth, seventh and eighth series was issued in the same manner. It can therefore be seen that Coalport-type porcelain bearing pattern numbers above 1000 cannot have been produced by the John Rose Company—a fact proved by the many existing factory pattern-books and marked examples.

Whilst collecting early Coalport porcelain teaware, it became apparent that, although several basic forms were produced, each different shape occurred with slight differences in the knob or handle, even though the porcelain body and the painted patterns were very similar. It was as if two different factories were copying each other's new shapes as they were issued. The differences in form are often very subtle and were, in many cases, missed before I began to look especially for them.

The existence of some pieces bearing pattern numbers in excess of 1000 proved conclusively that some of this Coalport-type ware could not have been produced by John Rose & Co. These high pattern numbers were at first very puzzling. Apart from Messrs Spode and the New Hall factory, no English porcelain factory of the obvious period of the pieces (*c.* 1800–15) had issued patterns in excess of 1000. Such small works at Pinxton, Mansfield were obviously out of the question on this count, and the porcelain body and potting characteristics of Spode and New Hall porcelain were quite different from the Coalport-type porcelain bearing these high numbers.

The discovery that Thomas Rose issued patterns up to at least 1419, as proved by the notations in the John Rose & Co pattern-book, offered the obvious explanation. The shapes and patterns were as close, in copy of each other, as were the sites of the two rival factories of Anstice, Horton & Rose and the John Rose concern.

Apart from the evidence of pattern numbers, early pre-1816 John Rose teaware can be identified and segregated from the others by comparing the porcelain with the documentary fragments—often unglazed—found at Caughley, where John Rose had his branch factory at this period.

Seven basic shapes of teaware were produced by Anstice, Horton & Rose prior to the closure early in 1814. In order that comparisons of form can be made, these have been illustrated on pages opposite those showing the same shapes produced by John Rose & Co. The basic John Rose teaware forms, as evidenced by factory wasters and moulds found on the pre-1815 Caughley site, have been set out on Pages 31–36. The Anstice porcelain has been shown to be very similar to the John Rose body, and by X-ray defraction analysis it has also proved to be a type of hard-paste porcelain.

The following account of Messrs Anstice, Horton & Thomas Rose's contemporary near-matching wares follows the order used in illustrating the porcelain on Pages 31–36.

Class A Teaware (Plates 36 and 37)

In the later Anstice teaware, which is more easily identified by reference to cross-entries in the John Rose pattern-book (see Page 56), two points stand out:

    (*a*) Anstice teapot and sucrier-cover knobs are heavy 'puddeny' versions of the well-modelled John Rose knobs.

    (*b*) Anstice teaware often bears a painted pattern number, whereas John Rose examples are normally not so marked.

These characteristics occur in the Class A teaware discussed below and illustrated in Plates 36 and 37. It is, of course, possible that the variations were made at John Rose's Coalport factory, while the standard better-designed and finished examples were made at the Caughley factory—either while Thomas Turner still managed the Caughley factory before the sale of the leases to John Rose and his partners in 1799 or soon after the new owners had taken over. This explanation seems rather improbable and, in view of the continuation of the two key characteristics into known but later Anstice, Horton & Thomas Rose teaware shapes,   57

I am of the opinion that this oval, often fluted, teaware originated at the Anstice, Horton & Thomas Rose factory.

Firstly, the examples most commonly found can readily be identified as originating from the Caughley factory (although the period is open to some doubt) by the discovery on the Caughley factory site of very many matching unglazed fragments, including the key well-modelled knob and the moulded spout (see Plate 37). This basic form occurs plain (without fluting), with straight fluting, and also with spiral fluting. This later spiral fluting sometimes shows a recessed line or slight groove at the highest point of each flute, giving a double-line effect.

The main variations in the teapots here attributed to the Anstice works are:

The knob is heavy-looking, standing higher than the John Rose knobs, and lacks the continuation of the fluting from the top of the knob to the underside. The stem on which the knob rests is also thicker than that on the John Rose covers.

General proportion of Anstice knob; compare with John Rose example reproduced on page 32

The teapot spout has twelve flutes running half-way up the spout from the body of the teapot, the line where these flutes cease being nearly vertical. The other (John Rose) version, matching the unglazed pieces found on the Caughley factory site, has only ten flutes and these end in a line moving some forty-five degrees from the vertical (see Plate 37).

The matching Class A oval covered sugar-basins—which are, again, found in the plain state (without moulded fluting), with straight flutes, or with spiral fluting—have the same heavy 'puddeny' knob as is found on the teapots, in contrast to the well-moulded neater John Rose knobs (see Page 32). The moulded ring-type handles applied at each end of the Anstice sucriers are of heavier gauge than the ring handles on John Rose examples and also stand out further from the body.

The creamers found with these basic Class A teapots and sucriers are of two types. An early and rare type has a circular body, which is gracefully patterned with an elegant 'S'-shaped handle (see Plate 36). The difference between the Anstice examples and the John Rose pieces lies in the shape of the top edge, as can be seen by comparing the example shown in Plate 36 with that included in Plate 37. The other, more normal types are of narrow oval form, with tall step-up handles (see Plate 39). These creamers, made by the Anstice firm and by the John Rose partnership, are very similar in general form; but the Anstice examples are slightly higher. To the top of the handle, the Anstice creamers are

$4\frac{1}{4}$ inches high. The John Rose examples vary between $3\frac{3}{4}$ and 4 inches high. A further point is that the Anstice handle starts about $\frac{9}{10}$ inch from the base, while the John Rose handles are set lower—some $\frac{2}{3}$ inch from the base (see Plate 39).

Apart from the above-mentioned differences, the examples now attributed to Messrs Anstice, Horton & Thomas Rose sometimes bear a painted pattern number (not found on early John Rose teaware). These pattern numbers are low (the teapot shown in Plate 37 is pattern number 8) and run up to about 100, indicating the first products of a new factory. Although the first John Rose pattern-book to be preserved starts in the 230s, the patterns appear to date from at least ten years after the probable date (*c.* 1800) of the Class A teaware.

I have been unable to trace Anstice teaware matching in form the John Rose Class B teaware shown in Plate 38. But as, in twenty years, I have found only three examples of this shaped John Rose teaware, it is extremely rare and was probably made only for a very limited period and may not have been copied by the Anstice firm.

Class C Teaware (Plate 41)

This teaware, dating from about 1803 and sometimes bearing pattern numbers up to about 400, does not match patterns of the same numbers in the John Rose pattern-book.

In plan, the Anstice oval teapots are slightly longer and narrower than the John Rose specimens, measuring $6\frac{1}{10} \times 4\frac{3}{10}$ inches against $5\frac{3}{4} \times 4\frac{2}{5}$ inches for the John Rose pots. The bases of the teapots have a low footrim, whereas the John Rose examples have a flat base. The handles are not of such a full curve as the John Rose handles; and the knob on the cover has a squat-looking oval knob, inferior to the elegant oval knob with sharply defined nipple found on the John Rose teapots. The differences can be seen by comparing Plate 40 with Plate 41 and from the drawings of the two different knobs, shown below.

John Rose Knob

Anstice Knob

The oval Anstice covered sugars are also longer than John Rose's (5 inches long as against $4\frac{3}{4}$ inches). They lack the raised rib running around the bottom of the John Rose sugar bowls some $\frac{1}{4}$ inch from the base. But the most striking difference lies in the knobs. Like the teapots, the Anstice knob is squat and fat in contrast to the elegant, long, narrow, oval knob on John Rose's examples (see drawings above).

The oval creamers in their plain form (without fluting or ribbing) are relatively easy to differentiate. The Anstice examples lack the raised bands found at the bottom and 2¼ inches up the body of John Rose's early creamers; but this distinction is blurred by the fact that John Rose creamers of this basic shape, when found with various ribbed designs, are also without these raised ribs. These creamers also occur with Class A teasets (see Page 57) and, as already explained, the handles on the Anstice creamers are higher than the John Rose handles, being 4¼ inches as against 3¾ to 4 inches high (see Plate 39).

There seems little or no difference between the forms of the cups and coffee-cans made by Anstice, Horton & Rose and those made by the John Rose Company. Some slight variations do occur, but they are not consistent and therefore do not constitute reliable pointers to origin. The differences in the teapots, covered sucriers and creamers are the most reliable means of differentiating between the porcelain of these two Coalport firms. However, as a general guide, it can be stated that quite often the Anstice examples have the pattern number boldly painted under the main pieces in numerals some ⅓ inch high, usually without any prefix such as 'N' or 'No'.

Class D Teaware (Plates 45–47)

This teaware is probably the most often met with of the early Coalport porcelain. The teapots have a prow-like spout, seemingly pulled out from the body, and the matching covered sucriers have moulded animal-head ornamental handles at each end. This is the teaware shown on the Baxter workbench in the 1810 watercolour drawing (see Plate 42). The shape was made at both the Anstice and the John Rose factories, with slight variations listed below. The John Rose examples are readily identified by reference to the many fragments found on the pre-1814 site, and the Anstice, Horton & Thomas Rose pieces can be checked by cross-references in the Coalport pattern-book to patterns produced by Thomas Rose. These basic teaware forms were in production at least by 1807, as specimens bearing this date are recorded.

The first version of Class D Coalport teaware occurs in four basic varieties: plain; with slightly shaped and ribbed body (see Plate 43); with straight fluting; or with spiral fluting. A further version has different spouts to the teapots, while the covered sugar and creamer forms remain the same.

The Anstice and John Rose versions of the prow teapots are very similar, the main differences occurring in the covers. The Anstice knob is of narrow, pointed, oval plan, about ¾ inch long (against the 1-inch long John Rose knobs). The John Rose knob is of an elegant slightly-faceted umbrella shape, whereas the Anstice knobs are heavy looking, with a horizontal top line broken by a nipple-like central projection. The drawings opposite, and Plates 44, 45, and 46, show these differing knobs to good effect. The covers to the Anstice teapots have a moulded line running round the cover some ¾ inch from the edge, whereas the John Rose examples do not have this feature. The thumb-rest on the top of the handle leaves the handle horizontally on the Anstice teapots but tilts upwards on John Rose teapots.

John Rose Knob

Anstice Knob

The matching oval covered sugar-bowls are quite easily distinguished. The Anstice knob is the same heavy, narrow oval one that occurs on the teapot covers, while the elegant faceted umbrella-like knobs occur on the John Rose sugar-bowls. The 'beard' of the moulded animal (or demon) head on the Anstice examples is a 'fully grown beard' filling the ring beneath the head, whereas the 'beard' on the John Rose animal-head handles is 'trimmed' to fill only a third of the ring (see Plate 47 and drawing).

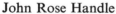

John Rose Handle

Anstice Handle

These oval sugar basins with relief moulded animal-head handles at each end are the standard ones found with teasets containing prow-spouted teapots. However, a further oval covered sugar was also made with applied turn-over grip handles protruding from each end (see drawing below). The same basic form was also made by the John Rose Company, but with a more graceful, slightly shaped handle and with the characteristic John Rose umbrella-shaped knob incorporating eight facets.

John Rose Handle

Anstice Handle

61

The matching creamers are remarkably similar, the Anstice examples being slightly narrower than the John Rose examples—2¼ inches or less across the widest part of the open top, against the 2½ inches of the John Rose creamers. The spout of the Anstice jug is slightly narrower than the John Rose examples, and the upward sweep of the body is cut off in a more pronounced manner.

A feature which helps to identify Anstice teaware of this 1807–12 period is the presence on some specimens of a small relief moulded circle under the teapot, covered sugar-bowl, or creamer.

There is a rare version of the prow-type teapot (see Plate 51). It has a twig ring knob to the cover and a simplified handle of plain loop shape without the stepped-in effect of the earlier handles. A very similar teapot was made by the John Rose Company, but with a different handle, incorporating the cover-holding lug (see Plate 49).

The matching covered sugar has entirely different moulded animal (lion)-head handles at each end (see Plate 51) and a ring twig handle matching that on the teapot. The matching creamers are very similar to those found with the normal version of prow-type teasets, except that some handles are the same as those on the new pot, with a simple curve (Plate 50) lacking the stepped-in effect found on the earlier creamers.

The teaware shown in Plate 60 would appear, on the evidence of the porcelain body and the shape of the creamer—which exactly matches that found with the previously mentioned tea services containing the prow-spouted teapots—to be a further but very rare form of Anstice, Horton & (Thomas) Rose teaware. Strangely, it is a shape not yet identified as being made by the John Rose Company, although almost the same teapot and covered sugar-basin shapes were employed by other manufacturers in the 1805–10 period.

A different version of the teaware with the prow-like spout to the teapots has an applied spout joined to the body with a slight bridge. The handle also is different, ending at the bottom with an upward curl (see Plate 41). There is a moulded border running around the bottom of the pot. Again, this form of teapot and matching teaset components was produced at both the Coalport factories; and a slightly different version, with different footrim and handle, was made by a so-far-unidentified factory.

Anstice teapot knobs now have nine facets, but the outline plan is oval; John Rose knobs have twelve shallow facets and the plan shows that their outline is not a cleanly drawn oval. Anstice covers have a recessed line running round the cover ¾ inch from the edge—a feature which does not occur on John Rose teapots. The scroll at the bottom of the handle of the Anstice teapots is more pronounced than that on the John Rose teapots—as if the Anstice handle terminal has been curved round on itself, giving a double thickness, whereas the John Rose handle ends with a short outward curve.

The oval covered sugars with the relief-moulded animal-head handles at each end, issued with the above-mentioned teapots, are of the same general form as those issued with the prow-like spouted teapots. However, a new form of knob was added, of umbrella form with nine facets against eight on John Rose examples (see drawings below), and having a moulded band running round

 Plan view of

John Rose   and   Anstice Knobs

$\frac{1}{4}$ inch up from the base, again to match the teapots (see Plate 54). The John Rose covered sugars found with this bridged style of teapot do not show the moulded bottom border and are, in fact, of exactly the same form as those found with the early teasets whose teapots have the prow-like spout without the bridge.

The new Anstice, Horton & Rose creamers have the new, simply curved handle with the slight outward scroll at the bottom end (matching the teapot handle) and two slight ears, one each side of the upward-turning thumb-rest at the top of the handle. They also have the moulded border at the base. The creamers found with the John Rose teasets, however, normally are of the old shape, with the stepped-in handle merging with the body at the lower end (see Plates 54 and 55). There is, however, a rare John Rose version of the normal Anstice creamer which has a wider spout, with the thumb-rest on the handle pointing forward (not slightly upwards as on the Anstice examples); and it does not show the two ear-like projections each side of the thumb-rest (see Plate 58). The John Rose examples also lack the double moulded border at the base.

Class E Teaware (Plates 61–2)

The form this new shaped teaware takes is radically different from all previous Coalport teaware. The new basic forms are shown in Plate 61.

Regarding the teapots, the knobs take the form of a fruit or flower bud and the handles are of grip type with an inward-curving projection above, into which the first finger readily fits. This handle appears to be fixed at its lower part by a mock screw or bolt, the head of which projects slightly. The spout has eight slight facets on its lower part. The contemporary John Rose teapots have a mock screw- or bolt-head at the top junction of the handle and the body as well as at the bottom junction, and the spout does not show the slight facets found on the Anstice teapots.

The matching covered sugars, with ear-like handles and bud knobs, would appear to be identical. I have not been able to discover any differences between Anstice and John Rose examples.

The creamers take two slightly different forms. In one the handle rises directly from the top back edge of the creamer; in the other it starts at a junction $\frac{1}{2}$ inch below the edge. So, again, both Anstice and John Rose examples would appear to be the same.

As explained on Page 35, in the John Rose section, the cups with this new teaware are of an entirely new form, the old graceful curved tea-cup with simple loop handle and the straight-sided coffee-can having been superseded by low, wide tea-cups and tall, narrow coffee-cups, the lower half being turned out with concave grooves. The handle has a thumb-grip which rises above the top edge of the cup (see Plates 61, 65, 69, 72, and 73).

Class F Teaware (Plates 63, 72, and 73)

The teapots—of rectangular form, with the corners and sides slightly shaped—are the first Coalport teapots not to be of oval plan. The knobs are of rectangular plan, whereas the John Rose knobs have canted cut-off corners. The moulded curved handle has a thumb-rest rising upwards from the handle; but the John Rose thumb-rest sweeps backwards from the top of the handle, almost horizontally.

The matching creamers from both the Anstice and the John Rose factories are very similar, the difference being mainly in the form of the moulded handle. The thumb-rest of the Anstice creamer handle matches that of the teapot, with the thumb-rest rising upwards from the side of the handle, whereas the John Rose creamer thumb-rest ripples off the top of the handle in a backward direction.

Cups found with these shapes normally have the concave, turned grooves near the base, with the thumb-rest of the handle rising above the top edge of the cup. Other services of this type have straight-sided cups with angular handles devoid of any thumb-rest (see Plate 63). Some services of this general type have plain angular bowls and extra pieces, such as covered muffin-dishes (see Plate 63).

A later variety of these basic teaware shapes occurs without the ornamental moulded handle and spout. Cross-references in the Coalport pattern-book prove that this simplified teaware shape was made by the Anstice, Horton & Thomas Rose partnership. All these shapes are shown in Plates 69–73, to which the reader should refer.

Class G Teaware (Plate 75)

This is the last so-far-discovered shape to have been made by the pre-February 1814 partnership of Anstice, Horton & Thomas Rose. The basic shapes are seen in Plate 75, which shows a part teaset with the painted pattern number 500. This design is drawn as number 297 in the John Rose pattern-book, with the contemporary note 'or 500 at Mr. Thos. Rose's', so proving the origin of this tea service. The same forms were, however, made by the John Rose Company (see Plate 74).

On the previous seven pages we have discussed the slight differences between Anstice, Horton & Thomas Rose teaware and those very similar forms made by John Rose and his partners. It is most improbable that the Anstice firm made only such teasets, and that they did not produce dessert and dinner services, jugs, mugs, vases, and other objects popular with other porcelain manufacturers.

On Page 45 I have identified early John Rose jugs. Similar jugs, which are probably examples from the Anstice factory, are also found with slight variations in the details of the moulding, usually in the handles. These are of simple loop form applied directly to the body, with the thumb-rest at the top of the handle pointing upwards (see Plate 105).

The handle on the John Rose examples (including a marked 'Coal-port' example and one dated January 1806) has a return kick under the top junction with the body, the thumb-rest leaving the back of the handle practically horizontally (Plate 104). Generally, the John Rose handle has a flattened top to the curve and the whole is set high on the side of the jug, so that the top of the handle is slightly higher than the rim. The Anstice examples have the raised thumb-rest level with the rim, with the top of the handle below the level of the jug rim, while the raised ribs under the spout are pronounced and number seven. There are, on the other hand, nine (or more on large jugs) shallow ribs under the spout of the John Rose jugs. In general, the Anstice jugs are slightly narrower and taller than the John Rose examples of the same basic shape. Although straight-sided mugs were probably made to match these jugs, as yet I have only been able to identify the John Rose examples (see Page 46 and Plate 109).

A further form of seemingly Anstice jug closely follows a John Rose shape, matching unglazed fragments found on the Caughley site. These are shown in Plates 106–8. The Anstice jugs have a stepped handle, terminating at its lower junction with the body in a shaped end, and the projecting grip from the top member of the handle is pointed downwards. The handle on John Rose jugs has moulded raised mock screw- or bolt-heads at the two junctions with the body (not present on the Anstice examples), and the lower terminal ends in a simple half-circle. The projecting grip takes the form of a scroll—not as downward or as pointed as in the Anstice examples (see Plate 106, which includes a half mould for the John Rose handle and also illustrates the mock bolt- or screw-heads).

Mugs were sometimes made to match these jugs. The finely enamelled and gilt initialled presentation jug shown in Plate 110 has a matching mug decorated in an identical manner, each obviously made and decorated by the same firm at the same time to accompany the other. Again, a very similar mug shape was made at the John Rose factories; and a John Rose specimen, decorated in London by Thomas Baxter, is dated 1809 (see Page 46 and Plate 110).

The characteristic ornately moulded handle was copied from Chinese porcelain of the 1780s and 1790s, and was used at Thomas Turner's factory at Caughley (taken over in 1799 by the John Rose partners). It has a raised heart-shaped panel near the top of the handle and a smaller one at the base of the handle. The Anstice moulded handle is almost identical with the John Rose handle, the most significant difference being in the mode of application to the body of the mug. The Anstice one is applied directly to the body, whereas the other is kept slightly away from the side of the mug by small pads of porcelain (see Plate 110).

The Anstice jugs and mugs are potentially of great importance. A dated example may well come to light indicating an early date for the establishment of the Anstice, Horton & Thomas Rose factory, for several of these appear to pre-date, by several years, the earliest reference we have to this firm in 1808.

65

I am sure that the Anstice works at Coalport produced much fine porcelain which has not as yet been identified, as it is entirely unmarked. I have initiated the research into this factory by identifying the teaware forms, two shapes of jugs and one form of mug. Many other pieces were probably made—such as vases, inkstands, spill-vases, pen-trays, and jardinières. Déjeuner services, supper sets, 'cabinet and ornamental vases', cups and cans and bowls, as well as dessert and dinner services, are mentioned in the January 1814 sale mentioned on page 54, which was in all probability the sale of the Anstice partners' stock before their dissolution of partnership on February 7th, 1814, the sale being advertised as being held 'on account of the Manufacturers and in consequence of a dissolution of Partnership' and which included tea and coffee equipages, and several superb and costly dinner and dessert services.

COALPORT PORCELAIN, 1815-1850 AND THE FACTORY PATTERN-BOOKS

At a period between 1815 and 1820 the standard Coalport porcelain was changed. As we learned on Page 28, the early Coalport body was of the hard-paste variety and was heavy in weight. The new body, however, is of soft paste—appearing open and floury in comparison with the dense early body—and the covering glaze is warm and gentle, though it may often display a minute network of fine cracks, termed 'crazing'.

A specimen bearing the 1820 'Society of Arts' mark (see Page 19,) gave the following analysis:[1]

Silica	42·88
Alumina	15·06
Lime	23·16
Phosphoric acid	16·30
	———
	97·40

The early examples of the 1820–30 period were somewhat heavily or thickly potted; but after this period the potting was trimmer, with plates and dishes of thinner gauge. The body also tended to become harder and more refined—in fact, similar to the standard mid-nineteenth-century English porcelain body.

---

[1] As given in Herbert Eccles and Bernard Rackham's *Analysed Specimens of English Porcelain* (V. & A. official publication, 1922).

Apart from the large circular 'Society of Arts' printed mark introduced in 1820, pre-1850 Coalport porcelain seldom bears a mark. The plates and dishes, however, often bear an impressed numeral indicating the size (see Page 17). Pattern numbers, often painted in a small, neat hand, can be of the greatest assistance in proving the provenance of this porcelain by comparison with the original factory pattern-books (see Pages 79–80 and Plate 160). The diamond-shaped Patent Office registration mark can also be of great help in identifying the Coalport shapes from 1845.

The identification of Coalport porcelain can best be carried out by comparison of the key shapes or the moulded decoration. These forms are illustrated in Plates 120–65, which are arranged in the same order as the pre-1815 porcelain—dinnerware, dessert services, and teaware, followed by ornamental articles.

A class of dinner-, dessert- and teaware bears an attractive relief-moulded design in the border, which is associated with the name Jones in the factory pattern-book. These moulded borders, shown in Colour Plate III, and Plates 120–3, 133–4, and 154, were also employed at other factories—notably at the Welsh Swansea and Nantgarw factories (see *An Illustrated Encyclopaedia of British Pottery and Porcelain*, 1966, Colour Plate IX and Plates 432–3); but the design may have originated, rather than have been copied, at Coalport—for at least one such moulded fragment has been found at the Caughley site abandoned in or before 1815. Parts of moulded dinnerware are shown in Plates 120–1, and some plates of this type reveal extremely fine floral painting (Colour Plate III). The basic moulded design was popular for some ten years from about 1815. The plate shown in Plate 123 is dated 1819, and many other specimens bear the post-1820 'Society of Arts' printed mark.

From about 1820 a new basic form of dinner service was in favour, at first concurrently with the moulded designs discussed above. The new plates had a tasteful moulded dentil edge; and the knobs of the tureens, small sauce-tureens, vegetable-dishes, etc, were modelled as fruit. The shape of these plates and the tureen is shown in Plates 124–5. A slightly later version has an oval tureen, and plates without the moulded dentil edging (see Plate 126). Coalport services of these types are normally unmarked, except for the pattern number painted in a small, neat manner.

The dinnerware shown in Plate 127 represents part of a fine, large service of the 1840–50 period decorated in maroon and gold. Some pieces bear the rare

JOHN ROSE & CO.
printed mark COALBROOKDALE The new form of moulded-edged plate
SHROPSHIRE

should be noted. A related design is found on services bearing the registration mark of December 1st, 1847, and an armorial decorated tureen and an oval platter from a dinner service bearing this registration mark are shown in Plate 129. A rather similar registered form of dinner-service shape is shown in Plate 128, with the tureen and vegetable-dish bearing the diamond-shaped registration mark of Jaunary 27th, 1845.

Dessert Services

The pair of superb fruit coolers shown in Plate 130 were part of the finest Coalport dessert set it has been my pleasure to see. My memory of it should be rather dim, for it was purchased by my father while I was still at school, and yet it is clearly fixed in my mind and I remember discussing the possibility of the service being Swansea. The body was pure and highly translucent; the flower painting seemed then, and even now, unequalled. However, the plates and dishes showed impressed numerals which we know occur on other examples of Coalport porcelain—examples which match designs in the factory pattern-books and, often, examples with the printed 1820 'Society of Arts' mark. The probable period of this set is 1815–20.

The fine dark blue ground, part dessert service (Plate 131) with hand-painted panels of flowers and birds is of the same period as the one mentioned above—that is, *c*. 1815–20. The shapes of the centrepiece and dishes are typical of the more expensive services of the period; and the pattern, or slight variations of it, are found on other Coalport porcelain. The service shown in Plate 132 is of the same 1815–20 period, but is of a less expensive nature. The same shape of handled dish was employed, but the centrepiece is simplified, the simple 'Japan' pattern with underglaze blue in conjunction with overglaze reds and greens being of the type painted by the lower-paid or apprentice workers.

The dessert-service dishes illustrated in Plates 133–4 (see also Colour Plate III) represent a range of fine Coalport porcelain, with the border designs relief moulded. The basic relief pattern—also, incidentally, found on dinner- and tea-ware—was introduced before 1815, as at least one example was found on the Caughley site. But this ware is normally associated with the 1815–25 period and several examples bear the printed 1820 'Society of Arts' mark. Similar relief-moulded border designs were used at other factories—at Swansea, Nantgarw, Derby and Davenport—but the Coalport examples normally have at least the impressed numeral marks (see Page 17). The quality of the flower and fruit painting found in the centre of this dessertware is most noticeable, and it is apparent that these services must have been the most expensive Coalport products of the period.

The simple but fine quality and tasteful dessert service shown in Plate 135 bears a rare style of scenic painting with some extremely rare seascapes. The pieces carry both the impressed numeral marks and the printed 1820 'Society of Arts' mark; and it is interesting to see that the indented-edged, slightly-lobed plate is continued some twenty years after its introduction (see Page 29).

Dessert services of the type shown in Plate 136 are often called Davenport, for an impressed fouled-anchor mark is found on some pieces. However, fractional pattern numbers (not employed at the Davenport factory) also appear, and in at least one instance this number agrees with the same design in the Coalport pattern-book. As long ago as 1862 Llewellynn Jewitt noted in the *Art Journal* that during the 1820s an impressed anchor mark was sometimes used—so the discovery cannot be termed new, although the fact is little known.

The service shown in Plate 137 represents a further class of Coalport dessert service, the design being basically a printed one, with the outline washed in with green enamel. The plates bear the impressed number 2, found on most Coalport plates from about 1815.

Plates 138 and 139 illustrate a dish and a covered sauce-tureen from 'Union' dessert sets—one of the staple moulded designs of the 1820–30 period. The handles of the dishes and tureens show relief-moulded emblems of the British Isles: a rose for England, a thistle for Scotland, and an Irish shamrock, hence the name 'Union'. Fine specimens were made in this 'Union' shape, most, but not all, painted with floral centres. The sample handled dessert-dish shown in Plate 138 was decorated outside the factory and bears the dated inscription 'Painted by Maria Hallen for her sister Mrs. Cottam, 1826.' The plate shown in Plate 140 represents a very rare class of Coalport dessert service of the 1820s. The relief-moulded bunches of grapes and vine leaves round the border also occur on Ridgway porcelain (see the *Illustrated Encyclopaedia of British Pottery and Porcelain*, Plates 477–8 and 480), but this plate bears the 1820 'Coalport Royal Society of Arts' mark and is of Coalport paste. The soft, fluid style of Coalport flower painting of the period can be seen to advantage here.

Coalport dessert services now discussed do not bear the 1820 'Society of Arts' mark and, in fact, bear only painted pattern numbers; but in many instances these numbers enable the design to be checked with the factory pattern-book.

The representative dessert-service components shown in Colour Plate IV are typical of the 1825–40 period, such services having no factory trade mark but only the pattern number. In this instance the pattern number is 2/601, which links with the factory pattern-book; but while this service is certainly of Coalport make, the Davenport and Ridgway factories made very similar shapes. Without going into details of slight differences in shape, it can be stated that the Davenport pattern numbers are not expressed in fractional form; and while Ridgway pattern numbers may be in fractional form, they are painted in a bold manner, some $\frac{1}{4}$ inch in height, whereas the Coalport pattern numbers are about half this size.

The covered tureen, plate, and dish shown in Plates 141–2 represent the standard dessert-service shapes of the 1830s, most of which are painted with floral centres, although landscapes and fruit subjects also occur. The fruit-painted plate and dish bear pattern number 2/893, which agrees with the drawing of this design in the factory pattern-book. The pattern-book entry also bears the notation 'Fruit by J. Birbeck' (see Page 103).

The services discussed above are normally of a soft paste and glaze, the latter showing a network of fine lines or 'crazing'. Subsequent sets from about 1840 are of a harder, more compact body, with a clear glaze normally free from crazing.

The dessert service shown in Colour Plate V illustrates typical shapes of the early 1840s. The centrepiece, or comport, stands $8\frac{1}{4}$ inches high but is rather foreshortened in the photograph. This service bears the painted pattern number 3/993, but, unfortunately, the pattern-book entry for this design does not appear to have been preserved. The same shapes can be seen in Plate 143, which shows the stem of the centrepiece or comport. This pattern is number 4/590, and the relevant page from the pattern-book is included in the illustration. The centres are 'flowers by Dixon' (see Page 108). The same shape of plate can also be seen in Plate 144. This example bears the pattern number 3/421, which agrees with the original drawing for this design in the pattern-book.

The fine service shown in Plate 145 is reproduced from an old photograph. Unfortunately, the number of the pattern was not recorded, but I have seen matching plates with the pattern number 4/412, a number which coincides with this design in the Coalport pattern-book. The contemporary notation 'Plants by Lawrance' is written against this design (see Page 116), but the basic shapes may be found with various styles of painted centres and panels.

The dessertware forms shown in Plate 147 date from December 1st, 1847, when these moulded-edged plates were registered at the Patent Office under the name of John Rose & Co of Coalport, and the pieces consequently bear the diamond-shaped registration mark (see Page 22). The pattern number on this particular service is 5/271, agreeing with this design in the Coalport pattern-book, which gives the additional information that the flowers were painted by Dixon. A detail of the flower painting is shown in Plate 146 (for information on Thomas Dixon see Page 108). Of course, these basic shapes of Coalport dessertware were also decorated with a variety of different patterns. Further basic dessert-service forms are shown in Plates 148–9. The openwork border design was registered on November 30th, 1849, and the diamond-shape registration mark will be found on specimens of these shapes.

The unglazed moulded fragments shown in Plate 150, representing teaware as well as parts of dessert plates, form a convenient link between this section and the following, which deals with teaware. These fragments were found in the mud in the River Severn, just below the factory—spoilt pieces which were thrown over the bank more than a hundred years ago, the river forming a most convenient dumping-ground.

Teaware, 1815–50

The part teaset illustrated in Plate 151 is moulded with sprays of flowers in relief, and is shown with an unglazed plate found in the River Severn just by the factory. The same relief-moulded design is drawn in the factory pattern-book against pattern number 988, where it is called 'New Embossed'. Several different patterns and backgrounds will be found with this 'new embossed' pattern during the period *c.* 1815–25.

The fine teapot featured in Plate 154 represents a further class of moulded design, rarely found on teaware, but obviously associated with the moulded dessertware discussed on Page 69 and illustrated in Colour Plate III; Plates 133 and 134. The description 'Jones' embossments' occurs in the pattern-book and may well refer to these relief-moulded designs.

The teapot, creamer and low covered sugar, shown in Plate 152, bear the circular 1820 'Society of Arts' mark, and represent one of the standard shapes of the 1820s. A variation is shown in Plate 153 with a low circular teapot, while further fine teaware shapes of the 1820s are depicted in Plates 155–60. The covered sugar-basin (Plate 157) with relief-moulded heads below the handles is a particularly rare shape, having the painted pattern number 961 which coincides with this design in the factory pattern-book. The elaborate handle to the cup is also the same as in the set (shown in Plate 156) of pattern 986, which again links with the original drawings. This cup shape is again seen in Plate 160 with the page of the pattern book open at the correct page, showing pattern 2/220 of about 1820–25. Another variation of this rare sugar-basin shape is shown with a matching creamer in Plate 158; these pieces bear the 1820 'Society of Arts' mark.

Coalport tea services rarely, if ever, included a coffee pot—although coffee cups were a regular feature of all sets. The covered jug shown in Plate 168 is probably a hot-water jug. While this shape is extremely rare, the pattern is very famous and is called the 'Indian Tree', based on a printed outline which was coloured over by hand. It is recorded that a whole section of the Coalport factory was devoted to the decoration of porcelain with this one design.

Factory tradition has it that the design was introduced in 1801, and one story tells how the pattern was copied from a piece of silk in the possession of an officer in the Shropshire Light Infantry. But I have never seen this pattern on Coalport objects that could be dated before 1820. I recently received a letter from Miss C. T. Herford, a descendant of A. Follett Osler (of the famous Birmingham glass manufacturers), informing me that, according to family tradition, some glassware returned from India was wrapped in a piece of paper bearing this design, which so appealed to the prosperous glass manufacturer that he asked the Coalport management to copy the design on to a teaset and some jugs—examples of the latter being retained in the family until recent times. Unfortunately, we have nothing to substantiate either the factory tradition or the Osler story, and perhaps rival traditions are held by other families.

To return to the chronological study of teaware forms, Plate 159 shows a further basic shape of Coalport teaware, with moulded design on the lower part of the main pieces and round the centre of the saucers. These shapes are of the early 1820s. The teaware shown in Plate 161 is slightly later, and from about 1830 the shapes became very rococo in feeling (see Plates 162–3). These unmarked post-1830 teasets are very often mistaken for Rockingham porcelain, but the pattern numbers and the original pattern-books prove their Coalport origin. Further Rockingham-type rococo-shaped teasets are shown in Plates 164–5. Their pattern numbers, 4/396 and 4/477, agree with the entries in the pattern-book, the low, wide teacups occurring in these teasets of the 1830s and 1840s.

Post-1815 Ornamental Ware

72 A large range of Coalport ornamental porcelain was made from 1815, and

although some discussed under this heading is not strictly ornamental, having various uses—as, for example, candlesticks or spill-vases—the term is here used to denote all porcelain other than tableware (dinner, dessert or tea sets).

Many examples from 1820 to about 1825 bear one of the self-explanatory circular 1820 'Society of Arts' marks (see Page 19) and little space need be used in describing this marked porcelain, examples of which are shown in Plates 169–70. Although the wall-pocket letter-rack shown in Plate 166 is marked, other of these rare and desirable items are unmarked and are found with various styles of decoration, including rich blue ground with reserve panels of flowers—a typical style that is shown in Plate 167 and is mainly associated with the Worcester factory.

Innumerable jugs and mugs are traditionally attributed to Coalport, most being painted with flowers or landscapes and some bearing initials or dates; but most of these presentation pieces are probably of Staffordshire origin. I know of only two certain Coalport jug or mug forms of the 1820–40 period, which is not to say that others were not made. I should be pleased to hear of others marked, or otherwise identifiable, Coalport jugs or mugs. The jug shown in Plate 174 is one made for Queen Victoria on or soon after her accession in 1837. This, like others still at Buckingham Palace, bears the initials 'V.R.' in gold on the front and the Buckingham Palace mark under the base. This basic shape may be found with other forms of decoration and in different sizes. Another, later, jug form is shown in Plate 173.

The mug illustrated in Plate 171 bears good printed views of the iron bridge just upstream from the Coalport factory and of the near-by Buildwas Abbey ruins. Again, the basic shape may be found in different sizes and with various styles of decoration.

Coalport porcelain from about 1825 to about 1850 was, in the main, unmarked (an exception occurring in some floral-encrusted porcelain discussed separately on Page 77). Consequently, many specimens are attributed to other factories. By fortunate chance, the design-book of John Rose's chief travelling salesman, William Hedley, has been preserved. This contains coloured drawings of many different vase and other ornamental forms, some of which are accompanied by notations giving details of the various sizes in which each shape was produced and also some prices. Small reproductions of the designs drawn in William Hedley's book are given in Plates 220–29 and some finished porcelain matching designs drawn in the design-book are illustrated in Plates 188–95. It will be observed that these designs included covered baskets, bowls with jugs, candlesticks and a candelabrum, cornucopia, a 'font', inkstands, jugs, a watch-stand, and many vases, both plain and ornamented with raised flowers. One group—two figures wearing cat masks (Plate 176)—was included.

The period of the designs drawn in the traveller's book appears to run from the late 1820s into the 1840s. The book was probably mainly used in the 1840s, but, of course, included drawings of the more popular earlier lines. It is inscribed at the front 'Willm Hedley, Madeley, near Wellington, Shropshire—Traveller for Mess. John Rose & Co., Coalport, near Ironbridge'. The local census returns,

73

compiled in April 1851, list William Hedley 'commercial traveller', aged fifty-two, giving a date of birth of about 1799.

The designs drawn in William Hedley's illustrated and costed book are reproduced in Plates 220–8. The various names, standard sizes and prices are listed below in the order that they appear in the book.

1. *'Brewer Vase'*

Plain	4 in	5s
	6 in	9s
	7½ in	10s 6d
	9¼ in	18s 6d
With raised	4 in	6s
flowers	6 in	10s 6d
	7½ in	12s 6d
	9¼ in.	21s

(See Colour Plate VII and Page 106 for details of Brewer)

2. *'Stick handled vase'*

Plain	7¼ in	12s 6d
	8½ in	15s
	10¼ in	21s (See Plate 190)
With raised	7¼ in	15s
flowers	8½ in	21s
	10¼ in	31s 6d

3. *'Tall Pastile, bouquet top'*

	9¾ in	12s 6d

4. *'Chelsea vase, flanged'*

	8 in	31s 6d

5. *'Oval Adelaide basket & cover'*

	8½ in	25s

6. *'Tall bellied Pastile & cover'*

Plain	7 in	12s 6d
With raised		
flowers	7 in	15s

7. *'New Cornucopia'* (See Plate 192)

Plain	6 in	12s 6d
With		
flowers	6 in	15s

8. *'Oval basket & cover'*

	4½ in	15s

9. *'Pastile, raised flowers'*

	7 in	15s

10. *'Dresden Pastile'*

	7 in	15s

11. No name given   10½ in   36s

(Wide double-handled vase; see Plate 189 for floral encrusted example)

12. *'Tall cross handled round basket & cover'* (See Plate 193)

	6 in	12s 6d
With raised		
flowers		15s

13. *'Chinese vase & cover'*

	14¾ in	4½ guineas

14. *'Cornucopia'*

	4½ in	4s 6d
	5½ in	7s
With raised	4½ in	6s
flowers	5½ in	8s

Coalport porcelain,
1815–1850 and the
factory pattern-books

15. *'New Font, raised flowers'*

	6½ in	3 guineas

16. *'New Poperee, raised flowers'*

	11½ in	3 guineas

17. *'Wigmore inks'*

	13½ in	36s
	15 in	42s

18. No name (bottle-shaped handled vase)

	13 in	27s 6d

19. No name (ornate handled vase)

	18 in	4½ guineas
With raised		
flowers	18 in	5 guineas

20. No name (handled vase)

No size given	36s

21. No name (ornate handled covered vase)

	18 in	4 guineas
With raised		
flowers	18 in	5 guineas

22. *'Sutherland Vase'*

No size given	52s 6d

23. No name (ornate handled covered vase)

		4 guineas
With raised flowers		5 guineas

(An example in the Victoria and Albert Museum is illustrated in G. Godden's *Victorian Porcelain*, 1961, Plate 3)

24. No name (handled vase)

	14¼ in	52s 6d

25. No name (handled vase)

	12 in	36s

26. *'Square top Beaker'* (flare-topped vase)

No size given		12s 6d
	7½ in	15s

27. *'3 Light candelabra'*

	15¼ in	2½ guineas
With raised		
flowers	15¼ in	3½ guineas

28. *'Fluted vase'*

	8¾ in	25s
No size given		31s 6d

29. *'Cabinet Ink', raised flowers*

	21s

30. *'Shepton [sic] Ink'*

	1st size	21s
	2nd size	25s
	3rd size	36s

(See Plate 194)

31(a). 'Oval basket & cover'   10s 6d
   (b). 'round basket & cover'   10s 6d

32.   'Two handle Cornucopia vase'
                              11 in   31s 6d

33.   'Cornucopia vase'
                              10 in   31s 6d

34.   'Stafford Ewer'   11 in   31s 6d

35.   No name (ornate handled vase)
      No size or price given
      (See Plate 188)
      (This vase, with Nos. 36 and 38, is on loose sheets in the main book; this sheet
      bears the watermark date 1845)

36.   No name (ornate handled covered vase)
      No size or price given
      (See note under No. 35)

37.   'Carter Vase'
                              10¾ in   42s
                              13¼ in   63s
      (See Plate 191)

38.   No name given (ornate handled vase)
      No size or price given
      (See note under No. 35)

39.   'Candlestick'
      No size or price given
      (This example of the same form as No. 41 is not reproduced)

40.   No name given (floral-encrusted vase, rather similar to No. 1)
      No size or price given

41.   'Candlestick' (same shape as No. 39)
                              6 in   9s
                              7 in   10s 6d
                              8 in   12s 6d

42.   No name (handled covered vase)
                              15 in   42s

43.   No name (tall covered vase)
      No size or price given

44.   No name (group of two figures with cat and monkey masks, see Plate 176)
                              8 in   18s

45(a). 'Chesterfield cologne'   28s
   (b). 'Pierced top match pot'   5s
      (A long gap occurs after this design; the following occur at the end of this
      traveller's design-book)

46.   'Braded ewer'   27s 6d

47.   'Brewer's jug, blue green & gold', handled and flowered
      No size or price given (see Plate 173)

48.   'Brewer's jug, green & gold'   6 guineas rate

49.   'Leafage jug blue, green & gold, handled'
                                                                     5 guineas rate

50. *'Leafage jug white & gold'*
(Same form as No. 49; No. 50 is not reproduced)
6 guineas rate

Ditto, gold edge only   2 guineas rate

51. *'New watch stand'*
8½ in   18*s*

52. *'Comport'*
No size or price given
(Same moulded edge is seen in Plate 147. A design registered in December 1847; this drawing is not reproduced)

53. *'Blenheim & leafage'* (Jug)   21*s* E.W.B. (each with bowl?)
(Same shape as No. 54; No. 53 is not reproduced)

54. *'Do. blue stripes and Dresden flowers'*
25*s* E.W.B.

55. *'Do. blue & gilt edge'*   31*s* 6*d*
Same shape as No. 54, not reproduced

56. *'Do. blue traced & Dresden flowers in compartments'*
27*s* 6*d*

57. *'Do. blue lines & gilt leaf'*, not reproduced
31*s* 6*d*

58. *'Octagon jug. Indian tree'*   36*s*

59. *'Wheat embossed, white & gold'*, not reproduced
6 guineas

Do. gold edge only   2 guineas

This documentary design-book with the several drawings and prices for richly decorated floral-encrusted porcelain leads us on to this important aspect of the Coalport styles of decoration. The floral-encrusted porcelain dates from about 1820 and, in keeping with the general policy of the period, most examples are unmarked. But some pieces of the 1820–30 period bear the following marks painted in underglaze blue:

C.D.   C.Dale   Coalport or Coalbrook Dale.

Marked examples are shown in Plates 177–83, but other examples of the same shapes may be found without factory marks. This is particularly true of the basket form illustrated in Plate 178. Most of these are painted with flowers—mainly compositions showing a tight bunch with one large bloom, often a tulip or rose, escaping from the top (see Plates 179–81, 183, 184, and 187). This characteristic grouping can also be seen on most of the drawings in William Hedley's design-books (see Plates 220–4).

Apart from the above-mentioned 'Coalport' or 'Coalbrook Dale' marks, some examples bear the Dresden crossed-swords mark; but this is more commonly found on Minton's essays in floral-encrusted porcelain. The ewer-shaped scent-bottle shown in Plate 184 has the initials and numerals 'W.T.36' in gold under the base. Similar marks occur on Minton floral-encrusted ware; but this scent-bottle has every appearance of being Coalport, as the flower painting matches that of other marked examples, and I picked up from the mud below the Coalport site an unglazed top section of such a scent-bottle. Most Coalport floral-encrusted porcelain made after 1830 is unmarked, and for many years it has been fashionable to attribute all such porcelain to the Coalport factory, but, in fact, nearly every porcelain manufacturer of the period made similar examples. The Minton factory produced an even larger range than the Coalport factory; but these Minton pieces have until recently been attributed in error to Coalport, and specimens are illustrated as Coalport in several reference-books.

In the case of Minton floral-encrusted porcelain, much contemporary information has been preserved—such as original drawings of the basic forms, estimates of cost for the various pieces, and even the names of the team of flowerers. Photographs of Minton drawings and finished objects are included in my *Illustrated Encyclopaedia of British Pottery and Porcelain*, 1966, and in my *Minton Pottery and Porcelain of the First Period, 1793–1850*, 1968. Some of these designs are also shown in Plates 234–7. It is noteworthy that no basic designs in the complete Minton records appear in William Hedley's book of Coalport forms.

Some charming and high-quality figures illustrated as Coalport in some reference-books are, in fact, of Minton make, and the drawings for these are contained in the Minton design-books. Sample illustrations of these drawings and finished figures are given in Plate 236 and in the two books mentioned above. Coalport figures are extremely rare, one group only being drawn in the traveller's design-book (see Page 73). The pair of figure candlesticks shown in Plate 175 bear the underglaze-blue 'Coalport' mark, but I do not know of any other figures or groups of the 1800–40 period that can be attributed to Coalport with confidence—although other models may subsequently be found. From the 1840s some parian busts, figures and groups were made; but even these are rare. A pair of busts depicting the Prince of Wales and Princess Alexandra bear the name mark 'John Rose & Co' with the date February 18th, 1864 . . . but post-1850 Coalport porcelain is discussed in Chapter VI.

As I have mentioned, several of the original John Rose pattern-books dating from the early 1800s have been preserved and retained by the various managements. The original records enable much early unmarked Coalport porcelain to be identified by comparison of the pattern number they bear with the original pattern-books. By this means different key shapes and, in some cases, the work of individual named artists can be identified.

Unfortunately, some books—including the first one, containing patterns preceding number 232—are missing. The following list shows which books are available, with the first and last number in each book. In addition to this basic information, other notes—including the approximate period of each book—have been added.

Sample pages from these books are reproduced in Plate 76, while check lists of pattern entries, including notations on the name of the artist responsible for painting certain patterns, are contained in Chapter VII.

CHECK LIST OF AVAILABLE COALPORT PATTERN BOOKS

First Book: c. 1800–10
Containing designs numbered 232 to 603 (with several missing). The page containing patterns 335, 336, and 337 bears the watermark date '1800'. Several designs have cross-references to the number of the same pattern at the rival factory of Messrs Anstice, Horton & (Thomas) Rose (see Page 56).

Second Book: c. 1811–20
Containing designs numbered 643 to 1000, then 2/1 to 2/170. Some pages bear watermark dates '1811' or '1812'. There are no cross-references to the same designs used by Messrs Anstice, Horton & (Thomas) Rose, a firm which closed in 1814 (see Chapter IV). Several designs drawn in this book are found on porcelain bearing the 1820 'Society of Arts' mark (see Page 19), and many patterns called for different colour borders. A check list of named colours noted in this pattern-book is given on Page 81.

Third Book: c. 1820–9
Containing designs numbered 2/171 to 2/508. Page showing design 2/182 bears the watermark date '1822'. Design number 2/444 has the date 'April 1st, 1829' added, and design number 2/507 (the next to last in this book) has the date 'August 1st, 1829' added.

Fourth Book: c. 1829–31
Containing designs numbered 2/522 to 2/670. Page bearing pattern 2/660, near the end of this book, is dated 'March 15th, 1831'.

Fifth Book: March 1831–c. 1832
Containing designs numbered 2/676 to 2/824. This book bears, in the front, the date 'March 18th, 31'. Design number 2/783 is dated 'April 27th, 1832'.

Sixth Book: c. 1832–3
Containing designs numbered 2/827 to 2/982. Design number 2/837, near the front of this book, is dated 'Dec. 18th, 1832'.

Seventh Book: c. 1833
Containing designs numbered 2/985 to 2/999.

Eighth Book: c. 1834–5
Containing designs numbered 3/2 to 3/133. Design 3/2 is drawn on paper bearing the watermark date '1833'.

Ninth Book: c. 1835
Containing designs numbered 3/134 to 3/161.

Tenth Book: c. 1836
Containing designs numbered 3/162 to 3/274.

Eleventh Book: c. 1836–7
Containing designs numbered 3/277 to 3/567. Some pages bear the watermark date '1836'.

Twelfth Book: c. 1837
Containing designs numbered 3/548 to 3/843. Some pages bear the watermark date '1836'.

Thirteenth Book: c. 1838
Containing designs numbered 3/846 to 3/999.

Fourteenth book: c. 1839–40
Containing designs numbered 4/1 to 4/338. Some pages bear the watermark date '1839'.

Fifteenth Book: c. 1840–1
Containing designs numbered 4/347 to 4/579.

Sixteenth Book: c. 1841–2
Containing designs numbered 4/583 to 4/706.

Seventeenth Book: c. 1843–5
Containing designs numbered 4/711 to 5/548. Some pages bear the watermark date '1843'.

Eighteenth Book: c. 1845–6
Containing designs numbered 5/166 to 5/548.

Nineteenth Book: c. 1847–8
Containing designs numbered 5/590 to 5/938.

Twentieth Book: c. 1848–50
Containing designs numbered 5/947 to 5/1000, then 6/1 to 6/251.

Twenty-first Book: c. 1850–5
Containing designs numbered 6/252 to 6/781.

Twenty-second Book: c. 1855–8
Containing designs numbered 6/784 to 7/324.

Twenty-third Book: c. 1859–60
Containing designs numbered 7/325 to 7/486.

Twenty-fourth Book: c. 1860+
Containing designs numbered 7/689 to 8/68.

No further books appear to have survived.

At the end of the nineteenth century the fractional system of numbering patterns was dropped in favour of progressive numbering, prefixed by letters indicating the type of article concerned (see Page 86).

CHECK LIST OF GROUND OR BORDER COLOURS MENTIONED IN THE *c.* 1811–20 PATTERN-BOOK CONTAINING DESIGNS 643 TO 2/170

Pattern	798	Light blue
	934	Purple
	935	Chrome green
	936	Ivory
	866	Blue ground
	872	Fawn ground
	877	Pink ground
	880	W. Bailey's green
	892	No. 2 green, W. Hancock's
	895	Pale rose
	918	Dark chrome
	919	No. 48 chrome
	933	Mistletoe ground
	938	Enamel blue
	976	Prussia blue, dark
	977	Apple green
	979	Yellow-green
	2/5	Wellington green
	2/10	Marone
	2/13	Bisque (kiln) blue
	2/39	Indigo blue
	2/43	Thomson's blue-green ground
	2/52	No. 10 Hancock's blue
	2/77	Buff
	2/80	S. Lawrenace's chrome green
	2/154	Celeste

Subsequent pattern-books list nearly every colour ever used on porcelain, and there is little point in listing the very many factory descriptions of post-1810 Coalport colours.

CHAPTER VI

COALPORT PORCELAIN FROM 1850

In general, Coalport porcelain tableware from 1850 to about 1875 is unmarked, like the earlier examples, although the ornamental pieces are often marked (see Pages 22–3). Pattern numbers in the fourth, fifth, sixth and seventh series may occur, expressed under these numbers in a small, neat hand. Certain moulded designs were registered at the Patent Office (see Page 22)—those registered in 1850 being illustrated in Plates 196–8—and, of course, these basic forms may be found decorated with a variety of designs. Other popular shapes registered in the late 1840s were also continued into the 1850s, and these often have potters' piece-rate signs in the form of letters or small star-like devices impressed into the underside. Similar potters' marks are found on other porcelain, but, in the case of Coalport marks, they are normally impressed twice on the same piece.

At the 1851 Exhibition 'John Rose & Co., Coalbrook Dale, Ironbridge, Shropshire' exhibited:

> Portions of porcelain embossed dinner services, crimson and gold, and turquoise and gold, etc.
>
> Dessert services, Rose du Barry, raised gold and flowers, embossed dessert services, green and gold, with plants, enamelled. Embossed services, celeste, gold and birds.
>
> China plates, various colours, with birds, plants, fruit, flowers, and heraldic decorations.
>
> Tea services—roses in gold ground, Victoria green and gold, turquoise ground and gold border, and white and gold.
>
> Small coffee sets, Rose du Barry, gold, etc. Celeste, gold, etc.
>
> Large porcelain egg-shell bowl and small pieces, various.
>
> Clock-case, gilt, with figures of Time and Cupid (Parian).
>
> Elevated flower-vase, supported by dolphins (Parian).
>
> Group of figures in parian, subject 'The Pleiades adorning Light'.

Group of figures in parian, 'Puck and his Companions'.

Pair of wrestling figures (Parian).

Basket, supported by three female figures (Parian).

Ornamental ewers (Parian).

Rose du Barry tripod epergne, with pierced basket, and representing the seasons, the cupids in parian.

Porcelain epergne, turquoise and gold, supported by sea-horses, executed in parian (see Plate 229).

Candlesticks.

Lotus vase, cream and sugar tureen.

Flower vases, turquoise and gold, supported by dolphins; also solid gold chased.

Lamp-pillar, pink and gold.

Apart from the above porcelain, exhibited under John Rose's name, fine Coalport ware was shown by Messrs A. B. & R. P. Daniell, the London retailers, whose premises in New Bond Street and Wigmore Street may be regarded as the Coalport Company's London shop. The 1851 Daniell exhibits included a plate that was a specimen from a rich service made to the order of Queen Victoria for the Emperor Nicholas of Russia, with various Russian orders and decorations. A similar plate now in the Victoria and Albert Museum is illustrated in my *Victorian Porcelain*, 1961, Plate 2. Messrs Daniells also showed 'dessert services, executed at the Coalbrook Dale china manufactory' which included a sumptuous one of a hundred and forty pieces with the Coalport Rose du Barry ground. The original engraving of an ice-pail from this service is reproduced in Plate 229, and the 1851 catalogue description reads:

> Ice pail in porcelain supported by dolphins, the handles of the sides and cover represent dolphins in graceful attitudes. The body of the ice pail is elaborately painted with groups of flowers and fruit. . . . The service contains two of these ice pails, and consists of about 140 pieces. It is now the property of the Right Hon. Lord Ashburton. The production of this celebrated colour, for the first time in this country (so famous at Sèvres during the reign of Louis XV) upon English porcelain, is deemed a great achievement.

The jury remarked on the excellence of the flower painting and gilding on this service and awarded the Coalport Company a Prize Medal. The rich ground colours on this porcelain of the 1850s were prepared by George Hancock (see Page 149).

The reader will have observed that no floral-encrusted porcelain was included in the Coalport display at the 1851 Exhibition. From this period onwards the vases and other ornamental objects lost their rococo floral style, and simpler classical or French forms came into favour. Whereas the earlier porcelain of the 1820–40 period tended to follow the lead given by the Dresden factory, porcelain from the 1840 period is clearly influenced by Sèvres ware in form, ground or border colours, and styles of decoration—such as exotic birds in landscapes. Plates 229–33 are reproductions from contemporary engravings of Coalport porcelain displayed in various international exhibitions held within twenty years from 1851. Finished ware of the same period is shown in Plates 199–205. The Sèvres-styled painting was mainly by John Randall—bird subjects; William Cook—fruit and flower compositions (Colour Plate IX); James Rouse—figure subjects, trophies, etc. Information about these and other Coalport artists is given in Chapter VII.

Apart from the ornate parian *tour de force* shown at the 1851 Exhibition, some forceful busts—including those of Wellington and Nelson—were made as well as portrait figures. A report dated April 1854 lists recent parian models as Aenon subjects from the Faerie Queen (modelled by Joseph Pitts), Britomart the Knight of Chastity releasing Amoret, the vision of the Red Cross Knight, and Sir Calepine rescuing Serena.

The Coalport management, like that of other factories, caused to be made high-quality copies of fashionable antique porcelain—noticeably, copies of decorative Sèvres and Chelsea models. Unlike the Minton policy of stopping short of reproducing the original mark, the Coalport copies often bear close imitations of the mark of the original. Joseph Marryat, in his *A History of Pottery and Porcelain, Mediaeval and Modern* of 1850 and 1857 (second edition), noted: 'We regret to have observed upon some recent specimens of this manufacture, marks of double L and anchor, in imitation of Sèvres and Chelsea.'

It would seem from the following newspaper report, under the heading 'Coalport', that the management received in 1854 several Sèvres designs direct from that manufactory:

> As evidence of the kind and international feeling now happily existing between France and England, it may be interesting to note that at the China Works in this country, a number of casts and drawings and other ornaments presented by the Royal Sèvres establishment have now been received for reproduction in this country. (*Eddowes Journal*, October 4th, 1854).

An ornate Chelsea-styled vase in the Victoria and Albert Museum, illustrated in my *Illustrated Encyclopaedia of British Pottery and Porcelain*, 1966, Plate 173, has the Chelsea anchor mark with the initial 'C' above. Some copies of the Sèvres mark also have the initial 'C' added, but by no means all Coalport copies have the initial added to the reproduction of the original mark. It is worth noting that some Chelsea-shaped vases are found with a reproduction of the Sèvres mark. Most Coalport Chelsea-styled ware is in the ornate, rich gold-anchor style, but some reproductions of earlier red-anchor-period Chelsea porcelain occur, and also covered bowls of cabbage-form. These latter articles, which have often been attributed to Chelsea, were probably made at Coalport by 1848, for a Minton letter dated January 5th, 1848 states: 'Herbert Minton & Co. do not make a Cabbage for the purpose of holding butter—the article is, they believe, made at Coalport . . .' Copies of the famous Chelsea 'Goat & Bee' small jug are also attributed to Coalport, and some may have had the Chelsea triangle mark engraved into the bottom.

From about 1851 to 1861 some of the finer Coalport porcelain was marked with a monogram of the initials 'C.B.D.' (Page 22)—a mark that was applied over the glaze in enamel colour or in gold and is found on ornamental or cabinet pieces rather than on tableware. Some fine classical figure decoration exists on pieces with this mark (Plate 199). In 1861 this monogram mark was superseded by the ampersand-like mark shown below, which incorporates the initials of the factories taken over by John Rose at an earlier period—Caughley, Swansea and Nantgarw; although the description 'taken over' as applied to the Swansea and Nantgarw factories is an exaggeration. The ampersand-shaped mark was also incorporated in various retailers' marks which, of course, prominently featured the name and address of the shop.

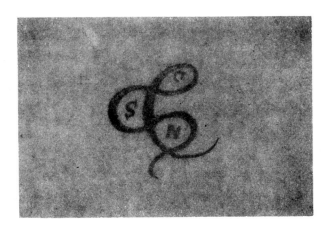

From about 1875 Coalport tableware began to be marked with the printed inscription COALPORT A.D. 1750. In 1881 a crown was added over this basic mark. Then, in 1891, the word 'England' appeared with the crown; and in the twentieth century, the words 'Made in England' replaced 'England'. These two marks were the standard ones employed from 1875 to 1939. They are to be found on hundreds of thousands of specimens, from inexpensive cups to ornate vases. The incorporation of the date 'A.D. 1750' in these marks has been the cause of much confusion to owners of Coalport porcelain bearing the standard marks, for they fondly imagine that their example was made in 1750. The right of this date to be incorporated in the mark is open to much doubt. It is the claimed date of the establishment of a *pottery* at Caughley, where Thomas Turner built his porcelain factory in the 1770s, which was taken over by John Rose and partners in 1799. Coalport porcelain dates from the 1790s (see Pages 4–9).

Apart from the printed marks listed above, most Coalport flatware—i.e. plates, dishes, saucers, etc.—from the 1900s bears impressed letters and numerals showing the date that each specimen was potted. These marks take the following form: 12 J 5 or 13 F 6, for example, denoting January 1905 and February 1906. It is not clear if the first numerals refer to the day of the month or if they are the reference number of the person who formed the article. The old fractional system of numbering the patterns had been dropped late in the nineteenth century and was replaced by progressive numbers ranging well above the old limit of 1000, reaching about 5000 by 1900. These new numbers had different letters placed in front, denoting the type of article—V on vases (a vase or goblet made for the 1902 Coronation bears the pattern number V.5148), X on dinnerware, Z on dessertware, Y on teaware. Some ornamental objects also bear painted size and model numbers—S/S 100, M/S 100, and L/S 100 referring, for instance, to small size, middle size and large size of design number 100.

Towards the close of the nineteenth century much fine jewelling was carried out, sometimes on a gold ground, sometimes occurring on teaware shapes 'registered' in January 1883. A writer in the trade paper *Pottery Gazette* noted in 1892:

> This ornamentation is exceedingly rich, and is shown on a great variety of fancy shapes. For the most part these are quite new models, and some of the tall handled vases are true artistic productions. The imitations of jewelled setting is very perfect, particularly the topaz and pearl. Some of the larger pieces—vases . . . have finely painted landscapes and other views on the side.

From about 1900 some of the Coalport artists were permitted to sign their work. Details of the different artists of the later period are listed in alphabetical order between Pages 100 and 130. The painting, often landscapes by Percy Simpson and J. Plant (Colour Plate X), is noteworthy, as is the fruit painting of F. H. Chivers or F. Howard. The work of E. O. (Ted) Ball and Arthur Perry is rightly sought after.

I have **already** stated that Coalport porcelain from about 1875 is nearly always clearly marked. As the main object of this book is to draw attention to the early unmarked porcelain and to assist in the identification of this neglected ware, space has not been used to show or discuss the often very richly decorated, high-quality post-1875 porcelain. Minor exceptions to this policy occur in Chapter VII, where details of some twentieth-century artists are given, and some purely representative late porcelain is shown in Plates 206–13.

In years to come other writers may wish to cover fully post-1875 Coalport porcelain. They should find pattern-books of the period preserved at the factory, and an interesting book showing post-1910 vase forms. But in this, the first reference book to deal exclusively with the history of Coalport, it has been felt right to concentrate on the earlier, unmarked specimens. One point of regret is that, although many of the Coalport pattern-books have been preserved, the old engraved copper-plates—many dating back to the Turner period at Caughley— would seem to have been sold for scrap in the 1950s. They were at the factory and seen by Mr Barrett before the publication of his book in 1951, but were apparently turned out before the company was sold to Messrs E. Brain & Co Ltd (see Page 92). Surely there should be some museum or other body willing to purchase such documentary material and save it from the scrap-heaps.

To turn to the managerial side, John Rose—one of the original partners of the 1790s—died in 1841. His name was, however, retained as the trade name of the company 'John Rose & Co' up to the spring of 1889, when a limited liability company was formed using the style 'Coalport China Company (John Rose & Co.) Limited'. John Rose was succeeded by Thomas Rose (probably the same person—that is, John's brother—who had been a partner in the rival firm of Anstice, Horton & Rose before 1814 [see Chapter IV] and who died in 1843), his son William Frederick Rose, and William Pugh, who had, in fact, been a partner since 1839. By 1862 William Pugh was the sole proprietor and remained so until his death in June 1875, when a Receiver (Thomas Gelson) was appointed to sort out the result of years of unbusinesslike stock-piling and haphazard manufacturing—whereby hundreds of saucers, for instance, were on hand without any matching cups.

In June 1880 Peter Schuyler Bruff, an East Anglian engineer with no knowledge of the ceramic industry, took over the Coalport factory, then available at a very advantageous price of £15,000. In 1888, when Peter Bruff's son Charles, on leave from India, visited the factory, he was influenced by the beauty of the valley of the River Severn and resolved to devote his life to restoring the Coalport factory to its former glories. He was appointed managing director of the new company and set-to on his self-appointed task, to use his own words:

to revive old designs with all the beauty and grace of once upon a time; to introduce new designs and patterns; to encourage originality and avoid imitation.

Peter Bruff remained in Ipswich and was kept informed of developments at Coalport by numerous letters from his son. One of the earliest letters from Charles has fortunately been preserved and is a most interesting document, setting forth the many malpractices he found at the factory. Extracts from this twelve-page letter, dated January 6th, 1889, are quoted below, but I have thought it charitable to leave out much of the material, as it throws a very unpleasant light on the situation at Coalport prior to 1889 and names are mentioned in unfavourable circumstances. The portion quoted below does, however, serve to show that to some extent the employees must have been responsible for the precarious state of the factory's finances and efficiency in the 1880s.

Coalport, Ironbridge, Salop.
6th Jany. 1889.

My dear Father,
I am commencing this Saturday evening . . . but I have dated to-morrow Sunday when it will be posted . . .
Last night I sat up devising schemes for piecework and other contrivances to prevent swindling in the manufacture . . . I have completed a

87

Muster and Acquittance Roll in one form, which I will have printed and bring into use at once, as I was horrified at the rotten system prevailing now and which was fully displayed at the payments today . . . I have consulted Benbow and he agrees about the necessity of having check numbers for the men and a lodge for them to pass through . . . I will have some numbers made at once in china, the size of a half crown, with our name and a number on each . . .

I think you will have to get someone in place of Mr. J . . . he has suppressed things from you which he should have told you—Today, just before payment when he knew I would find out, he informs me that Foreman Piper receives £1.12. a month in addition to his fortnightly pay of £4.4.0. and Foreman Brocksidge £2.8.0. per month in addition to his fortnightly pay of £3.16.0. Mr. J . . . states Mr. Gelson (the former manager and Receiver) gave these extras about a year ago to keep the men quiet, as they are jealous of each other. Piper now fondly imagines he is above Brocksidge as he receives £4.4.0. against his £3.16.0. but to quiet Brocksidge, Mr. Gelson gives him £2.8.0. extra against Piper's £1.12.0. These extra sums are paid on the Monday following pay-day in Mr. J . . .'s office . . .

I have taken possesssion of the Post Bag key, so as to control all letters—I shall go down to the Works now before breakfast, so as to open letters and give orders. I wish I had someone to assist me, I could trust, as next week I want to be mainly in the Works, but must under present circumstances devote much time to Office . . .

With regard to payment of wages yesterday, I fear the system hitherto pursued will prove to be another method of fraud successfully practised but which will be remedied before another pay day. I allude to the custom of paying 3 men under one number and only one person appearing to receive. By the new method each employee will have a number and must appear in person to receive . . .

Your allusion this morning (in a letter just received) as to work proceeding during Mr. Gelson's abstention, you need not be under the slightest apprehension—I will see they are all fully employed and I intend making each Foreman submit a daily return of work on hand and in progress.

I find I must close this long and I fear very painful letter to you as the Post leaves earlier on Sunday—Tell Bab I am so busy I cannot write today & give my love to all.

Hoping you are well,
I remain,
Your affect. son,
C. P. Bruff.

P.S. Bruff, Esq. Ipswich.

This letter shows that Charles Bruff brought a fresh mind to the task of bringing the Coalport works to its old glories. He was full of new ideas which must have at first made him very unpopular with the staff, who, it would appear, had enjoyed a damaging lack of responsibility and discipline under the Receiver appointed after William Pugh's death. However, the workpeople soon realized that Charles Bruff's policies were the only ones capable of ensuring the continuance of the Coalport factory, their one source of livelihood. Sir Compton Mackenzie, in his little book *The House of Coalport, 1750–1950*, 1951, prints in Chapter III several reminiscences of former Coalport employees who testified to the generosity and good citizenship of the Bruffs.

One of Charles Bruff's first tasks was to engage a new art director, choosing Thomas John Bott—a very talented ceramic artist, who had been trained at the Worcester Royal Porcelain Company and who had practised his art with great success in London and in the Staffordshire Potteries (see Page 104). It is interesting to see from Bott's correspondence that he wrote to Peter Bruff at Ipswich rather than to Charles Bruff at the Coalport factory—which suggests that the elder Bruff took more than a passing interest in the factory and did not leave all decisions to his son.

The complaints outlined in Charles Bruff's letters to his father were, however, matched by complaints from the workmen; and it would appear that Thomas John Bott, on taking up the post of art director, had to contend with some unrest among the workpeople. An enlightening letter, addressed to Mr Bruff and dated June 27th, 1889, sets out the demands of the gilders and printers; but perhaps the most interesting section of the letter is the list of signatories:

Sir,

We the undersigned being gilders and printers in your employ request that you consider our condition. Our branch of the trade being the worst paid for. Without there is some alteration we shall be compelled to give you a months notice from next Wednesday.

The following is what we require—

1) Count of ware same as Worcester (here follows a pencilled note 'shall be altered').

2) The same pay per hours as Worcester (pencilled note 'further explanation required').

3) That all existing patterns be re-estimated and priced at a rate to pay a medium workman a fair wage (here follows a pencilled note 'where possible to be considered and concession made').

We hope that these requests of ours will meet with your mature consideration; as it is only what is fair to yourself and us as men & master.

Signed (here follows individual signatures)

Sam Bednall	John Aston
Edwin Tagg	George Bebb
Christopher Skitt	William Smith
George Jones	John Richards

Thomas Wilkes

Robert Lowe

John Parhon (?)

George Boughey

Daniel Fone

John Boden

Edwin Brown

William Rogers

Harry Piper

John Oswell

Alick Ward

Joseph Birbeck

George Langford

James Richard

William Abbotts

William Hassall

Albert Taylor

Harry Evans

Stanley Worrall

John Shelley

Arthur Harrison

William Allen

Moreton Wilton

H. J. James

The late Alfred Langford, later to become art director at Coalport, was apprenticed in the printing department under Mr Brocksidge in 1899. Mr Langford wrote of these times:

> Along with other boys we worked from 7.30 in the morning until 6 at night, we had to get the coal in and light the stove pots before we came. From 6 we walked to Coalbrookdale School of Art. The wage was not great just 2/6d per week, shilling [rise?] every 12 months, in Winter we had to pay 2 pence a week . . . for the gas light.
>
> Charles Bruff made many improvements including central heating which was a Godsend for us. He had to get an Art Director, this was given to T. J. Bott. At that particular time Bott was painting for Brown-Westhead, Moore & Co., at Stoke-on-Trent (see Page 105) . . .

Mr Langford, born in January 1885, attended the local Coalbrookdale School of Art and was apprenticed at the Coalport works at the age of fourteen. He worked under Thomas Brocksidge, sketching out designs for the engravers; but he also relates 'we apprentices had to give a hand in all small decoration, such as on pin trays, toy cups and saucers, knobs for walking sticks, etc. . . .' Alfred Langford remained with the Coalport firm, moving with it to Stoke in 1926. He succeeded Thomas John Bott as art director in 1932, a post he held until the Second World War and its restrictions made unnecessary the talents of an art director. After the war Mr Langford worked for Messrs Booths and for the Crown Staffordshire Porcelain Co Ltd, until he retired in 1959 and returned to his native county of Shropshire, where he died in March 1968. The inclusion in this book of these details of Mr Langford's relatively recent ceramic career is relevant, for he had always shown a deep interest in the history of the works and had kept many letters and newscuttings relating to the later period, which have enabled me to add several items of new information to this chapter for the benefit of present and future collectors.

The Coalport management did not believe in advertising their ware during the latter part of the nineteenth century and the first part of the twentieth

century, feeling that the quality of their products was widely known. One of the few trade notices of the Coalport scene was published as an article—'A Brief visit to Coalport'—in the *Pottery Gazette* of October 1906. Some interesting extracts from this article are reproduced below:

Coalport is alike one of the most charmingly situated and one of the most inaccessible places that could be imagined. It is far away from any industrial centre, and its picturesque appearance in the beautiful valley of the Severn causes a stranger to wonder how any lover of nature could have desecrated the scene by first establishing a factory of any kind there . . . I have headed this article 'A Brief Visit to Coalport', I mean, of course, to the Coalport China Works. There was, however, no necessity to say so because the China Works are Coalport . . . there is nothing, practically nothing else there to interest anyone but the china factory, and nearly everyone in and around Coalport is either employed or is connected with someone else who is employed at it . . .

It was my good fortune to meet all these gentlemen (Charles C. Bruff, Chairman of the 'Coalport China Company', Mr. A. N. Bruff-Garrett, J. C. Cheadle (Secretary) and T. J. Bott—Art Director).

Mr. Bruff is a perfect compendium of information on all that pertains to the factory and the productions of Coalport. The works have been greatly enlarged, and a considerable portion of them has been rebuilt, and new and improved machinery and appliances have been introduced since the incorporation of the Company (in 1889). Every provision seems to be made for the health, convenience, and comfort of the employees. The artists and decorators work under most pleasant conditions. Light and well ventilated work-rooms look over the river Severn to the woodland scenery on the opposite banks. Every place and every person looks clean and fresh. There are about five hundred employed altogether . . .

The ancient and the modern mingle at Coalport in the most harmonious fashion. There are old cottages, some inhabited, and others converted into workshops, and in line with them there are substantial showrooms and artists' rooms built but a few years ago . . . The new premises are neat in appearance and conveniently arranged and fitted. A little distance away there are some new ovens built in the most effective modern style, and in the midst of them there is an oven of quite another stamp. It is claimed that this is the oldest pottery oven now working, and it looks it. The Company are self-reliant to a very great extent . . . they prepare their own raw materials, even calcining and grinding of bone. The river runs close to their premises, and they have a siding connecting with the railway. The Company do not use lead in their glazes, so that they do not come under the compensation rules . . .

As an evidence of the good feeling that exists between the principals and their employees, there was a remarkable demonstration to welcome the Managing Director, Mr. Charles C. Bruff, on his return from a visit to the United States. The whole was the spontaneous work of the employees themselves, who arranged it as a surprise to their principal. They decorated the approach to the works, and presented him with an appropriate address of welcome artistically illuminated by one of the staff and handsomely framed. But what Mr. Bruff prizes above all is an album beautifully bound in vellum and containing the signatures of every employee on the works, men and women, boys and girls . . . Coalport china has a world-wide reputation and its merits and special features are well-known to our readers.

The front part of the factory facing the road was rebuilt by 1902, although many of the old buildings at the rear, near the river bank, were retained and, in fact, still remain today. The early part of the twentieth century was such a difficult time for the pottery industry—especially for a firm left on its own, away from the centre of the industry in Staffordshire—that costs had to be cut and wages lowered, resulting in a strike in 1923. Charles Bruff was now losing thousands each year.

In 1924 the Coalport Company was sold to Cauldon Potteries Limited, the well-known Staffordshire company, and in 1926 the Coalport factory was closed, production being continued at Shelton in the Staffordshire Potteries. Many of the Coalport personnel made the trip to the new works by special bus (Plate 214). In 1936 a further change was made, when both the Coalport and the Cauldon concerns were moved to Messrs George Jones & Son's large five-acre Crescent Potteries at Stoke. In 1947 Mr S. T. Harrison and his son, Stanley, became proprietors of the George Jones Company which included the Coalport china division. The postwar years presented many new difficulties for the ceramic industry, when restrictions were placed on goods made for the home trade and, as we all know only too well, costs were rising year by year. In July 1958 Mr Harrison decided to close down the old Crescent Pottery, where the 'Coalport' porcelain had been made since 1936.

Fortunately, this is not the end of the Coalport story. In October 1958 Messrs E. Brain & Co Ltd, manufacturers of the famous 'Foley China', took over the concern. Mr E. W. Brain, the new managing director, has related to me how he first became interested in Coalport some twenty years before he actually purchased the Company. In 1939 his Territorial regiment was posted to Ironbridge, just upstream from Coalport; and, like Charles Bruff some fifty years previously, 'Bill' Brain was taken with the charming situation of the Coalport factory in the lush valley of the River Severn. He resolved to purchase the Coalport Company if and when the opportunity arose and to continue and build up on its former glories. The continuance of the Coalport tradition today may well have depended upon the chance drafting of a Territorial officer in 1939.

Mr Brain became so enthusiastic about the potentialities of the Coalport tradition that the old Foley name was soon discontinued in favour of the new Coalport image. Apart from revivals of old tableware patterns, sometimes slightly amended to suit modern taste or production methods, a new line of charming porcelain cottages—originally pastille-burners for scenting a room—has been introduced (Plate 215), as have limited editions of 'Coalbrook Dale' floral-encrusted porcelain (Plate 216). These *tours de force* have enjoyed conspicuous success on both sides of the Atlantic: a success which has been supported by the sales of the 'bread and butter' lines—the well-designed, tasteful tableware.

In July 1967 the Coalport company joined forces with the Wedgwood group so that, with the resources of this large company, the task of bringing back the name of Coalport to its former glorious position in the history of English fine porcelain would be accomplished even more efficiently. The name 'Coalport' will, of course, be retained. In closing this chapter and the short résumé of recent changes of ownership, I wish to record again my debt to Mr Brain for his interest in my researches and for his generosity in lending me many of the original factory pattern-books, so enabling me to check many of my attributions against the original factory records. He has recently retired, having done much to continue the story of Coalport fine china, a product to be found on the tables of discerning folk the world over, as well as in the cabinets of collectors.

CHAPTER VII

COALPORT ARTISTS

A brief check list of Coalport artists, their subjects and working periods, will be found on Pages 100–30. Pattern numbers that can be attributed to individual artists are given on Pages 130–36.

Very little is known about the early, pre-1815, Coalport artists. Of these, the gilders of the 1797–1815 period are, however, probably more worthy of note—for the fine and tastefully designed gold ornamentation shows more individual talent than the popular 'Japan' patterns with their bold designs in red and green enamel, in conjunction with areas of underglaze blue.

The name of one 'Japan' painter is recorded by John Haslem (*The Old Derby China Factory*, 1876) while writing of Derby artists and gilders:

> George Mellor, a gilder and Japan painter, was apprenticed at Derby but left in 1796, before the expiration of his apprenticeship, and went to Pinxton, where he worked under Billingsley until 1799, he then got employed at Coalport and remained there until 1811 . . .

The recently discovered Pinxton factory records show that George Mellor's first wage was paid in November 1796, his last in January, 1799, his standard wage being 1*s* 2*d* a day (*The Pinxton China Factory*, 1963, by C. L. Exley). The facts link well with Haslem's information. Haslem continued: 'On leaving he (George Mellor) worked in the Potteries, a few years; afterwards he returned to Derby, where he was employed with little intermission until about 1830. He died in Derby in 1861, in his eighty-fifth year.' George Mellor's name is included in the 1841 Derby census return, which gives the information that he was born at Derby. In 1841 he was in the age group 60 to 64, and was then a china dealer in Victoria Street. His date of birth was about 1776, so that he was aged approximately twenty-three to thirty-five during his twelve years' employment at the Coalport factory.

The obvious popularity of the early Coalport 'Japan' patterns and the number of surviving specimens suggests that several painters must have been employed on these gaily decorated services, of whom only the name of George Mellor has been recorded.

During the evening of October 23rd, 1799, the ferry taking forty-one of the Coalport employees to their homes on the opposite bank of the River Severn was overturned and twenty-eight were drowned (see Page 9). The names of the drowned personnel were recorded, the thirteen men being: William Beard, John Cheil, James Farnsworth, Benjamin Gosnal, John Jones, John Leigh, Robert Lowe, George Lynn, Richard Mountford, Joseph Poole, George Sheat, Charles Walker, and Benjamin Wyld. Unfortunately, from the collector's point of view, their calling—painter, gilder, turner, kilnman, etc.—was not recorded, so that we do not know how many of these persons were artists.

Several books state that Charles Walker was a leading Coalport painter, and illustrate a damaged and partly finished casket and cover, painted with figure subject and floral panels, as a piece Walker was decorating before he was drowned. This specimen, however, is clearly—in shape and style of decoration—of a period some thirty or forty years after the 1799 accident. (A further unfinished piece attributed to Walker is part of a vase, seemingly of French hardpaste porcelain.) This does not mean that Charles Walker was not an early Coalport artist, but simply that the so-called documentary specimen of his work is open to the gravest doubt.

While factory-decorated Coalport porcelain of the period prior to 1850 is always unsigned, some decorative specimens of the 1800–20 period do bear, on occasions, such names as Thomas Baxter, Donovon, W. Fletcher, or Thomas Pardoe. These are the names of independent decorators (and retailers) who purchased undecorated Coalport porcelain for their own requirements. They are not factory artists, and for further information on these decorators see Pages 136–9.

An early marked 'Coalbrookdale' plate in the Victoria and Albert Museum has in the past been attributed to the much-travelled former Derby flower painter William Billingsley. It is known that Billingsley did visit Coalport in 1811 in connection with the building of a new kiln, and he was reputedly at Coalport from *c.* 1820 until his death in 1828 at the age of 70. But it is not known if he decorated Coalport porcelain. The plate in the Victoria and Albert Museum which has been attributed to him would certainly seem to pre-date his recorded visit by several years.

John Haslem, in his *The Old Derby China Factory*, 1876, states that Henry L. Pratt, a former Derby ceramic painter as well as a noted oil painter, worked at Coalport. But his name does not occur in surviving Coalport records, and the legend that he worked at Coalport may have arisen from a misreading of Pratt's obituary notice which appeared in the *Staffordshire Sentinel* on March 8th, 1873. This states that his *oil* paintings were to be found in Derby, Birmingham and Coalport. Regarding his *ceramic* painting, the obituary mentions only the Derby factory and Messrs Minton. It is not disputed that Pratt was in the Coalport district, for a daughter, Ann Elizabeth, was born at near-by Ironbridge, *c.* 1850.

Having disposed of some improbables, we can refer to artists whose names are recorded in contemporary documents. The most important of these sources is the original factory pattern-book, where, from about 1825, the names of some artists are recorded against patterns which they painted. It must be understood that only a small percentage of the drawings in the factory pattern-books have the painter's name added (and some books and individual pages are missing); but when they do occur they are of the utmost value in gauging the painter's speciality and, in some cases, in tracing specimens of his work. The numbers of the patterns known to have been painted by each artist are given under his name and are repeated in the progressive list printed on Pages 130–6.

A further source of information on painters is the fact that many of the Coalport personnel went on strike in November 1833 over the right to join or form a union. On March 3rd, 1834, the loyal employees who had remained at work presented John Rose with an address setting out their reasons for remaining at work and acknowledging 'the extreme generosity of Mr. Rose, in striving to find, in bad times, employment for a surplus number of hands, to the detriment of his own pocket and to the injury of old workmen'. The following persons—probably the leading, well-established hands—signed this loyal address. To the names of some of the signatories I have added their occupation (gleaned from census returns) and references to pages containing further information on the artists and gilders.

George Aston	
William Aston	
Thomas Bagshaw	'china painter'
Joseph Birbeck	'china painter', see Page 103.
John Culliss	
Thomas Dixon	'china painter', see Page 108.
B. T. Goodwin	
John Greatbatch	'china potter' (maker?)
Joseph Harper	
Thomas Hayward	
John Hughes	'china painter'
Edward Jones	'china painter', see Page 114.
John Jones	'china painter' or gilder, see Page 114.
John Leighton	'china painter', see Page 116.
George Mansell	'china painter'
Abraham Milner	'china gilder', see Page 117.
Enoch Nevitt	
Josiah Patten	'china painter', see Page 119.
John Poole	
James Rouse	'china painter', see Page 123.
J. H. Smith	
Thomas Speak	'china painter', see Page 125.
Henry Stephan	'china potter'
Peter Stephan	'artist modeller', see Page 127.
William Stephan	'china potter'
Hamlet Stevens	'china painter', see Page 128.
W. Street	'china gilder', see Page 129.
William Worrall	

A further undated list has been preserved. This is quoted below and would seem to have been prepared by someone having first-hand knowledge of the Coalport artists of the 1840–60 period. The sheet bears a subheading 'List of Painters from 1840':

> . . . Mr. J. Birbeck succeeded to be Foreman about 1844.
> William Street was the designer and superintended the apprentices.
> Mr. Randall. Sèvres Birds.
> William Trevis. Flowers.
> Josiah Pattern. Crests & Flowers & Wild flowers.
> John Williams. Sèvres flowers & groups.
> Thomas Dixon. Flowers.
> Hamlet Stevens. Sèvres flowers & Chelsea groups & flies.
> Cecil Jones ⎱ These left Coalport about 1846 or 1848
> Stephen Lawrence ⎰ to work at Wordsley on Glass.
> William Cook. Sèvres flowers—on dessert comports (?) & baskets for the 1851 Exhibition, also painted the Arms of the Emperor of Russia's Dessert Service.
> Jabez Aston. Fruit & Plants.
> John Parker. Groups of Flowers & a good copyist.
> Samuel Powell. Flowers.
> Thomas Steele. Landscapes.
> Edward Jones. Foreman of Paintresses at Ropewalk. (Presumably a separate department for the female painters.)
> John Leighton. Foreman of Woman Gilders & Japanners.
> W. Sneyd ⎱ Engravers.
> Jessie Pepper ⎰
>
> Others came from the (Staffordshire) Potteries and Worcester and worked for a time, but the list given above refers to the old Coalport workmen.
>
> Some of a more recent period were Arthur Bowdler who sat next to Mr. Cook, William Dixon, who left and went to Minton (? this word is indistinct), William Stevens.

Of the painters given as of a 'more recent period', Arthur Bowdler and William Dixon were included in the 1859 wages list (see Page 98). Bowdler was born in 1842, and Dixon in 1833. William Stevens was born in about 1830 and his name is included in the 1851 census returns as a 'China painter'. It would appear that this undated and unsigned list was drawn up in the 1850s or 1860s at the latest.

Other vital sources of information on the Coalport artists are the census returns of 1841, 1851, and 1861, which give in most cases the ages and occupations of the local inhabitants—and also, in the case of the 1851 and 1861 returns, their place of birth.

A painters' wage list of 1859 has fortunately been preserved, and has proved a most helpful guide to the later Coalport artists. This hitherto unpublished list is headed 'Messrs. John Rose & Compy. Coalport. Painters Bills from 29th Jany 1859 (for 14 days)', and includes the names of seventy-three Coalport painters or gilders with their wages for that period. The full list is given in alphabetical order on Pages 99–100.

While many painters were no doubt apprentices or youths drawing a very low wage, it is surprising the number of highly paid and presumably talented artists or gilders named here who are not mentioned as Coalport artists in earlier books on this factory. I have included the named decorators who drew £1 10s 0d or more, for these painters must have been regular artists or gilders of standing. The list is given in descending order of wages received, and cross-references have been added so that the reader can quickly find detailed information on each person listed. The descriptions 'artists' or 'gilders' have in most cases been extracted from the local census returns taken in 1851 and 1861.

Joseph Birbeck & Co	£6 5s 0d	(artist?)	See Page 103.
Francis Birbeck	£5 10s 0d	(artist)	See Page 103.
John Harvey & Co	£4 14s 0d	(ground layer)	See Page 112.
William Cook	£4 0s 0d	(artist)	See Page 107.
Joseph Birbeck, Senr	£3 10s 0d	(artist)	See Page 103.
William Street	£3 3s 0d	(gilder)	See Page 129.
James Rouse, Senr	£2 14s 0d	(artist)	See Page 123.
John Randall	£2 10s 0d	(artist)	See Page 122.
Daniel Lucas	£2 10s 0d	(artist)	See Page 117.
Henry Pedley	£2 10s 0d	(artist)	See Page 119.
John Benbow	£2 10s 0d	(artist)	See Page 102.
Henry Evans	£2 5s 0d	(artist)	See Page 110.
Philip Birbeck	£2 5s 0d	(artist)	See Page 103.
William Steele	£2 4s 8½d	(gilder?)	See Page 127.
James Rouse, Junr	£2 2s 0d	(artist)	See Page 123.
Thomas Edwin Pugh	£2 0s 0d	(artist)	See Page 121.
Thomas Dixon	£2 0s 0d	(artist)	See Page 108.
Joshua Jones	£2 0s 0d	(artist)	See Page 114.
William Dixon	£2 0s 0d	(artist)	See Page 108.
William Evans	£2 0s 0d	(gilder)	See Page 110.
Edwin Pattern (or Patten)	£2 0s 0d	(artist)	See Page 119.
Hamlet Stevens	£2 0s 0d	(artist)	See Page 128.
William Trevis	£2 0s 0d	(artist)	See Page 129.
John Bennett	£1 16s 0d	(artist)	See Page 103.
Benjamin Potts	£1 16s 0d	(gilder)	See Page 121.
George Adams	£1 14s 0d	(gilder)	See Page 101.
John Davies	£1 14s 0d	(——)	No other record.
John Fall	£1 10s 0d	(artist)	See Page 110.
William Jenks	£1 10s 0d	(gilder)	See Page 113.
Richard Spendlove	£1 10s 0d	(artist)	See Page 126.

The complete list of persons included in the list of Coalport 'Painters Bills from 29th Jany 1859' has been rearranged, for easy reference, in alphabetical order:

George Adams	£1 14s 0d	See Page 101.
Jabez Aston	no amount recorded[1]	See Page 101.
John Aston	no amount recorded[1]	See Page 101.
John Bagshaw	£1 5s 0d	See Page 102.
James Ball	£1 8s 0d	See Page 102.
Thomas Ball	£1 8s 0d	See Page 102.
John Benbow	£2 10s 0d	See Page 102.
John Bennett	£1 16s 0d	See Page 103.
Francis Birbeck	£5 10s 0d	See Page 103.
Joseph Birbeck, Senr	£3 10s 0d	See Page 103.
Joseph Birbeck & Co	£6 5s 0d	See Page 104.
Philip Birbeck	£2 5s 0d	See Page 103.
Arthur Bowdler	12s 0d	See Page 105.
Edwin Brown	£1 4s 0d	
Richard Caswell	12s 0d	See Page 106.
Joseph Chew	3s 6d	
William Churchman	£1 8s 0d	See Page 106.
William Cook(e)	£4 0s 0d	See Page 107.
John Davies	£1 14s 0d	
Samuel Davies	£1 5s 0d	
Thomas Dixon	£2 0s 0d	See Page 108.
William Dixon	£2 0s 0d	See Page 108.
John Downes	4s 0d	See Page 109.
Robert Eaton	6s 0d	See Page 109.
William Ellis	10s 0d	See Page 109.
Aquila Evans	10s 0d	See Page 109.
Frederick Evans	£1 10s 0d	See Page 109.
Henry Evans	£2 5s 0d	See Page 110.
William Evans	£2 0s 0d	See Page 110.
John Fall	£1 10s 0d	See Page 110.
James Glover	8s 0d	See Page 110.
John Harper	no amount recorded[1]	See Page 111.
James Hartshorne	10s 0d	See Page 111.
John Harvey & Co	£4 14s 0d	See Page 112.
Holland Harvey	10s 0d	
John Heighway	12s 0d	See Page 112.
Thomas Hodgkiss	£1 10s 0d	See Page 112.
Edwin Howells	£1 8s 0d	See Page 112.
William Jenks	£1 10s 0d	See Page 113.
Alfred Jones	£1 5s 0d	See Page 113.

[1] The artists were obviously on the Coalport payroll at this period, but on account of illness, etc, no work had been carried out in the period covered by this one preserved list.

John Jones	£1 8s 0d		See Page 114.
Joshua Jones	£2 0s 0d		See Page 114.
Levi Jones	no amount recorded		
William Jones	no amount recorded		See Page 114.
Frederick Love	12s 0d		See Page 116.
Robert Lowe	10s 0d		See Page 116.
Daniel Lucas	£2 10s 0d		See Page 117.
John Merrington	18s 0d		
Richard Owen, Senr	16s 0d		See Page 118.
Richard Owen, Junr	4s 0d		
Edwin Pattern	£2 0s 0d		See Page 119.
Josiah Pattern	£1 7s 0d		See Page 119.
Henry Pedley	£2 10s 0d		See Page 119.
John Poole	18s 0d		
William Pope	£1 8s 0d		See Page 121.
Benjamin Potts	£1 16s 0d		See Page 121.
Thomas Potts	9s 0d		
Thomas Edwin Pugh	£2 0s 0d		See Page 121.
John Randall	£2 10s 0d		See Page 122.
James Richards	9s 0d		See Page 123.
Robert Roden	£1 0s 0d		
James Rouse, Senr	£2 14s 0d		See Page 123.
James Rouse, Junr	£2 2s 0d		See Page 123.
William Rouse	£1 7s 0d		See Page 124.
Edward Soulsby	£1 0s 0d		See Page 125.
Thomas Speak	£1 7s 0d		See Page 125.
Samuel Spencer	16s 0d		See Page 126.
Richard Spendlove	£1 10s 0d		See Page 126.
George Stanway	£1 4s 0d		See Page 126.
William Steele	£2 4s 8½d		See Page 127.
Hamlet Stevens	£2 0s 0d		See Page 128.
William Street	£3 3s 0d		See Page 129.
William Trevis	£2 0s 0d		See Page 129.

Information on the later Coalport artists has been gathered from the persons concerned or from their fellow artists. From about 1890 the leading artists signed their work, and examples are therefore of documentary interest.

The following list of Coalport artists, gilders and modellers is arranged in alphabetical order:

ROBERT FREDERICK ABRAHAM. Painter. c. 1855–62
Robert Frederick Abraham was born in London in 1827, reputedly studied in Paris and Antwerp, and exhibited at the Royal Academy from 1846 to 1851. He had moved from London to Coalport by 1855, for his daughter was born at near-by Madeley.

Abraham's ceramic painting on Coalport porcelain was shown at the 1862 Exhibition, a contemporary account of his work reading in part:

> The principal painter of the present day . . . is Mr. Abrahams . . . The softness of touch, the purity and delicacy of feeling, and the sunny mellowness of tone, as well as the chasteness of design and correctness of drawing, produced on the best pieces of this gentleman's productions, show him to be a thorough artist, and place him high above others in this difficult art.

Abraham's figure paintings are often in the style of William Etty, but he also favoured Cupid subjects. Other Abraham compositions comprise classical figures delicately painted. It is regrettable that this artist left Coalport after seven or eight years. His name is included in the April 1861 census returns, but soon after this he joined the Hill Pottery in Staffordshire and in 1865 was appointed art director at Copelands, a post he held for many years.

GEORGE ADAMS. Gilder. *c.* 1851+

George Adams was born at Broseley in about 1833. He is included in the 1859 artists' and gilders' wages list, and is listed in the 1861 census returns as a 'china painter'; but both the 1871 and the 1881 returns list him as a 'china gilder'.

JABEY ASTON. Flower painter. *c.* 1820–75

Aston was born at Ironbridge, near Coalport, in about 1799. He was a very talented fruit and flower painter who served the Coalport management over a long period. It is highly probable that he painted some of the powerful floral and fruit studies which occur on porcelain of the 1820s without pattern numbers.

The first reference to Jabey Aston in the pattern-book occurs under design 2/717, 'Flowers by Jabey Aston'. Other named references include: 2/964, 'Jabey Aston's flowers'; 3/195, 'Save (Sèvres) group by Jabez Aston'; 3/210, 'Fruit by Aston'; 3/234, 'Fruit in centre by J. Aston'; 3/421, 'Plants painted by J. Aston' (see Plate 144); 3/432, 'Fruit by J^{by.} Aston'; 3/433, 'Fruit by Mr. Aston'; 3/436, 'Fruit by J. Aston'. Other Aston patterns were: 3/135, 3/583, 3/596, 3/601, 3/603, 3/724, 3/725, 3/726, 5/249, 5/273, 6/422, 6/558, 6/582, 6/672, 6/676, 6/741, and 7/389.

His name is included in the local census returns of 1841, 1851, and 1861, and also in the 1859 wage list (but no payment is recorded). Some fine plaques painted with fruit and flowers are signed and dated, one example bearing the date 1867. Rather surprisingly, Llewellynn Jewitt, writing ten years later, records that Jabey Aston was still employed at Coalport, being one of the 'principal artists'. The 1859 painters' and gilders' wage list also includes the name John Aston (see next entry).

JOHN ASTON. Gilder, heraldic artist. *c.* 1859+

John Aston was born in the Coalport district in about 1846. The name is included in the 1859 wage list for painters and gilders and in the 1881 census return he is described as a 'China gilder, Heraldic artist'.

WILLIAM ROBERT ASTON. Painter. *c.* 1860+

William Robert Aston is listed as a locally born 'porcelain painter', aged thirty, in the 1861 Coalport census returns; but no other references have been traced relating to him. Details of Jabez Aston are given on Page 101.

JAMES or JOHN BAGSHAW. Painter or gilder. *c.* 1850+

James Bagshaw was born at Broseley in about 1827. In the 1851 census returns he was listed as a 'china painter'. However, the 1859 wages list gives only John Bagshaw. The 1861 census return lists John Bagshaw 'china gilder', the place and date of birth agreeing with those of James Bagshaw in the 1851 returns. The initial and name 'J. Bagshaw' appears against design 7/379 in the pattern-books.

EDWARD (TED) BALL. Landscape painter. Late nineteenth century

Edward Ball was the leading Coalport landscape painter late in the nineteenth century, who worked into the twentieth century. His work is often signed 'E. BALL', 'E. O. BALL', or 'T. BALL' (see Plate 207).

Earlier Coalport artists bearing the name Ball include James, Michael, and Thomas Ball (see below), but no other details are available on these artists or gilders.

JAMES BALL. Painter(?). *c.* 1851+

James Ball was born at Westminster in about 1822. His name is included in the 1851 and 1861 census returns as a 'china painter', and it appears in the 1859 wages list. He was still employed in 1881. Patterns 5/378, 7/341, 7/408, 7/411, 7/412, 7/414, 7/460, 7/464, and 7/468 have Ball's name noted against them.

THOMAS BALL. Gilder and/or painter. *c.* 1850+

Thomas Ball was born at Broseley, near Coalport, in about 1821. His name is included in the 1841, 1851, 1861, 1871, and 1881 census returns. In those of 1861, 1871, and 1881 he is described as a 'gilder on china', and in the earlier returns as a 'china painter'. It is therefore possible that he was both a painter and a gilder. In the 1859 return, the wage of £1 8s 0d is recorded against his name.

JOHN BEARD. Garden scenery subjects. *c.* 1850+

John Beard was born at Broseley in about 1836. In the 1851 census returns he is described as an 'apprentice china painter'. His name is given against designs 4/580, 4/587, 4/598, and 4/606 in the pattern-book. Pattern 4/580 has the notation 'Garden Scenery by Beard'. This artist should not be confused with the two Derby-trained artists of the same name who worked in Staffordshire from the 1830s.

JOHN BENBOW. Landscape painter. *c.* 1835+

John Benbow was born at Broseley in about 1813, his name being included in the Coalport 1841, 1851, and 1861 census returns as a 'china painter'. He was also included in the 1859 wages returns, with the high wage of £2 10s 0d (the same as that earned by such well-known artists as John Randall and Daniel Lucas).

John Benbow's name is, however, mentioned only once in the available pattern-books—3/730 'Landscape by John Benbow'.

JOHN BENNETT. Painter. *c.* 1850+

John Bennett, born at Broseley in about 1834, is included as a 'china painter' in the local censuses of 1851 and 1861, and is in the 1859 wages list.

WILLIAM BILLINGSLEY. Gilder. *c.* 1830+

William Billingsley, who was born in Shropshire in about 1807, is one of the few persons to be described in the Coalport 1841 census returns as a 'china gilder'. He should not be confused with the celebrated flower painter of the same name.

FRANCIS BIRBECK. Gilder or artist. *c.* 1840+

Although little is known of him, Francis Birbeck drew the highest wage for an individual artist in the January 1859 wage list—£5 10s 0d against £4, £2 14s 0d and £2 10s 0d for such well-known artists as William Cook, James Rouse, and John Randall.

The 1841, 1851, and 1861 census returns record him as a 'china painter' or 'artist', the son of Joseph Birbeck the painter. He was born at Madeley, near Coalport, in about 1822. A 'Mr. Birbeck' is mentioned in contemporary reports of the Coalport exhibits at the 1862 Exhibition, and previous writers have assumed this reference to relate to the better-known Joseph Birbeck. The Coalport artist and local historian John Randall wrote that 'Mr. Francis Birbeck was happy in the production of gems and in the art of gilding', so the possibility exists that Francis Birbeck was one of Coalport's finest gilders—a fact which would account for the absence of references to him in the factory pattern-books.

PHILIP BIRBECK. Painter. *c.* 1850

Philip Birbeck was born at Coalport in about 1832. His name is included in the 1859 wages list with the above-average remuneration of £2 5s 0d. However, he would appear to have enjoyed other interests, for the 1861 census returns list him as 'Licensed Victualler and china painter' at the Elephant and Castle, High Street, Broseley.

JOSEPH BIRBECK. Flower painter, etc. *c.* 1820+

Joseph Birbeck was born in Worcester in about 1798. He was probably trained at the Chamberlain factory, where several artists named Birbeck were employed, including a Joseph Birbeck. Birbeck had moved to Coalport by the 1820s, as his name occurs at this period in the pattern-book; and a son (also Joseph) was born at near-by Madeley in 1831. Recorded Birbeck tableware patterns are: 2/242, 'Roses by Birbeck'; 2/893, 'Fruit by J. Birbeck' (Plate 142); 3/108, 'Flowers by

Mr. Birbeck'; 3/113, 'Flowers by J. Birbeck'; also designs 3/119, 3/128, 3/160 (see Plate 219c), 3/266, 3/336, 3/344, and 3/437.

Joseph Birbeck worked for a long period at the Coalport factory. The undated list quoted on Page 97 notes that 'Mr. J. Birbeck succeeded to be Foreman' in about 1844; his name appears in the 1833/4 loyal address, in the 1841 and 1851 census returns, and in the 1859 wage list. But in 1861 he is recorded as 'over-looker, Coalport Works'—a fact that suggests he had then ceased painting. The 1851 census returns list his two sons, Joseph and Thomas, as china painters. Other Coalport painters of the 1851 period named Birbeck include Francis (aged 29), Philip (aged 21) and William (aged 26).

The 1859 wages list includes Joseph Birbeck's name and a further entry 'Joseph Birbeck & Co.', indicating a small team of workmen, perhaps of ground layers, gilders or printers.

In support of the suggestion that this entry might have related to printers, there is the fact that pattern 3/609, 'Flowers by Birbeck'; 3/610, 'Birds by Birbeck', and 3/612, 'Plants by Birbeck', appear to be printed outline designs, while the next pattern, 3/613, has the note 'Flowers by Birbeck's girls'. The signatories to the gilders' and printers' 1889 letter of complaint contains the name Joseph Birbeck—a fact that, with the above information, strongly suggests that Joseph Birbeck, Junior, was a printer or engraver from about 1850 to at least 1889.

WILLIAM BIRBECK. Landscape artist. c. 1840+

William Birbeck was born at Broseley in about 1825, the son of Joseph Birbeck, also a Coalport painter (see Page 103). Although William Birbeck's name is included as a 'china painter' in the 1841 and 1851 census returns, it does not appear in the 1859 wage list or in the 1861 census returns; though in the Shelton (Staffordshire) 1851 census returns he is included, with his wife Harriet and son John H. Birbeck, who was born at Coalport in 1853. After leaving Coalport, between 1853 and 1859, William Birbeck emigrated to France, returning, however, to England by 1861 and working for Messrs Copelands at Stoke-on-Trent. He died in the 1880s.

William Birbeck would seem to have succeeded Steel as the leading Coalport landscape painter (see Page 126). Design 5/740 in the factory pattern-book is inscribed 'Scotch View by W. Birbeck'; Pattern 5/846, 'Landscape by W. Birbeck', and Pattern 6/336, 'Landscape by W. Birbeck'.

BENJAMIN BLOORE. Gilder. c. 1820+(?)

The 1851 Coalport census returns list Benjamin Bloore as 'late china gilder, pauper, defective vision', aged sixty-nine, born at Marylebone, London. He may have been employed at the Coalport factory over a long period, but no details are recorded.

THOMAS JOHN BOTT. Art director. c. 1889–1932

T. J. Bott, the son of the famous Worcester enamel painter Thomas Bott, was born in 1854 and died in 1932. After training in the Limoges enamel style of painting on a dark blue ground under his father at Worcester, he left that city in about 1886 and was employed in London and in Hanley by Messrs Brown-Westhead, Moore & Co. His paintings for this firm were shown at the 1889 Paris Exhibition and highly praised. Also in 1889 Bott became art director at Coalport—a post he held until his death at the age of seventy-seven. While at Coalport, Thomas John Bott did very little painting, although his style of white enamel painting on a dark blue ground was sometimes employed. F. A. Barrett states that a vase by this artist was exhibited at the 1862 Exhibition—a statement which does not link up with Thomas John Bott's known date of birth, 1854. The vase illustrated by Mr Barrett as being painted by T. J. Bott would appear to be of a date some thirty years before he joined Coalport's staff. Thomas John Bott was succeeded by Mr Alfred Langford (see Page 90).

ARTHUR BOWDLER. Painter. *c.* 1859+

Arthur Bowdler was born at Madeley, near Coalport, in about 1842. He was a junior, or apprentice, in January 1859, as his name appears in the wages list of that period as drawing only 12*s*. His name is included in the 1861, 1871, and 1881 census returns as a 'china painter'. He painted mainly floral subjects and had been trained by William Cook; but he also painted snowscapes and crests. His name is also mentioned in contemporary accounts of the 1878 and 1897 periods, but he appears to have retired or died by 1913. John Randall referred to him as a skilful flower painter.

THOMAS BRENTNALL. Flower painter. *c.* 1821–35

John Haslem, the Derby ceramic artist and historian, wrote 'About 1821 Mr. Bloor discharged one landscape and four flower painters, all of whom readily found employment at Coalport. They had all been apprenticed at Derby and were clever hands . . . The names of the flower painters were William Cresswell, Thomas Brentnall, James Farnsworth and William Hall, and of the landscape painter, Jesse Mountford.'

Of Thomas Brentnall, John Haslem further recorded: 'Brentnall, on leaving Coalport, worked at several manufactories in Staffordshire, the latter part of his time for Messrs. Ridgway, of Cauldon Place. He died about 1869 aged 70. Brentnall excelled as a flower painter . . .' Llewellynn Jewitt, in his *Ceramic Art of Great Britain*, 1878 and 1883, lists 'Brentnall, who was a clever flower painter' as an artist at the Rockingham factory in Yorkshire.

The census returns help to trace and date the movements of Thomas Brentnall. He was born at Derby in about 1800 or 1803. His son Henry was born at Broseley, near Coalport, in about 1824 (his wife, Harriet, being a local Broseley girl). By *c.* 1836 he had moved to Yorkshire, where his son Alfred was born. By June 1841 he had moved to Staffordshire (being included in the Shelton census return), where a further son, Thomas, was born in 1847. Thomas Brentnall was still employed at Hanley as a 'china painter' in 1861, probably then working for Ridgways. Thomas Brentnall, Senior, was at Coalport from *c.* 1821 to the 1830s. His name occurs only once in the factory pattern-books, against Pattern 912—

'Flowers by Mr. Brentnall', but the whole pattern is crossed through and the note 'No. 886 to be done for this' added.

Brentnall was probably responsible for some of the finest early Coalport flower painting on the fine porcelain bearing the 1820 'Society of Arts' mark (see Page 19, Colour Plate III; and Plates 133 and 140).

FRANCIS BREWER. Modeller. c. 1835–50s

Francis Brewer was born at Derby in about 1814. His name is not included in the signatories to the 1833 Coalport strike notice, but he is recorded in the June 1841 census returns as a china modeller. It has been recorded that he was a modeller at the near-by Madeley factory, which closed in 1840; but this was, in the main, a decorating establishment, giving little scope to a modeller.

Brewer moved to the Coalport factory, probably in the late 1830s, as the first vase drawn in the traveller's pattern-book (see Page 74 and Colour Plate VII) is called 'Brewer's vase'; and there is also a jug called 'Brewer's jug' (see Plate 173), indicating that the design was the work of this modeller. Francis Brewer remained at Coalport until at least 1844, as children were born to his wife, Annie, at Coalport in 1841 and 1844.

In 1861 Francis Brewer was at Fenton, in the Staffordshire Potteries, making china and parian ornaments. It is not known at what period between 1844 and 1861 he left Coalport, but it is evident that, with Peter Stephan, he was responsible for the fine Coalport vase and other forms during the 1830s and 1840s.

BRINDLEY. Flower painter. c. 1840s

Design number 4/461 in the factory pattern-book has the notation 'Flowers by Brindley', but no other information has been traced relating to him.

CARTWRIGHT. Apprentice painter early in the twentieth century.

RICHARD M. CASWELL. Gilder. c. 1859+

Richard M. Caswell was born at Madeley, near Coalport, in about 1841. His name is given in the 1861, 1871 and 1881 census returns as a 'gilder on china'. He was employed at the Coalport factory, probably as an apprentice, in 1859. The 1859 wages list shows that he drew the low wage of 12s.

FREDERICK H. CHIVERS. Fruit and flower painter. c. 1906–14

F. H. Chivers was first employed painting fruit and flower patterns for the Royal Worcester Company. He joined the Coalport staff in about 1906 and remained there until called up in the First World War. As at Worcester, Chivers specialized in fruit and flower subjects and painted some fine vases and very ornate plates. He was a slow worker and his work was in demand. After the war, Chivers was employed at the King Street, Derby, works. His work is normally signed.

WILLIAM CHURCHMAN. Gilder. c. 1825–60s

106 The name of William Churchman—who was born at Broseley, near Coalport,

in about 1816—is included in the 1841, 1851, 1861, and 1871 census returns, in the latter of which he is listed as a 'china gilder'. His name is also given in the 1859 wages list, but does not occur in the 1889 letter of complaint (see Page 89).

WILLIAM COOK. Flower painter. *c.* 1843–76

William Cook, one of the best-known Coalport artists, drew the second highest individual wage recorded in the 1859 wages list. He was born at Burslem in the Staffordshire Potteries in about 1800, and reputedly worked at Messrs Robins and Randall's decorating establishment in London and at Thomas Martin Randall's similar establishment at Madeley, near the Coalport factory. A daughter, Jane Margaret, was born to William Cook's wife, Jane, in June 1841, at which time the family lived in Camden Town, London. Two years later a son (also William) was born to them at Madeley, so that the date for his move to Shropshire can be fixed to the 1841–3 period.

Cook, whose work is painted in rich, vivid, wet-looking enamels, specialized in Sèvres-type floral panels reserved in the borders of plates and dishes. Fine floral groups, often including fruit, appear in the centre of fine plates. His finest work is found on vases and other ornamental pieces (see Colour Plate IX and Plate 202). His groups, which often also include a cluster of small fine-leafed flowers washed over with one colour, can be readily recognized although his plates, vases and other factory-decorated ware are not signed, but some rare signed plaques may be found. Cook's flower and fruit compositions very often appear on the same piece as John Randall's bird compositions. For example, a vase may have panels by both artists, or a plate may have a bird centre by Randall and flower panels in the border by Cook, or vice versa. William Cook received wide praise in the nineteenth century, a writer in the *Pottery Gazette* going so far as to state that Cook 'excelled all others in painting flowers and fruit in the soft delicate manner of old Sèvres, and his imitations are probably to say the least, equal to anything ever turned out of the original manufactory . . .'

As far as is known, William Cook worked at the Coalport factory up to the time of his death in 1876—so he was employed there for over thirty years. Jewitt and other writers have spelt the name Cook with a final 'e', but signed watercolour drawings show the signature as 'Cook', a spelling confirmed by the census returns and by his daughter's birth certificate.

Cook's name appears only once in the available pattern-books, against design number 6/761, 'Cook's small sprigs', but most of his flower and fruit painting occurs on non-repetitive cabinet plates, vases, etc, that are not given in the records of standard repetitive designs. Cook reputedly also painted the ornate crests on the Coalport service made for the Emperor of Russia in 1845 (see *Victorian Porcelain*, Plate 2).

H. COOPER. Painter

The initial and name H. Cooper is given against design 7/351 in the factory pattern-books, but no other details are available.

WILLIAM CORDEN

A signed example of William Corden's portrait painting occurs on a porcelain plaque bearing the rare incised mark 'J. Rose & Co. Coalport.' This example is dated 1822, but there is no firm evidence that this Derby-trained ceramic painter worked at the Coalport factory. It seems that these blank porcelain plaques were supplied to independent decorators, as a further marked plaque bears the signature of the Worcester painter E. Doe.

WILLIAM CRESSWELL. Flower painter. *c.* 1821–35

William Cresswell was apprenticed at the Derby factory as a flower painter, from where—according to John Haslem—he was dismissed in about 1821 and, with other Derby painters, went to Coalport (see under Thomas Brentnall). Apparently he left Coalport (before the 1841 census) and painted in France, returning to England and the Staffordshire Potteries in 1848.

The available Coalport pattern-books do not include Cresswell's name, but this is to be expected in the 1820s when no artist's name is noted in these books.

JOHN DIXON. Painter

John Dixon, born at Broseley, near Coalport, in about 1831, is listed in the 1861 census returns as a 'painter on porcelain', but no further information has been recorded.

THOMAS DIXON. Fruit and flower painter. *c.* 1820–70s

Thomas Dixon was born at Broseley, near Coalport, in about 1798. His wife, Sarah, and three daughters were all employed at the Coalport factory as burnishers of the gilding; and from about 1845 his sons John and William were employed as china painters.

Thomas Dixon spent all his working life at Coalport and was responsible for most of the best flower painting on Coalport porcelain from about 1820, or before, until the 1870s. Designs drawn in the available factory pattern-books with Dixon's name added are: 2/921, 2/995, 3/72, 3/125, 3/296, 3/335, 3/462, 3/507, 3/510, 3/517, 3/582, 3/597, 3/769, 3/770, 3/788, 3/789, 3/806, 3/811, 3/898, 3/926, 3/932, 3/945, 3/974, 3/980, 3/982, 3/992, 3/994, 4/42, 4/46, 4/268, 4/299, 4/300, 4/383, 4/514, 4/511, 4/590 (see Plate 143), 4/603, 4/656, 5/218, 5/271 (see Plate 147), 5/414, 5/499, 5/547, 5/707, 5/713, 6/88, 6/89, 6/90, 6/314, 6/313, 6/327, 6/338, 6/339, 6/355, 6/409, 6/469, 4/764, 4/767, 4/793, 4/810, 4/812, 4/836, 4/930, 4/967, 5/6, 5/138, 5/140. Some of these list only the name Dixon, without forename or initial: e.g. 'Purple Geranium by Dixon'. Some designs—3/161 and 3/166—feature birds: 'Birds by Dixon'. But before Thomas Dixon's sons came of working age, in about 1845, Thomas would seem to have been the only artist named Dixon employed at Coalport.

Thomas Dixon's name is included in the 1833–4 loyal address, the 1841 and 1851 Coalport census returns, and the 1859 list of painters' wages, as well as the 1871 census returns. His son William is listed as a 'Porcelain painter' in the 1851 and 1861 census returns. William was born at Broseley in about 1833 and, apart from the census returns of 1851 and 1861, he is also included in the 1859 wages list.

DONOVAN. See Page 137.

JOHN DOWNES. Painter. *c.* 1859+
John Downes's name is included in the 1859 wages list, but as the remuneration was only 4*s* it can be assumed that he was then an apprentice. The initial and name 'J. Downes' appears against designs 7/419, 7/420, 7/421, 7/452 in the factory pattern-book.

CHARLES DYAS. Painter. *c.* 1820s+
Charles Dyas was born at Madeley, near Coalport, in about 1800. Although he was employed at Coalport over a very long period, very little is known about him. The name is included in the 1841 and 1881 census returns as a 'china painter', but it is possible that he was really a china printer.

ROBERT EATON. Painter. *c.* 1859+
Robert Eaton's name is included in the 1859 wages list, his low remuneration —6*s*—pointing to the fact that at that period he was a junior or inexperienced painter. He later matured to be a talented flower and fruit painter, as several signed plaques are known—one of which is in the Victoria and Albert Museum, Allen Collection, number 403. A marked Davenport plate signed Robert Eaton and dated 1887 has been recorded, but this is likely to have been decorated by Eaton in his own time or painted by another artist of the same name.
A Robert Eaton, 'painter on china', born in Derby, *c.* 1844, was included in the 1861 Stoke census returns as a nephew of the painter Henry Pedley. It is difficult to gauge when Eaton was at Coalport and when in Staffordshire.

WILLIAM ELLIS. Painter. *c.* 1859+
William Ellis, whose name is included in the 1861 census returns as a 'china painter', was born in about 1841. His name also occurs in the 1859 wages list, but with the low apprentice wage of 10*s*.

AQUILA EVANS. Painter or gilder. *c.* 1855+
Aquila Evans was born at Broseley in about 1840, the daughter of William Evans, 'china gilder'. Her name is recorded in the 1859 wages list with the low (apprentice) remuneration of 10*s*. The name again occurs in the factory pattern-book against design number 7/348, but in the 1861 and 1871 census returns she is listed as a 'gilder on china'.

FREDERICK EVANS. Gilder. *c.* 1850+
Born at Broseley, near Coalport, in about 1832, his name is included in the 1859 wages list and in the 1861 census returns, where he is listed as a 'china gilder'.

HENRY EVANS. Artist. *c.* 1845+

Henry Evans, the son of the Coalport gilder William Evans (see below), was born at Broseley in about 1832, being classed as a 'china painter' in the 1851 census returns and mentioned in the 1859 wages list.

WILLIAM EVANS. Gilder. *c.* 1840–70s

The 1841 census returns include a 'china painter' named William Evans, in the age group 35 to 39, of Irish birth. The 1861 census return records William Evans's age as 56, giving a date of birth of about 1805; and in 1861 he was described as 'Gilder on china, accountant and land surveyor'. The 1871 returns also list him as a gilder. His wife, Mary, was born at Broseley, as was their daughter Aquila (in about 1840), a 'gilder on china' (see Page 109), William Evans's name appears again in the 1859 wages list, but no further information about him has been traced.

FALL. Landscape painter. *c.* 1840s

Design number 6/408 in the factory pattern-book of the late 1840s or early 1850s bears the notation 'Landscape by Mr. Fall'. A John Fall is included in the 1859 wages list, but no other information would seem to be recorded.

JAMES FARNSWORTH. Flower painter. *c.* 1821–35?

James Farnsworth, a Derby-trained flower painter, left Derby for Coalport in about 1821 (see Page 105, under Thomas Brentnall). No contemporary record of this artist at Coalport has been recorded, his name not being included in the 1841 or 1851 census returns.

W. FLETCHER. See Page 137.

JAMES GLOVER. Painter?. *c.* 1860

The 1861 and 1871 census returns included the name of James Glover, who was born at Broseley in about 1843. His name also appears in the 1859 wages list, but the low remuneration of 8*s* indicates that at this period he was an apprentice. His name is written against designs 7/377 and 7/391 in the pattern-books.

EDWIN GREEN. Flower painter. *c.* 1840+

Edwin Green, born in about 1821, is included in the 1841 census return, but not in that of 1851 or 1861, or in the 1859 painters' wages list.

Pattern 3/455, a single specimen flower, was 'painted by Green', and pattern 3/483 depicts 'Plants by Green'.

EDWIN GRIFFITHS. Gilder or painter. *c.* 1835+

Edwin Griffiths's name is included in the 1841 census returns as a 'china painter' in the 25 to 29 age group, but the only other reference to him occurs in the factory pattern-book against design 3/721—'this plate was gilt by Edwin Griffiths'. It must be noted that it was the practice of some gilders to describe themselves as china painters, for nearly all the Derby gilders are termed painters in the Derby census returns.

WILLIAM HALL. Flower painter. *c.* 1821–30

John Haslem recorded that this Derby-trained flower painter left Derby for Coalport in about 1821 (see Page 105, under Thomas Brentnall). Haslem further records: 'Hall found employment in the Staffordshire Potteries, after he left Coalport, and for part of the time was foreman at Messrs. Alcocks. He also worked for Alderman Copeland at Stoke-upon-Trent. He died in February, 1861, aged 61. The year after leaving Derby, and when at Coalport, he painted a plate with a basket of flowers in the centre, which he presented to Mr. Thomason; it is now in the possession of the writer (Haslem), and gives a favourable impression of Hall's talent. The plate has the painter's initials at the back, with the date—1822.' This plate is described in the 1879 catalogue of the Haslem collection as: 'Embossed plate, probably Coalport; insects and gilding in border, basket of flowers standing in a landscape in centre.'

Haslem's information that William Hall went to the Staffordshire Potteries after leaving Coalport is confirmed by the 1841 and 1851 Staffordshire census returns. These also confirm his date of birth as 1800 and show he was born in Staffordshire. A son, John, was born in Shelton in about 1831, showing that his time at Coalport was ten years or less from 1821. Consequently, his name is not recorded in the Coalport pattern-books, which do not include painters' names at this period.

JOHN HARPER. Landscape painter. *c.* 1835+

Born in 1812, Harper's name is included in the 1841 census return as a 'china painter', and in the 1859 wages list. His name has been associated with landscape paintings, but does not appear in the factory pattern-books. The 1871 census returns list a further china painter of this name, then aged 29, giving a date of birth of about 1842. He is also listed in the 1881 returns.

J. HARPER. Painter. Twentieth century

Landscape painter in the early part of the present century.

JAMES E. HARTSHORNE. Painter. *c.* 1859+

James Hartshorne, born at Broseley in about 1842, drew the low wage of 10*s* in the 1859 wages list, indicating that he was at that period an apprentice. At a later date he specialized in animal subjects, his work being included in the 1871 Exhibition and featured in contemporary engravings (see Plate 230). In the 1870s his name was included in the short lists of principal artists working at Coalport. Apart from cattle and other animal subjects, he probably painted flowers and figure compositions.

JOHN HARVEY & CO

This team drew £4 14s 0d in wages during the period covered by the 1859 wages list, but no further information has been traced to indicate the speciality of John Harvey and his team. It is, however, likely that this was a ground-laying team, responsible for the fine coloured grounds and borders on tableware, as well as vases, etc. This aspect of the factory's decoration is not separately listed in any available record.

A John Harvey, 'china painter', was included in the 1861 census returns, being then aged 33 and having been born at Broseley, near Coalport.

RICHARD HARVEY. Flower painter. c. 1840+

Richard Harvey was born in Shropshire between 1822 and 1826. The sole reference to him in the available Coalport pattern-book is against design 3/630— 'Flowers by R. Harvey'. His name is included in the 1841 Coalport census returns as a 'china painter'.

JOHN HEIGHWAY. Gilder. c. 1840+

John Heighway (or Haighway), whose name is included in the 1841, 1851, and 1861 census returns and in the 1859 wages list, was born at Broseley, near Coalport, in about 1823. In the 1851 census he is described as a 'china gilder'; and in the 1861 census as 'Hairdresser & china gilder'!

THOMAS HODGKISS. Gilder. c. 1830+

Born at Broseley, near Coalport, in about 1808, Hodgkiss's name appears in the 1841, 1851, and 1861 census returns and in the 1859 Coalport wages list. In the 1851 census he is described as a 'china gilder'.

EDWIN HOWELLS. Bird painter and gilder. c. 1840+

Edwin Howells was born at Broseley in about 1821. His name is included, as a 'china painter', in the 1841 and 1851 census returns, and also occurs in the 1859 wages list. But in the 1861 census return he is described as 'artist, china gilder'. The 1871 returns also give the description 'china gilder'.

Pattern 4/210 of the 1840s includes 'Howell's birds', and design 5/324 in the pattern-book has the notation 'E. Howells' birds'. Freely drawn Chelsea-type exotic birds in landscapes are probably painted by Howells, although they have been attributed to Mottershead in the past (see Page 118).

HOWILL. Painter

Franklin A. Barrett mentions that an artist named Howill succeeded John Randall in the 1880s as a bird painter. Although I have been unable to substantiate this, there may be a connection between Mr Barrett's Howill and the Edwin Howells included in the 1859 wages list (see above). This artist was also a bird painter, as proved by the pattern-book entry '5/324 E. Howell's birds'. However, a former Coalport artist mentioned to me in correspondence a flower painter named Fred Howitt who may be Mr Barrett's Howill.

F. HOWARD

This artist specialized in fruit painting, but also painted flowers and birds (see Plate 207). He was employed for many years from the early 1900s. His best work is normally signed.

H. HUGHES

Apprentice painter of birds, etc, early in the present century.

WILLIAM JENKS. Gilder. *c.* 1815–70s

William Jenks was born in about 1791. His name is included in the 1841 and 1851 census returns, and also in the 1859 wages list. The 1851 census returns list him as a 'china gilder'; and since the 1871 census returns surprisingly list him— then aged 80—as still a 'china gilder', it would seem that he was one of the most senior Coalport gilders.

ALFRED JONES. Gilder. *c.* 1845+

Alfred Jones was the son of Edward Jones, a Coalport painter. His mother, Maria, was a burnisher of gold. Alfred was born at Broseley, near Coalport, in about 1825, his name being included in the 1851 census returns as a 'china gilder'. He is also included in the 1859 wages list and the 1861 and 1871 census returns. His younger brother, John, was aged 15 in 1851 (see Page 114) and is also listed as a gilder; and three of Alfred's sisters were employed as gold burnishers.

CECIL JONES. Flower painter. *c.* 1820–45

Cecil Jones was born near Coalport in about 1799, for his age was given as 42 in the 1841 census returns. By the 1820s, he had established himself as one of John Rose's leading flower painters. Entries referring to his patterns painted on tableware read: 2/139, 'Flowers by C. Jones'; 2/241, 'Flowers by Jones'; 2/997, 'Group (of flowers) by Cecil Jones'; 3/145, 'Flowers by C. Jones'; 3/177, 'Flowers by C. Jones'; 3/184, 'Flowers by Cecil Jones'; 3/460, 'Painted by C. Jones'. His name also appears against patterns 3/461, 3/506 (a fruit pattern), 3/776, 3/778, 3/798, 3/834, 3/885, 3/978, and 4/391. Apart from these table-service designs, it is highly probable that he painted some of the finest Coalport ornamental porcelain, vases and other ware of the 1820s and 1830s. A unique signed and dated 1815 porcelain plaque by Cecil Jones shows his early talent.

Cecil Jones's name is not included in the 1851 or 1861 census returns, nor does it appear in the 1859 wages list, so that he would seem to have ceased work at Coalport in the 1840s. The list of artists on Page 97 notes that Jones left Coalport in about 1846 or 1848 to work at Wordsley on glass. It will be observed that in the references to this artist in the factory pattern-book his name or initial is given because other painters were employed with the name Jones: Cecil's son, Augustus; Edward Jones; Edwin Jones; Frederick Jones; and John Jones—all described as 'china painters' in the Coalport 1841 census returns.

EDWARD JONES. Painter. *c.* 1830s+

A signatory to the 1833 strike notice (see Page 96), Edward Jones was born at Broseley, near Coalport, in about 1799, his name being included as a 'china painter' in the 1841 and 1851 census returns. In the returns of April 1861 he is described as 'Overlooker of china paintresses' (a similar expression is used on the undated list quoted on Page 97), so that at this period he had ceased to decorate Coalport porcelain.

I have been unable to ascertain the speciality of this artist, but his family certainly played a considerable part in the decoration of Coalport porcelain, and he was himself still employed in 1871. The 1851 census returns give the following members of the family and their occupations:

Edward Jones	aged 52	china painter
Maria Jones	aged 51	burnisher of gold
Celina Jones	aged 30	burnisher of gold
Alfred Jones	aged 26	china gilder (see Page 113)
Emma Jones	aged 21	burnisher of gold
Rebecca Jones	aged 20	warehouse woman
John Jones	aged 15	china gilder (see two below)
Mary Jones	aged 12	burnisher of gold

JOHN JONES. Painter or gilder. *c.* 1815+

John Jones is described in the 1841, 1851, and 1861 census returns as a 'china painter' and the name is included in the 1833–34 loyal address as well as in the 1859 wages list. He was born at Broseley in about 1788; and although the available pattern-books do not mention him, he may—notwithstanding the census statements—have been a gilder, not a painter. The 1851 census return does, however, include another John Jones, 'china gilder' (see following entry).

JOHN JONES. Gilder. *c.* 1855+

John Jones was born in about 1836 at Broseley, near Coalport, the son of Edward Jones, a Coalport painter. His name is included as a 'china gilder' in the 1851, 1871 and 1881 census returns and in the 1859 wages list, which shows that he drew the wage of £1 8s 0d.

JOSHUA JONES. Artist or gilder. *c.* 1840–60 and *c.* 1880

Joshua Jones was born at Worcester in about 1811. He is listed as a 'china painter' in the 1851 Coalport census returns and is included in the 1859 wages list with the average remuneration of £2 0s 0d. But by 1861 he had moved to Stoke and was described as a 'china gilder'; and in the 1881 Coalport census returns he again appears as a 'china gilder'.

WILLIAM JONES. Painter or gilder. *c.* 1850+

William Jones's name is included in the 1859 wages list. A William Jones is included in the 1841 census returns as the youngest son of Cecil Jones the china painter. His age was given as 11, so that at the time of the 1859 wages list he would have been about 29; but a William Jones, 'china painter', aged 21, is included in the 1861 census returns (see below).

WILLIAM JONES. Painter. *c.* 1859+

This William Jones was born at Broseley, near Coalport, in about 1840. His name is included, as a 'china painter', in the 1861 census returns; and it appears in the 1859 wages list, but no remuneration is recorded.

Patterns numbered 7/329, 7/334, 7/352, 7/385, 7/388, and 7/395 have the name 'W. Jones' noted against them.

NORMAN W. KEATES. Fruit and flower painter. *c.* 1960

Norman Keates was born in 1893. From 1907 to 1917, when he joined the army, he was employed at the Royal Doulton factory at Burslem. He rejoined Doultons after the war and remained with them up to 1960, when he joined the Coalport China Company. He painted fine fruit and flower subjects for the Coalport Company. His work is signed 'N. W. Keates'.

THOMAS KEELING. Figure painter. Early twentieth century

Tom Keeling painted figure (and cat) subjects for the Coalport Company early in the present century. The finest example of Coalport ceramic painting I have ever seen was by Tom Keeling. He also worked for Copelands at Stoke.

KELSHALL. Flower and fruit painter. *c.* 1830–40

Kelshall's (or Kelsall's) name occurs in the Coalport pattern-book in the early 1830s: 2/533, 'Fruit by Kelshall'; 2/584; 2/712, 'Flowers by Kelshall' (see Plate 219); and also patterns 2/787 and 2/815. Like other flower painters, Kelshall also painted fruit. His name is not included in the Coalport 1841, 1851, or 1861 census returns and he must be presumed to have left the district. A Thomas Kelshall 'artist (china painter)' was included in the 1851 census return for Burslem in the Staffordshire Potteries, but it is not known if this is the same person as the Coalport flower painter.

JOHN LATHAM. Flower painter. *c.* 1825

John Latham, who was born at Coalport in about 1801, reputedly painted Worcester and Nantgarw porcrlain before 1820. The sole reference to an artist of this name in the Coalport pattern-book appears under design 2/261 (of the mid- or late 1820s): 'Seive (Sèvres) groups by Jno Latham.' After leaving the Coalport works, Latham painted white porcelain on his own account at near-by Ironbridge. In 1862 the Victoria and Albert Museum (to use its present-day title) acquired a Minton plate, decorated with butterflies and foliage, painted by a John Latham. John Latham's name is included in the Shelton (Staffordshire) census returns of 1861.

STEPHEN LAWRANCE. Fruit and flower painter. *c*. 1820–45

Born in about 1797, Stephen Lawrance's name first occurs in the Coalport pattern-book under design 2/80 of the 1815–20 period, but the note is confusing because of the lack of punctuation. The basic design has panels of landscapes, and the note reads: '3 compartments in saucer, 2 (in) cup S. Laurance chrome green ground.' Design 2/83 has panels of birds in branches and has the same type of unpunctuated note—'3 compartments saucer S. Laurance chrome green ground', so that it is not clear if the chrome green ground was associated with Stephen Lawrance or the painted panels. Design 2/237 of the 1820s is clearer: 'Fruit and Flowers by Stephen Lawrance in the centre.' Other flower patterns by this artist were 3/274, 3/453, 3/779, 3/782, 3/886, 4/233, 4/257 (a garden view), 4/271, 4/283, 4/288, 4/311, 4/412, 4/791, 4/805, 4/811, and 5/213. The signed and dated (1826) plaque illustrated in Plate 172 clearly shows the talent of this Coalport flower painter. His name is included in the 1841 census, but not in the 1851 or 1861 census returns or in the 1859 painters' wages list. The seemingly authoritative list of Coalport painters quoted on Page 97 notes that Stephen Lawrance left Coalport in about 1846 or 1848 to work at Wordsley on glass.

JOHN LEIGHTON. Painter or gilder(?). *c*. 1830+

John Leighton, a signatory to the 1833–4 loyal address (see Page 96), was born early in the nineteenth century and his name is included in the 1841 Coalport census returns as a china painter in the age group 35 to 39. The seemingly authoritative but undated list of Coalport painters, quoted on Page 97, states that Leighton was 'Foreman of Women gilders and japanners'. The name does not appear in the 1851 or 1861 Coalport census returns, but an Edward Leighton is included in the 1881 census as a 'china painter', then aged 51.

FRANCIS LOCKETT. Flower painter. *c*. 1840s

Francis Lockett's name is given against several floral designs in the Coalport pattern-book of the late 1840s: 6/292, 'small groups by F. Lockett', also 6/293, 6/295, 6/296, 6/319, 'Plant by F. Lockett', 6/322, 6/323, 6/370, 6/371, 6/380, 'Plants by Francis Lockett', 6/394, 6/400, 6/420, 6/445, 6/447, but I have been unable to trace any information on this artist.

FREDERICK LOVE. Painter. *c*. 1855+

Frederick Love was born at Broseley, near Coalport, in about 1838. His name is included in the 1859 wages list with the low, apprentice remuneration of 12*s*. His name appears in the 1861 census returns as a 'china painter'.

ROBERT LOWE. Painter or gilder. *c*. 1855+

Robert Lowe was born at Broseley in about 1841, his name being included in the 1859 wages list with the low, apprentice remuneration of 10*s*. In the 1861 census returns he was described as a 'china painter', but in the 1889 letter, quoted on Page 89, there is the signature of Robert Lowe as a gilder of printer.

DANIEL LUCAS, JUNIOR. Landscape and flower painter. *c.* 1845–60

Daniel Lucas, Junior was the third son of Daniel Lucas, the well-known Derby landscape painter. He was born at Derby in about 1818; and he learned the art of china painting from his father.

John Haslem, the Derby artist and historian, writing in or before 1876, noted: 'On leaving (Derby) he worked for many years at Coalport. Afterwards he was employed at Messrs. Copelands, at Stoke. He now resides at Longton, in the Potteries, having a small establishment there, where, assisted by his sons, he paints landscapes and otherwise decorates china for different manufacturers.'

Designs numbered 6/607, 'Views by Lucas', 6/648, 'Plant by Lucas', 6/745, and 6/747 are by Daniel Lucas.

I have not traced Daniel Lucas's name in the 1841 census returns for either the Derby or Coalport districts, but it does occur in the 1859 Coalport wages list. He must have left soon after this period, for his name is not in the 1861 census returns and he painted Copeland vases shown at the 1862 Exhibition (see *Victorian Porcelain*, 1961, Page 50).

BERTRAM MACKENNAL. Modeller. *c.* 1890+

(Sir) Bertram Mackennal was born in 1863. He won fame for his work on the Statue of Liberty for Australia, and for his Statue of Sarah Bernhardt in Paris; but for a period late in the nineteenth century he was employed as a modeller at the Coalport factory.

JOSEPH MANSFIELD. Gilder. *c.* 1820–9

Joseph Mansfield, who was born at Madeley in about 1803, married a local Broseley girl and was presumably employed at the Coalport works from about 1820 to a period before 1829. But it is his later career which is recorded, rather than his training at Coalport.

Llewellynn Jewitt, in his *Ceramic Art of Great Britain*, 1878, speaks of Mansfield as 'the principal embosser and chaser in gold' at the Rockingham Porcelain factory. The 1851 and 1861 Shelton census returns permit us to gauge, within limits, Joseph Mansfield's movements by the birth of his several children. Henry was born *c.* 1829 at Swinton, Yorkshire, indicating that the Coalport family had then moved to Swinton, near the Rockingham factory. Elizabeth, Mary and George were also born in Yorkshire in about 1833, 1836, and 1837; but Jane and Ann were born at Burslem, Staffordshire, in *c.* 1841 and 1843.

GEORGE MELLOR. Gilder and 'Japan' painter. *c.* 1799–1811. See Page 94

ABRAHAM MILNER. Gilder. *c.* 1820–50s

Abraham Milner was born in about 1787. He is one of the few Coalport hands to be described as a 'china gilder' in the 1841 census returns. His name appears also in the 1851 returns, but not on the 1859 wages list or 1861 census returns. Milner must have been employed at the Coalport factory for most of the first half of the nineteenth century, and he was also one of the signatories to the 1833–4 loyal address.

J. MIST. See Page 138

MORTLOCK. See Page 138

MOTTERSHEAD. Bird painter. *c.* 1830s
   Pattern number 3/347 has the notation 'Birds by Mottershead'. No other information is available, and a class of freely painted long-legged exotic birds painted in landscape has been attributed to this artist. However, the period of most of these pieces in the Chelsea style appears to be some fifteen years or more later than the reference to Mottershead in the pattern-book. Moreover, the 1841, 1851, and 1861 census returns do not include this artist's name.

JESSE MOUNTFORD. Landscape painter. *c.* 1821–34
   John Haslem recorded in his *The Old Derby China Factory* . . . , 1876, that Jesse Mountford was a landscape artist at the Derby factory (where his father was enamel kiln fireman) before being discharged with other artists in about 1821. Haslem further states: 'Mountford worked at Coalport about fifteen years [after leaving Derby in 1821]. On leaving, he was employed as a landscape painter for twenty-five years at Messrs. Davenport's, Longport, near Burslem, dying there in 1861. He was an expert brother of the angle, and when at Coalport . . . was wont to exercise his skill successfully on his walks to and from the works . . .'
   Jesse Mountford's name appears against tableware pattern numbers 2/808 and 2/923; but this talented Derby-trained landscape painter probably painted much ornamental ware and other patterns not especially noted in the available records. Mountford had left Coalport by 1835, for his third child, Jesse, was born in Staffordshire at this period.
   The 1841 and 1851 Staffordshire census returns throw fresh light on Jesse Mountford. He was born at Hanley in the Staffordshire Potteries in about 1799 (being fifty-two in 1851). Children John and Maria were born in Shropshire in about 1826 and 1831, Jesse and Elijah in Shelton, Staffordshire, in 1835 and 1836. In the 1851 census Jesse Mountford, Junior, was also described as a 'Painter of China'. A Davenport porcelain plaque signed by Jesse Mountford, Senior, is illustrated in my *Victorian Porcelain*, 1961, Plate 99, and is dated 1851.

CHARLES MUSS. See Page 138

RICHARD OWEN. Gilder. *c.* 1855+
   Richard Owen was born at Madeley, near Coalport, in about 1837. His name is included as a 'china gilder' in the 1861, 1871 and 1881 census returns and is
also included in the 1859 wages list.

CHARLES PALMERE. Figure painter. *c.* 1870

This talented figure painter decorated Coalport vases shown at the 1871 Exhibition. The Worcester Company also employed an artist named Palmere, but his Christian name is not recorded—so one does not know if the Coalport Palmere was the same person as the Worcester painter of this name.

THOMAS PARDOE. See Page 139

JOHN PARKER. Shell, feather and flower painter. *c.* 1820–40s

John Parker was born in Shropshire in about 1786. Shell painting in the Coalport pattern-book under numbers 3/284, 3/287, 3/365, and 4/265 was carried out by him. Pattern 4/274 features feathers 'by Parker'.

John Parker's name is included in the 1841 census return, but not in the 1851 or 1861 census returns, or in the 1859 wages list—facts which indicate that he died or left the Coalport works in the 1840s. The undated list of Coalport painters quoted on Page 97 notes that Parker painted 'Groups of flowers and a good copyist'.

A John Parker or Barker is recorded as a shell painter on Barr, Flight & Barr Worcester porcelain of the 1807–13 period. It is possible (but not certain) that this is the same shell painter as that later at Coalport.

EDWIN PATTERN. Gilder. *c.* 1845+

Edwin Pattern was the first son of Josiah Pattern, the Coalport artist (see below). Edwin was born at Broseley in about 1828. His name is included in the 1851 and 1861 census returns, and in the 1859 wages list his remuneration was given as £2. Pattern number 7/328 has the name E. Pattern against the design.

JOSIAH PATTERN (OR PATTEN). Flower painter. *c.* 1820–60s

This local artist's name is recorded in the 1841, 1851, and 1861 census returns. The last gives his age as 62 (he was therefore born in about 1799). He had two sons, both described as 'china painters'—Edwin, aged 23 in 1851 (see above), and Josiah, aged 21 in 1851.

Josiah Pattern (or Patten)'s name first appears in the Coalport factory pattern-book against design number 934, of the 1815–20 period. He is the first artist to be mentioned by name in these books and he must have shown talent at an early age. Most of his designs are of flowers, but he also painted fruit and crests. His name appears in the 1833–4 loyal address, the census returns and the 1859 wages list. He must be considered one of the Coalport factory's leading artists from about 1820 to at least 1861.

Designs painted by Josiah Pattern include: 934, 935, 957, 3/112, 3/128, 3/511, 3/512, 3/514, and 6/578.

HENRY PEDLEY. Painter(?). *c.* 1830–60

He is included in the 1859 Coalport painters' wages list, which records his remuneration as £2 10s 0d—a very high one, being the same as that drawn by

John Randall and by Daniel Lucas. I have been unable to trace further references to him at Coalport, apart from notations in the factory pattern-book against designs 6/418, 'Plants by Pedley', and 6/419, 'Two birds by Pedley'; but the Allen Collection at the Victoria and Albert Museum contains a plaque signed 'Hy. Pedley'. This is painted with various types of birds, named on the reverse. The Allen Collection Catalogue reference notes that: 'Henry Pedley worked at Copeland's Factory, Stoke-upon-Trent, and at the Old Hall Factory, Hanley . . .' Following up the reference to Henry Pedley at Stoke-on-Trent, we note that the 1851 Stoke census does include a Derby-born china painter named Henry Pedley, then aged 45. He is again listed in the 1861 Stoke census, with children born in the Potteries in c. 1837 and 1838, a second son being born in France in about 1840. There is no proof that this plaque was painted by the same artist as is included in the 1859 Coalport wages list, but the probability exists.

ARTHUR PERRY. Painter. c. 1899+

This versatile and travelled artist has imparted to me much interesting information on the Coalport (also Copeland and Doulton) artists of the late nineteenth and early twentieth century. He was born at Stoke-on-Trent in 1871. After an initial spell at Copeland's works, he joined the Coalport Company in about 1899 and remained there for five and a half years before returning to Copelands. Subsequently he was employed at Doultons for nearly twenty years. Arthur Perry could paint most subjects, but he is best known for his bird or fish studies.

GEORGE PERRY. Flower painter. c. 1840+

George Perry, born in about 1820, is described as a 'china painter' in the 1841 census returns. The name Perry appears against design 3/977 in the factory pattern-book, 'Flowers in centre by Perry', but no other information has been forthcoming. At a later date Arthur Perry excelled in painting landscape, fish, and game subjects (see above).

PIPER. Landscape painter. c. 1830s

Coalport patterns 3/950, 3/962, 3/963, 3/983 of the late 1830s were painted with landscapes by Piper, according to notations in the factory pattern-book, but I have been unable to trace any details of him. An Alfred Piper, 'china painter', was included in the 1851 census; but as he was then only 14 he could not have painted the designs of the 1835–40 period.

ALFRED PIPER. Painter or gilder. c. 1860+

Alfred Piper was born at Madeley, near Coalport, in about 1835. His name is included as a 'china painter' in the 1851 and 1861 census, but the 1871 return has the description 'Porcelain or China Gilder'. Patterns numbered 7/335, 7/336, and 7/339 have 'Alfred Piper' noted against the designs. The name does not appear in the 1881 returns.

ENOCH PIPER. Gilder or painter. *c.* 1850s+

Enoch Piper was born at Madeley, near Coalport, in about 1834, and was the elder brother of Alfred Piper (see above). His name is included in the 1851, 1861 and 1871 census returns as a 'china painter', but the 1881 returns use the description 'china gilder'. In the 1881 census returns two further painters named Piper are listed—Henry E. Piper, aged 22, and William L. Piper, aged 27.

JOHN H. PLANT. Painter. Twentieth century

This talented landscape, fish and animal painter practised his art at Coalport as well as at several other centres of the ceramic industry in the twentieth century. His signed work is found on marked porcelain of several firms, notably Messrs Doultons. See Colour Plate X for a typical example of Plant's landscape painting.

WILLIAM POPE. Gilder or painter. *c.* 1830s+

William Pope was born at Broseley, near Coalport, in about 1810. His name is included in the local census returns of 1841, 1851, 1861, 1871, and 1881. In all but the last two he is listed as a 'china painter'; but this is changed to 'china gilder' in the fuller returns of 1871 and 1881. In the 1859 wages list the average sum of £1 8s 0d is recorded against his name.

BENJAMIN POTTS. Gilder. *c.* 1830–60

Benjamin Potts was born at Broseley, near Coalport, in about 1806. His name is included in the 1841, 1851, and 1861 census returns and in the 1859 wages list, where his remuneration is given as £1 16s 0d—an above-average wage. The 1851 and 1861 census returns listed Benjamin Potts as a 'china gilder', and judging by his wage in 1859 he was amongst the top flight of Coalport gilders. The 1861 census returns also list Benjamin's son, Thomas Potts, who was then aged 17, as a 'gilder on china'.

SAMUEL POWELL. Flower painter. *c.* 1840+

Samuel Powell, born in Derbyshire in about 1770, married a Broseley girl who was later employed as a gold burnisher at Coalport. His name is included in the 1841 and 1851 Coalport census returns, and the undated list of Coalport painters given on Page 97 lists Powell as a flower painter. His name is not included in the 1859 wages list or the 1861 census, and he would appear to have retired or died between 1851 and January 1859.

EDWARD PUGH. Gilder. *c.* 1840s

Edward Pugh's name is included in the 1841 census, where his occupation is given as 'china gilder', in the age group 20 to 24. His name does not appear in the 1851 or 1861 census returns, and no further details are known of this Coalport gilder.

THOMAS PUGH. Landscape painter. *c.* 1830s+

The early Coalport pattern-books show many patterns painted with landscape centres or with panels of landscapes. Regrettably, only three of these landscape designs bear a notation of the artist's name. One of these patterns, 3/479 of the mid- or late 1830s, is inscribed 'Landscape by Pugh'.

The 1841 Coalport census returns include two 'china painters' named Thomas Pugh—one aged 24 and one in the age group 25 to 29. The 1851 census return includes only one Thomas Pugh. The name Thomas Edwin Pugh occurs in the 1859 list of painters' wages, where the amount of £2 is entered. It must be added that not all Coalport landscape designs were painted by Thomas Pugh, other landscape painters being John Benbow, Daniel Lucas, Jesse Mountford, Piper, and Thomas or William Steele.

ENOS RABY. Ground layer and/or gilder. *c.* 1840+

Enos Raby was born at Madeley in about 1796 and was employed at Thomas Martin Randall's decorating establishment at Madeley prior to 1840. Mr W. Turner, in an article on Madeley porcelain and workmen published in the *Connoisseur* magazine in November and December 1908, stated that Raby was ground layer, colourman and gilder to Randall at Madeley.

The 1851 census returns list Enos Raby as a 'china painter', so the possibility exists that Raby was employed at the near-by Coalport factory after the closure of the Madeley establishment. His experience as a 'ground layer' (the operative responsible for laying an even ground colour on ornately decorated Sèvres-type porcelain) would have been valuable to the Coalport management. I have been unable to trace his name in the 1861 census returns.

JOHN RANDALL. Bird painter. *c.* 1835–81

Born at Broseley, near Coalport, in 1810, at the age of 18 John Randall was apprenticed to his uncle, Thomas Martin Randall, who decorated English and French porcelain in the Sèvres manner, at first in London and then at Madeley, close by Coalport. Randall subsequently painted at the Rockingham factory, but joined the Coalport staff in 1835.

Randall's name first occurs in the Coalport pattern-book under design 2/973, 'Birds by Randall'. Subsequent pattern numbers are: 3/25, 3/60, 3/269, 3/278, 3/279, 3/283, 3/290, 3/294, 3/360, 3/395, 3/404, 3/420, 3/883, 3/951, 3/961, 3/997, 4/245, 4/253, 4/281, 4/385, 5/77, 5/244 (see Plate 219, D), 6/343, 6/673, 6/679, 6/687, 6/689, and 6/692. Most of these designs feature panels of Sèvres-type exotic birds in landscape. Apart from these tableware patterns, John Randall decorated some of the finest Coalport vases and other ornamental objects (see Colour Plate IX). Randall's bird painting is often found on the same object as William Cook's flower painting.

In the 1860s John Randall largely forsook the Sèvres style of bird painting for naturalistic studies of birds—often birds of prey—in their natural surroundings, documentary examples of which are shown in Plate 204. In 1881 failing eyesight forced John Randall to give up ceramic painting after a career of over fifty years. Subsequently Randall wrote several books on the neighbourhood. His *History of Madeley* and *The Clay Industries* give most valuable first-hand information. John Randall's name was included in the 1841, 1851, 1861, and 1871 Coalport census returns as a 'china painter'; and he is included in the 1859 painters' wages list, which shows that at this period he was one of the highest-paid artists.

JAMES RICHARD. Painter or gilder. *c.* 1859+

Described as a 'china painter' in the 1861 census returns, James Richard—the son of John Richard, a Coalport 'china potter'—was born at Broseley, near Coalport, in about 1841. His name also appears in the 1859 Coalport artists' wages list, but as he drew the low wage of 9*s* he was probably then an apprentice. The 1871 census returns list James Richard as a 'china gilder', but in 1881 he was described as a 'china painter'. Patterns numbered 7/325, 7/326, 7/327, and 7/418 have Richard's name noted against them. In 1889 the name is given as a gilder or printer (see the letter quoted on Page 89).

ROBENS. Apprentice painter early in the twentieth century.

EDWARD ROUSE. Painter. *c.* 1860+

Edward Rouse was the younger son of James Rouse, senior (see below). Born at Madeley, near Coalport, in about 1846, his name is included as a 'china painter' in the 1861 census returns.

JAMES ROUSE, SENIOR. Flower and figure painter. *c.* 1833–60s

James Rouse was born at Derby in about 1805. He was trained at the Derby factory as a flower painter, but left for Staffordshire in the 1820s. He had moved to Coalport by 1833, for his second son, James, was born at near-by Madeley at this period; and James Rouse was one of the signatories to the 1833–4 loyal address. For the ensuing thirty years James Rouse painted a variety of Coalport porcelain with figure and Cupid subjects as well as with fruit and flower studies. On his own admission he painted Coalport porcelain in the Nantgarw manner: presumably, this Nantgarw-styled ware was decorated with floral designs.

James Rouse's work was shown at the 1851 and 1862 International Exhibitions. The Coalport factory pattern-book records only two tableware designs as being painted by Rouse—numbers 5/278 and 7/327. Most of his time was devoted to decorating the fine ornamental porcelain—vases, etc. Three of James Rouse's sons—William (see Page 124), James, and Edward—were also employed as china painters at the Coalport factory. In the 1859 wages list James Rouse drew the high wage of £2 14*s* 0*d*.

In the 1860s Rouse left Coalport. At first he was employed in Birmingham enamelling for jewellers and goldsmiths; but he returned to his native Derby in 1875. There he painted for the small works in King Street before leaving in October 1882 to join the staff of the new Royal Crown Derby factory. His later Derby work is sometimes fully signed (see *Victorian Porcelain*, 1961, Plate 29), but his painting on Coalport porcelain is not signed.

JAMES ROUSE, JUNIOR. Figure subjects. *c.* 1855+

James Rouse, Junior, was the second son of the flower and figure painter of the same name. He was born at Madeley, near Coalport, in about 1833. His name is included in the 1859 wages list, where he drew £2 2s 0d against his father's £2 14s 0d. The name also occurs in the 1861 Coalport census returns.

On the evidence of signed Derby porcelain, completed after he left Coalport, James Rouse, Junior, was a figure subject painter. He probably left Coalport with his father in the 1860s.

WILLIAM ROUSE. Flower painter. c. 1840+

William Rouse was born at Derby in about 1824, the son of James Rouse, the celebrated and talented ceramic artist. William Rouse's name is included in both the 1841 and 1851 Coalport census returns and in the 1859 wages list, but not in the 1861 census returns.

Flower patterns 4/753, 4/773, 4/910, 4/949, 4/954, 5/325, 5/509, 6/315, and 6/385 of the late 1840s or early 1850s are by William Rouse.

JOSIAH RUSHTON. Figure painter. Late nineteenth century

Josiah Rushton was a talented figure painter at the Royal Worcester factory from c. 1854 to c. 1871, who decorated Coalport plates for the Chicago Exhibition of 1893 with eighteenth-century court beauties.

GEORGE EDMUND SALE. Painter. c. 1850+

George Sale was born at Madeley, near Coalport, in about 1833. His name is included as a 'Porcelain Painter' in the 1861 census returns.

The 1851 Staffordshire census returns show George Sale, born at Madeley, as the son of a 'potter Painter' called Enoch Sale, whose name is also included in the 1841 Staffordshire census return. George Sale therefore went to Coalport between the time of the 1851 and 1861 censuses. No further information has been recorded.

RICHARD SAMPSON. Painter. c. 1860

Richard Sampson was born at Hanley, Staffordshire, in about 1833. His name is included as a 'china painter' in the 1861 Coalport census return, but no other information is available.

EUGENE SIEFFERT. See Page 139

PERCY SIMPSON. Painter. 1901–56

Percy Simpson was the son of Thomas Simpson (see over), a former Coalport artist and manager. Percy Simpson commenced his ceramic painting career at the Coalport works in 1901, retiring in February 1956. Simpson, trained under Arthur Perry, painted the finest Coalport fish, game, and landscape subjects, and his signed work is rightly prized in many public and private collections. For many years he held the postion of art director at Coalport; and he is one of the very few ceramic artists who spent their working life at one factory (see Plates 208 and 213).

THOMAS SIMPSON. Painter. 1890–1934

Thomas Simpson was the father of Percy Simpson (see previous entry), and joined the Coalport Company in 1890. He painted various subjects, including floral and bird motifs, for many years being manager of the Coalport works, where he remained until he died in 1934.

JOHN SMITH. Painter(?). *c.* 1830+

The 1841 census returns include John Smith, 'artist', in the age group 40 to 44, with a son of the same name, aged 14, described as a 'china painter'. The only reference to John Smith in the factory records is the indistinct note against the 1820s pattern 2/169, 'Landscape, Smith', which perhaps relates to John Smith, Senior. A 'J. H. Smith' was a signatory to the 1833–4 loyal address.

EDWARD SOULSBY. Gilder. *c.* 1830+

Edward Soulsby was born at Madeley, near Coalport, in about 1805. His name is included in the 1841, 1851, and 1861 census returns and in the 1859 wages list. The 1851 census returns describe him as a 'china gilder'. His wife was employed as grinder of colours and his daugher Hannah as a coloured-ground layer. In 1861 his son William (then aged 19) was described in the census returns as a 'china painter' (see below).

WILLIAM SOULSBY. Painter or gilder. *c.* 1860+

William Soulsby was born at Madeley, near Coalport, in about 1842, the son of Edward Soulsby, the Coalport artist (see above), and his name was included as a 'china painter' in the 1861 Coalport census returns, although the 1871 returns gives 'china gilder'. The name Soulsby appears against late pattern numbers 7/389, 7/488, and 7/459.

SOUTHAN. Apprentice painter early in the twentieth century

E. SPARKES. Flower painter. *c.* 1830s

Sparkes's name first appears under pattern 3/74 of the early 1830s—'Flowers by E. Sparks'—the name being spelt with or without the final 'e'. Other Sparkes patterns were 3/123, 3/296, 3/339, 3/355, 3/472, and 3/620. I have been unable to trace Sparkes's name in the 1841 or 1851 census returns; and as his name is not included in the 1859 wages list, his period of employment would seem to have been confined to the 1830s.

SPARKUM. Painter. *c.* 1830s

The name written against pattern number 3/66 of the early 1830s appears to be Sparkum, but no other record has been traced concerning this painter and the name may have been intended for Sparkes—a painter mentioned several times on following pages in the pattern books.

THOMAS SPEAK(E). Gilder. *c.* 1830–60

Thomas Speak(e) was born at Willey, near Coalport, in about 1797. His name 125 is included in the 1833–4 loyal address, and in the 1851 and 1861 census returns he is described as a 'china gilder'. He was also included in the 1859 wages list.

Designs numbered 6/690 and 6/966 in the Coalport pattern-book of the late 1840s have the notation 'small vermicelli by Speak'.

SAMUEL SPENCER. Gilder. *c.* 1859

Samuel Spencer was born in about 1840. He was described as a 'china gilder' in the Coalport 1861 census returns; and his name appears in the 1859 wages list, where the low wage of 16*s* is recorded against his name. He did not sign the 1889 letter relating to the wages of gilders and printers.

RICHARD SPENDLOVE. Gilder(?). *c.* 1830+

Richard Spendlove was born in Shropshire in about 1805. A daughter was born at Broseley, near Coalport, in *c.* 1834, and a son at Mettlach in Prussia in 1842. But the family had returned to Coalport by 1844, for children were born at Madeley in *c.* 1844, 1849, and 1859.

Richard Spendlove's name is included in the 1859 wages list, where the remuneration is given as £1 10*s* 0*d*. His name also occurs in the 1861 and 1871 Coalport census returns, that of 1871 using the description 'china gilder'; but other details are lacking.

GEORGE STANWAY, Senior. Painter. *c.* 1815–50s

George Stanway, born in Staffordshire in about 1784, is included in the 1841 and 1851 census returns as a 'china painter'; but he had been in the Coalport district from at least 1816, for his son George was born at Madeley at this period.

George Stanway, senior, was not included in the 1859 wages list, or in the 1861 census returns.

GEORGE STANWAY, Junior. Painter and gilder. *c.* 1835+

George Stanway was born at Madeley, near Coalport, in about 1817, the 1841 census returns showing that he was the son of a Staffordshire-born 'china painter' of the same name, aged 67 in 1851. The 1841, 1851, and 1861 census returns all list George Stanway, junior. The 1861 returns give him as a 'china gilder'; but the earlier records use the term 'china painter', one which on many occasions embraced gilders as well as true painters. His name is included in the 1859 wages list, when he drew an average wage of £1 4*s* 0*d*.

THOMAS STEEL(E). Landscape painter. *c.* 1835–45

The name Steele appears in the Coalport pattern-books as a landscape painter, e.g. 'Scotch views in centre by Steele'. The pattern numbers with Steele's name added are 3/929, 3/948, 3/996, 4/1, 4/3, 4/7, 4/9, 4/269, 4/272, 4/278, 4/279, 4/599, 4/604, and 4/605 of the late 1830s and 1840s.

This may relate to Thomas Steel (son of the famous fruit and flower painter of the same name). John Haslem, in his *Old Derby China Factory*, 1876, stated:

'Thomas, the youngest (son of Thomas Steel) gave promise of making a clever landscape painter but he died at Coalport in early life.'

The 1841 Coalport census returns include a 'china painter' named Thomas Steel in the age group 25 to 29, not born in Shropshire. He married a local girl, Elizabeth, and a son, Thomas, was born to them in 1838 at Coalport. Thomas Steel, the Coalport landscape painter, is not included in the 1851 census returns, nor does he appear in the 1859 wages return—so he must have died between 1841 and 1851.

A slight complication arises from the fact that no Christian name was used in the Coalport pattern-book references to this landscape artist, for, apart from the reference to Thomas in the 1841 census returns, there is also a William Steel(e), 'china painter' (see next entry).

WILLIAM STEEL(E). Painter or gilder. c. 1830s–60s

William Steel(e) was born at Worcester in about 1818, the son of James Steel, a glover. His name is included in the 1841, 1851, and 1861 census returns, where in 1851 he is listed as a 'china gilder', but in 1861 as a 'china painter and organist'. In the 1859 wages list he drew the high wage of £2 4s 8½d.

PETER STEPHAN. Modeller. c. 1830+

Peter Stephan was born in Staffordshire in about 1796 and, according to Llewellynn Jewitt (*The Ceramic Art of Great Britain*, 1878 and 1883), was the son of Pierre Stephan, a Frenchman at one time at Chelsea and at Derby and afterwards of Jackfield, 'where he had a small pottery, produced some striking good arabesque patterns in blue printing . . . He also made encaustic tiles . . .' Pierre Stephan, 'modeller and china or porcelaine repairer', entered into an agreement with Duesbury of the Derby factory in the eighteenth century.

John Haslem, the Derby painter and historian, devotes a page and a half of his book *The Old Derby China Factory*, 1876, to this family. After noting that Stephan modelled for Wedgwoods in 1774, and commenting on the quality of his models of portrait statuettes of generals and admirals of the 1775–90 period, Haslem continues:

> Stephan probably left Derby shortly before the close of the last century (the eighteenth), and was afterwards employed at Coalport. His descendants, of whom there are several still employed (in the 1870s) as workers in clay in the Staffordshire Potteries, now spell the name Strephan. A grandson worked for several years at the present Derby factory for Mr. Hancock, who exhibited at his stall in the Derby Exhibition in 1870, some large vases and other ornaments, profusely covered with flowers in biscuit, in which kind of modelling Stephan greatly excelled . . .'

Haslem therefore suggests that Stephan, senior, went to Coalport after leaving Derby 'shortly before the close of the last (eighteenth) century'. But the 1851 census reports, which give the place of birth of his son, Peter, as 'Staffordshire Potteries' (the 1861 returns give 'Stoke'), indicate that at the time of

Peter's birth, in about 1796, Stephan, senior, was in Staffordshire, not at Derby or Coalport—a fact that is confirmed by Staffordshire Directories of 1795 and 1802. The Stephans would appear to have supplied models to many manufacturers, for in January 1793 Chamberlain of Worcester paid £6 5s 0d to a John Charles Stephan 'for models'.

Peter Stephan went to Coalport from Staffordshire in about 1830 or before, as his name is added to the November 1833 strike notice (see Page 96) with William (born Staffordshire, c. 1798) and Henry (born Staffordshire, c. 1801) Stephan. If we can assume that William was the younger brother of Peter Stephan (born Staffordshire, c. 1796), and that they came to Coalport together, then the Stephans were at Coalport by 1830, when William's eldest son, Edwin, was born at near-by Broseley.

Peter Stephan is termed 'artist modeller at china manufactory' in the 1851 and 1861 Coalport census returns. From at least 1830 to the 1860s Peter Stephan (with Francis Brewer) must have modelled the Coalport factory's finest porcelain—like the ornate vase forms, inkstands, and centrepieces—as well as the relief-moulded dinner-, dessert- and teaware. The name Stephan appears in Exhibition reports appertaining to Coalport porcelain in the 1860s and 1870s, and writers have assumed that these references relate to Peter Stephan. However, the name is perpetuated in the 1861 census by 'Alfred Stephan, china modeller, aged 28'. It must be remembered that Peter Stephan was born in about 1796 and, if living in the 1870s, must have been of an advanced age.

The 1861 census returns give information on Peter Stephan's family. His wife, Susanna, was born at Madeley in about 1811 and was described as 'former china painter'; a daughter, Hannah, was born at Broseley in about 1842; a son, George, in about 1844—an 'apprentice china potter'; and another son, Edward— 'apprentice china potter'—in about 1847.

HAMLET STEVENS. Flower painter. c. 1825–80s

Hamlet Stevens was born at Hanley in the Staffordshire Potteries in about 1802. He married a Coalport girl who bore him two children, William Henry and George (aged 21 and 20 in 1851), both of whom were also employed as china painters at the Coalport factory. Hamlet Stevens was one of the signatories to the loyal address issued at the time of the strike lasting from November 1833 to March 1834, and his name is included in the 1841, 1851, 1861, 1871, and 1881 census returns and in the January 1859 wages list.

Stevens's name appears in the Coalport factory pattern-books against designs: 3/481, 3/482, 5/339, 5/498 ('growing flowers by H. Stevens'), 7/353, 7/430, and 7/434. The undated list of Coalport artists quoted on Page 97 gives Stevens's specialities as 'Sèvres flowers & Chelsea groups (of flowers) & flies'.

WILLIAM STEVENS. Painter(?) c. 1850+

William Henry Stevens, the son of Hamlet Stevens the artist (see above), was
born at Broseley, near Coalport, in about 1830. His name is included as a 'china

painter' in the 1851 and 1871 census, and the name 'Wm. Stevens' is given against design number 7/387 in the factory pattern-book.

WILLIAM STREET. Gilder and designer. *c. 1820s–60s*

William Street was born at Willey, near Coalport, in about 1796. He was employed at Coalport in the 1830s, as he was a signatory to the loyal address at the time of the 1833–4 strike. His name appears as a 'china gilder' in the 1841 census returns, and he is included in the 1851 and 1861 census returns and the 1859 wages list, where he is recorded as drawing the very high wage of £3 3s 0d. William Street was undoubtedly one of the leading Coalport gilders over a long period, possibly from about 1820 to the 1860s. The undated list quoted on Page 97 states that William Street 'was the designer and superintended the apprentices'.

TATLER. Bird and flower painter. *c. 1830s+*

Pattern number 3/947 in the Coalport pattern-books bears the note 'Birds in centre by Tatler'. Other Tatler patterns are 4/389, 'Flowers by Tatler'; 4/392, 'Flowers by Tatler', and 4/403, 'Groups by Tatler'.

The 1841 census returns include 'Elijah Tatler, china painter' in the age group 20 to 24, but I have been unable to trace other references to this artist.

TAYLOR. Bird painter(?). *c. 1820s–30s*

I have been unable to trace a china painter named Taylor in the 1841 or 1851 census returns, but the name appears in the factory pattern-books against designs 2/138, 2/140 and 3/289. These are of bird subjects: 'Birds by Taylor'— the drawing of pattern 3/289 showing birds in branches of a tree. Nothing further is recorded about this artist of the 1820–30 period, and it could be that the notation was intended to relate to Tatler, not Taylor (see above entry).

TOULOUSE. Flower and fruit painter. *c. 1840s*

'Flowers by Toulouse' is the notation against pattern 4/762 of the mid-1840s, 'Botanical Plant by Toulouse' against design 4/744, 'Fruit & flowers . . . by Toulouse' against pattern 4/781, and 'Regular groups by Toulouse' against designs 4/966, 5/275 and 5/301; but no other information has been traced. A John Toulouse was a china painter at the Worcester factory. He may have moved to Coalport, but evidence on this point is lacking.

WILLIAM TREVES. Flower painter. *c. 1820s+*

William Treves was born at Broseley in about 1799. He is described as a 'china painter' in the 1841, 1851, and 1861 census returns; and his name is also included in the 1859 wages list, where his wage is given as £2—an above-average remuneration.

References to Treves are few in the factory pattern-books although, judging by his age, he should have been painting Coalport porcelain from the 1820s. The first recorded reference to his work is against pattern 3/332 of the 1830s. Subsequent Treves floral designs are 4/962, 6/3, 6/4, 6/5, 6/91, 6/459, 6/514, 6/619, 6/750, and 7/436.

J. VAILLANT. See Page 139.

WILLIAM WALKER. Gilder. *c.* 1840+
William Walker was born at Broseley, near Coalport, in about 1822. His name is included in the 1841 and 1851 census returns, and in the latter he is described as a 'china gilder'.

W. (BILL) WATERSON
Born *c.* 1890, he was an apprentice painter from about 1906 to *c.* 1913, when he emigrated to America. The service shown in Plate 211 is painted with bird subjects signed by W. Waterson and H. Hughes.

JOHN 'JACKEY' WILLIAMS. Flower painter. *c.* 1830–60s
John Williams was born at Madeley, near Coalport, in about 1807. His name is included in the 1841 and 1851 census returns, but does not appear in the 1859 painters' wages list. Pattern numbers 2/920, 3/116, 3/209 (featuring shell motifs 'painted by Jackey Williams'), 3/312, of the early 1830s, and pattern 5/362 of the late 1840s have notes in the factory pattern-book: 'Flowers by J. Williams', 'Plants and single flower by Williams', or 'Flowers by Mr. Jno. Williams'.

GEORGE WRIGHT. Gilder. *c.* 1820s+
George Wright, born about 1796, is included in the 1841 Coalport census as a 'china gilder', but no further details are known.

CHECK LIST OF PATTERNS WHICH HAVE THE NAMES OF INDIVIDUAL ARTISTS MARKED AGAINST THEM IN THE ORIGINAL FACTORY PATTERN-BOOKS

It must be understood that most designs drawn in the available Coalport pattern-books do NOT have the name of the specialist painter responsible for the main part of the design noted against the entry, and that no names are recorded against the first nine hundred and eleven patterns.

Where names are recorded, it may be taken as reasonably certain that the pattern was painted by the artist whose name is recorded against it in the pattern book. Names are not given against designs drawn in the first pattern-book.

Second Pattern-book, containing designs 643 to 2/170 (some pages and designs are missing) of the period *c.* 1811–20

912	T. Brentnall (entry crossed through)
934	J. Pattern
935	J. Pattern
957	J. Pattern

2/80	S. Lawrence
2/83	S. Lawrence
2/138	Taylor
2/139	C. Jones
2/140	Taylor
2/169	J. Smith

Third Pattern-book, containing designs 2/171 to 2/508 of the period *c.* 1820–9

2/237	S. Lawrance
2/240	Taylor
2/241	C. Jones
2/242	J. Birbeck
2/261	J. Latham
2/289	Taylor

Fourth Pattern-book, containing designs 2/522 to 2/670 of the period *c.* 1829–31

2/533	Kelshall
2/584	Kelshall

Fifth Pattern-book, containing designs 2/676 to 2/824 of the period *c.* 1831–2

2/712	Kelshall
2/717	J. Aston
2/787	Kelshall
2/808	J. Mountford
2/815	Kelshall

Sixth Pattern-book, containing designs 2/827 to 2/982 of the period *c.* 1832–3

2/893	J. Birbeck
2/920	J. Williams
2/921	T. Dixon
2/923	J. Mountford
2/964	J. Aston
2/973	J. Randall

Seventh Pattern-book, containing designs 2/985 to 2/999 of the period *c.* 1833

2/995	T. Dixon
2/997	C. Jones

Eighth Pattern-book, containing designs 3/2 to 3/133 of the period *c.* 1834–5

3/25	J. Randall
3/60	J. Randall
3/72	T. Dixon
3/74	E. Sparkes
3/108	J. Birbeck
3/112	J. Pattern

3/113   J. Birbeck
3/116   J. Williams
3/119   J. Birbeck
3/123   E. Sparkes
3/125   T. Dixon
3/128   J. Pattern

Ninth Pattern-book, containing designs 3/134 to 3/161 of the period *c.* 1835

3/135   J. Aston
3/145   C. Jones
3/160   J. Birbeck
3/161   T. Dixon

Tenth Pattern-book, containing designs 3/162 to 3/274 of the period *c.* 1836

3/166   T. Dixon
3/177   C. Jones
3/184   C. Jones
3/195   J. Aston
3/209   J. Williams
3/210   J. Aston
3/234   J. Aston
3/266   J. Birbeck
3/269   J. Randall
3/274   S. Lawrance

Eleventh Pattern-book, containing patterns 3/277 to 3/567 of the period *c.* 1836–7

3/278   J. Randall
3/279   J. Randall
3/281   J. Randall
3/283   J. Randall
3/284   J. Parker
3/287   J. Parker
3/289   Taylor
3/290   J. Randall
3/294   J. Randall
3/296   Parker
3/312   T. Williams
3/332   W. Treves
3/335   T. Dixon
3/336   J. Birbeck
3/339   E. Sparkes
3/343   Mountford
3/344   J. Birbeck
3/347   Mottershead

3/355   E. Sparkes

3/360	J. Randall
3/365	J. Parker
3/395	J. Randall
3/404	J. Randall
3/420	J. Randall
3/421	J. Aston
3/432	J. Aston
3/433	J. Aston
3/436	J. Aston
3/437	J. Birbeck
3/453	S. Lawrance
3/455	E. Green
3/460	C. Jones
3/461	C. Jones
3/462	T. Dixon
3/472	E. Sparkes
3/479	T. Pugh
3/481	H. Stevens
3/482	H. Stevens
3/483	E. Green
3/506	C. Jones
3/507	T. Dixon
3/510	T. Dixon
3/511	J. Pattern
3/512	J. Pattern
3/514	J. Pattern

Twelfth Pattern-book, containing designs 3/548 to 3/843 of the period *c.* 1837

3/582	T. Dixon
3/583	J. Aston
3/596	J. Aston
3/597	T. Dixon
3/601	J. Aston
3/603	J. Aston
3/609	Birbeck ⎫
3/610	Birbeck ⎬ see Page 104
3/612	Birbeck ⎭
3/620	E. Sparkes
3/630	R. Harvey
3/721	E. Griffiths
3/724	J. Aston
3/725	J. Aston
3/726	J. Aston
3/730	J. Benbow
3/769	T. Dixon

Coalport artists	3/770	T. Dixon
	3/776	C. Jones
	3/778	C. Jones
	3/779	S. Lawrance
	3/782	S. Lawrance
	3/788	T. Dixon
	3/789	T. Dixon
	3/806	T. Dixon
	3/811	T. Dixon
	3/834	C. Jones

Thirteenth Pattern-book, containing designs 3/846 to 3/999 of the period *c.* 1838

	3/883	J. Randall
	3/885	C. Jones
	3/886	S. Lawrance
	3/898	T. Dixon
	3/926	T. Dixon
	3/929	T. Steel
	3/932	T. Dixon
	3/945	T. Dixon
	3/947	Tatler
	3/948	T. Steel
	3/950	Piper
	3/951	J. Randall
	3/961	J. Randall
	3/962	Piper
	3/963	Piper
	3/974	T. Dixon
	3/977	G. Perry
	3/978	C. Jones
	3/980	T. Dixon
	3/982	T. Dixon
	3/983	Piper
	3/992	T. Dixon
	3/994	T. Dixon
	3/996	T. Steel
	3/997	J. Randall

Fourteenth Pattern-book, containing designs 4/1 to 4/338 of the period *c.* 1839–40

	4/1	T. Steel
	4/3	T. Steel
	4/7	T. Steel
	4/9	T. Steel
	4/42	T. Dixon
	4/46	T. Dixon

4/210	E. Howells
4/233	S. Lawrance
4/245	J. Randall
4/253	J. Randall
4/257	S. Lawrance
4/265	J. Parker
4/268	T. Dixon
4/269	T. Steel
4/271	S. Lawrance
4/272	T. Steel
4/274	J. Parker
4/278	T. Steel
4/279	T. Steel
4/281	J. Randall
4/283	S. Lawrance
4/288	S. Lawrance
4/299	T. Dixon
4/300	T. Dixon
4/311	S. Lawrance

Fifteenth Pattern-book, containing designs 4/347 to 4/579 of the period *c.* 1840–1

4/383	T. Dixon
4/385	J. Randall
4/389	Tatler
4/391	C. Jones
4/392	Tatler
4/403	Tatler
4/412	S. Lawrance
4/461	Brindley
4/514	T. Dixon
4/571	T. Dixon
4/580	Beard

Sixteenth Pattern-book, containing designs 4/583 to 4/706 of the period *c.* 1841–2

4/587	J. Beard
4/590	T. Dixon
4/594	J. Beard
4/598	J. Beard
4/599	T. Steel
4/063	T. Dixon
4/604	T. Steel
4/605	T. Steel
4/606	J. Beard
4/656	T. Dixon

Seventeenth Pattern-book, containing designs 4/711 to 5/165 of the period *c.* 1843–5

4/744	Toulouse
4/753	W. Rouse
4/762	Toulouse
4/764	Dixon
4/767	Dixon
4/773	W. Rouse
4/781	Toulouse
4/791	Lawrance
4/793	Dixon
4/805	Lawrance
4/810	Dixon
4/811	Lawrance
4/812	Dixon
4/836	Dixon
4/910	W. Rouse
4/930	Dixon
4/949	W. Rouse
4/954	W. Rouse
4/962	Treves
4/966	Toulouse
4/967	Dixon
4/997	Toulouse
5/6	Dixon
5/31	Rouse
5/77	J. Randall
5/138	Dixon
5/140	Dixon

OUTSIDE PAINTERS
INDEPENDENT DECORATORS
AND DEALERS

During the early part of the nineteenth century the Coalport factories supplied blanks, or undecorated porcelain, to mainly independent decorators and dealers who painted them in their own manner or to suit the requirements of their customers. Fortunately, several of these non-factory decorated pieces are signed and sometimes dated.

The most interesting firm of decorators is undoubtedly that of Thomas Baxter (father and son) at their studio at 1 Goldsmith Street, Gough Square, Clerkenwell, London, in the *c.* 1797–1814 period. The interior of this studio (Plate 42) is depicted in a watercolour drawing (now in the Victoria and Albert Museum) by Thomas Baxter, junior, which was completed in 1810 and was included in the Royal Academy Exhibition of 1811. Its importance relevant to this book is that on a notice hanging on the wall can be clearly read the heading 'New Price List. Coalport White China' (the complete list is not given—only dashes appearing below the heading). This list shows that the Baxter studio at least was interested in Coalport white china and that by 1810 at least two such price lists had been issued, making clear that this aspect of the Coalport trade was an important one.

The Baxter watercolour drawing of 1810 shows a good range of teaware with certain peculiarities. It is my contention that this teaware is Coalport of the 1805–15 period (see Pages 42–3, Colour Plate II and Plates 43 and 44), and that furthermore—unless evidence such as factory marks points to the contrary—all pre-1815 Baxter-signed ceramic painting on obviously English porcelain is of Coalport manufacture rather than Worcester, as has been supposed in the past. Such pieces are illustrated in Plates 91–5. I have been unable to trace companion pieces bearing the mark of any other factory, as all pieces are unmarked and link up with other Coalport ware.

Thomas Baxter, senior, was born c. 1760, and his son in February 1782. Thomas Baxter, junior, was trained under his father at London and examples of his painting were exhibited at Royal Academy exhibitions between 1802 and 1812, the subjects including fruit, flowers and shell compositions. Signed figure subjects are also recorded, showing that he was a very talented painter in all branches of ceramic decoration. However, the 1810 watercolour drawing shows that simple border motifs were added by other hands at Baxter's London decorating studio, not all the work being that of the Baxters.

In or before 1814 Thomas Baxter, junior, moved to Worcester, where he ran a school for painting, training several ceramic artists. He also painted for the Worcester Porcelain Company—then run by Messrs Flight Barr & Barr—where all his work is likely to have been marked with one of several self-explanatory name marks or with the impressed initial marks 'F.B.B.' under a crown. Thomas Baxter, junior, subsequently painted at the Swansea factory and at the Chamberlain factory at Worcester. He died in 1821. Signed Baxter ceramic painting bearing dates (or being datable) between c. 1805 and 1814 is very likely to have been carried out on Coalport blanks, although it was decorated at London and not at the factory.

DONOVAN

James Donovan, of George's Quay, Dublin, imported and sometimes decorated English pottery and porcelain before reselling it. He purchased porcelain from several factories and his name mark can be found on marked Derby porcelain of the 1790–1810 period and on early marked Minton porcelain. It also occurs on Coalport porcelain of the 1805–20 period; but it is difficult to decide if the object was entirely decorated by Donovan in Dublin or if he only added his name to factory-decorated examples. James Donovan and his son operated from c. 1770 to c. 1829.

W. FLETCHER

Little is known of this figure painter. Two Coalport-type lobed-edged plates of the 1805–15 period bear the inscription 'W. Fletcher, junr. Del. et Pinx'

(Allen Collection, No. 515 and 516, Victoria and Albert Museum). A signed plaque was sold in Sotheby's in 1954. The Allen Collection Catalogue suggests that he may have been an amateur, but the quality of the painting and the rich, ornate gilt borders indicate that W. Fletcher was an independent commercial decorator of china.

MIST

James Mist had a retail establishment at 82 Fleet Street, London. The first directory entry occurs in 1810, and he was declared bankrupt in 1815. His written name-and-address marks occur on porcelain of the 1810–15 period, including a Coalport oval sucrier of the type depicted in Thomas Baxter's 1810 watercolour drawing (see Plate 42).

MORTLOCKS

Messrs. Mortlocks were one of the foremost London china retailers throughout the nineteenth century, the full period being from c. 1746 to c. 1930. In directories up to and including 1806, the address 'Staffordshire Warehouse, 250 Oxford Street' is given. In directories from 1808 to 1838 the reference to Staffordshire is deleted and the description 'Colebrookdale China Manufacturers' takes its place. From about 1808 Messrs Mortlocks' Oxford Street premises must have been the main London outlet for Coalport porcelain. This may well account for the dearth of marks, for all retailers of the period were loath to permit the ware they sold to bear the maker's name. When a firm such as Wedgwoods, Spode, or the Derby or Worcester porcelain companies had their own retail establishments their ware invariably bore a clear factory mark—the opposite being the case when ware was sold through an independent retailer. Coalport porcelain sold for Mortlocks in 1820 is listed on page 146.

CHARLES MUSS

Charles Muss was born in 1779. Jewitt states that he painted at the Caughley factory, but it is more likely—to judge from his date of birth—that he painted Coalport porcelain. A contemporary view of the Coalport factory, engraved in nineteenth-century reference books, is credited to Muss. His painting on porcelain reputedly consisted of landscapes and figures in sepia and purple monochrome, but no documentary signed specimens have been recorded. In 1800 Charles Muss exhibited at the Royal Academy a painting of Dunkeld Cathedral. In 1802 and 1803, and from 1817 to 1823, he exhibited various enamels, mainly portraits, a London address being given, indicating that at these periods he was not at Coalport.

Charles Muss and his father also ran a decorating establishment in London, where both probably decorated Coalport as well as other porcelain. Later, Charles Muss turned his attention to enamel painting on metal and was patronized by Royalty—George IV giving £1,500 for an example said to be the largest enamel ever painted on metal, measuring 21 inches by 15 inches. Charles Muss died in 1824.

THOMAS PARDOE

Thomas Pardoe was a talented flower painter employed at the Derby porcelain factory in the 1780s, who later migrated to the Worcester factory and then to Swansea. This factory-decorated ware is not signed, but in 1809 Thomas Pardoe established himself as an independent decorator at Bristol. Such ware often bears name-and-address marks, and some rare pieces are also dated. Marks such as 'Pardoe. 28 Bath Street, Bristol' indicate a period between *c.* 1812 and 1816 when the artist was at this address. From about 1821 Pardoe was at Nantgarw, where he died in July 1823.

While decorating on his own account at Bristol between 1809 and *c.* 1821 Thomas Pardoe seems to have used chiefly Coalport blanks—in particular, the typical 1810-type lobed plates (see Page 29).

SHARPUS

Messrs R. & E. Sharpus were London retailers at 13 Cockspur Street from *c.* 1801 (several later changes in title are recorded in directories). A trade card of *c.* 1806 describes this firm as 'Colebrookdale China & Art Glass Manufacturers'. Among porcelain available for retail sale or for export are listed 'Table services, Dessert set, Tea Equipages, Sandwich Sets, Dejunees Etc. of every description. Elegant chimney ornaments in vases, urns, tripods, garden pots, cabinet cups etc. . . .' Many of these objects must have been of Coalport manufacture; but like most retailers, Sharpus purchased their stock from many sources. However, the description Colebrookdale China (& Art Glass) Manufacturers does indicate that by this date (1806) Coalport ware had gained a good reputation in London and that R. & E. Sharpus largely stocked this porcelain. A slightly later (*c.* 1812) card of Edward Sharpus bears the same description.

EUGENE SIEFFERT

This talented French figure painter decorated some Coalport porcelain for Messrs Daniells in the second half of the nineteenth century. His stippled miniature style of painting is very fine and is signed 'E. Sieffert' or with the initials 'E.S.' The porcelain, if of Coalport origin, bears a Daniell retailer's mark. Sieffert's signed painting is, however, to be found on French porcelain and on Messrs Brown-Westhead, Moore & Co's ware.

VAILLANT

Some Coalport-type porcelain of the 1805–15 period bears rather laboured figure paintings which are signed on the reverse 'Vaillant pinx'. The 1810-type teaset shown in Plate 44 with some pieces initialled 'J.V.' and dated 1807 could well be by the same hand, as the enamel colours are the same and the same rather amateurish style is evident.

CHAPTER VIII

COALPORT-TYPE PORCELAIN

In previous chapters I have sought to show what was made at Coalport; but it is just as important to explain what was *not* made at Coalport, for many specimens have been incorrectly attributed in previous books.

The Coalport series of pattern numbers offers a good guide to attribution, and porcelain bearing pattern numbers outside the Coalport range cannot have originated from John Rose's factory. The Coalport series range from 1 to 1000, continuing 2/1 to 2/1000, then 3/1 to 3/1000 and so on through at least eight series. It therefore follows that porcelain of the pre-1870 period bearing pattern numbers above 1000[1] or with a letter prefix, such as B/100, cannot be Coalport. The Coalport pattern numbers are normally painted in a small, neat hand; and they do not have the prefix 'No' or 'N' which are to be seen before the pattern numbers on the porcelain of some other factories.

In the second half of the nineteenth century the old system of fractional pattern numbers was discontinued and progressive numbering, reaching about 5000 by 1900, was employed. Letter prefixes were also introduced—V for vases, X and Z for dinner- and dessertware, and Y prefixing teaware pattern numbers. This information does not invalidate the points made in the previous paragraph, as this later ware bears the standard 'Coalport' crowned printed mark and is unlikely to be mistaken for the products of other factories.

FLORAL-ENCRUSTED PORCELAIN

For very many years, most fine-quality floral-encrusted porcelain of the 1820–40 period has been termed 'Coalbrookdale'. In fact, most major factories of the period produced this decorated class of porcelain, as is proved by marked specimens or surviving factory pattern-books.

Recent research has shown that much unmarked 'Coalbrookdale'-type porcelain was produced at the Minton factory and not at Coalport. Certain forms featured as typically Coalport in several reference books, are shown by the contemporary Minton shape books to have been produced by Mintons. Some pages from the Minton books are reproduced in Plates 234–7.

[1] The pre-1814 porcelain produced at the Coalport works of Anstice, Horton & Thomas Rose may bear progressive pattern numbers up to at least 1419 (see Chapter IV).

These Minton designs include a globular covered vase which normally bears a named view on one side and a flower panel on the other side, most specimens being richly encrusted with raised flowers. They do not bear a factory mark, but a mock-Dresden crossed-swords mark in blue is often present. This form is described as 'Globe Potpourri—raised flowers' against the drawing of this article in the Minton shape book. The Minton cost-estimate book shows that these so-called Coalport covered bowls were made in at least three different sizes, and a few factory costs gleaned from the Minton estimate book may be of interest. The landscape painting cost 7s; the flower painting, 5s 6d; 1s 6d worth of gold was employed, which cost 1s to apply and 4½d to burnish; and women were employed to colour the applied porcelain flowers at a cost of 1s 6d per 'Globe potpourri'. Examples of these Minton articles, classed as 'Coalport' or 'Coalbrookdale', will be found illustrated in G. B. Hughes's *Victorian Pottery and Porcelain*, 1959, Plate 61, and in several other books and magazine articles.

Various very imposing plates or pierced dishes containing fruit and flowers in full relief are invariably termed 'Coalport'. Again, most examples are Minton, and both models normally found are drawn in the Minton shape book (in fact, the moulds for these fine pieces were retained at the Minton factory until 1926). The Minton estimate book again shows that these superb plates of fruit and flowers were made in three different sizes, the Minton cost entry No. 102 reading: 'Plate of fruit & flowers 9 ins. round, rims perforated. Painting—the fruit & flowers coloured by women (at cost of 5/11d per piece), forget-me-nots painted on the underside and flies, coloured. Gilding, slight upon the pierced work (1/3d worth of gold, which cost 8d to apply and 8d to burnish).' Many examples bear a blue mock-Dresden crossed-swords mark, as does much other Minton floral-encrusted porcelain. The attribution of these plates of porcelain fruit and flowers is complicated by an example in the Victoria and Albert Museum which bears the name 'Coalport' in gold. Although one would hesitate to assert that this mark was added later by someone seeking to prove the believed origin of these articles, it should be pointed out that gilt 'marks' are relatively easy to apply, as the article does not require to be refired at a very high temperature to fix the gold.

The Minton shape book includes much floral-encrusted porcelain, typical examples from this original source book being reproduced in Plates 231 and 232, which include several forms attributed to the Coalport factory in some reference books. For finished examples of Minton's floral-encrusted porcelain, the reader is referred to the writer's *Illustrated Encyclopaedia of British Pottery and Porcelain*, 1966, and *Minton Pottery and Porcelain of the First Period, 1793–1850*, 1968.

VASES, ETC

Just as floral-encrusted porcelain of Minton manufacture is often called 'Coalport', so various vase forms are often termed 'Coalport' in error. Some of the troublesome so-called 'Coalport' shapes are shown in Plate 234, and these are reproduced from the original Minton shape book.

FIGURES

Many fine-quality figures of the 1820s and 1830s are also called 'Coalport' by authors, auctioneers, collectors, and dealers. Only one is featured in the available Coalport travellers' pattern-book, but the so-called Coalport figures do appear in the Minton design books and some related ones bear Minton marks. Two illustrated in Plates 119 and 120 of Franklin A. Barrett's *Caughley and Coalport Porcelain*, 1951, are Minton, but are described as 'typical of the finely finished and brilliantly decorated figures made at Coalport . . .'

When Mr Barrett wrote the above he was, of course, repeating a widely accepted belief, and he had not had the opportunity to examine the Minton factory records where this porcelain is featured—so no blame whatever attaches to him. Nevertheless, the present writer feels that these errors of attribution must be pointed out.

Plate 237 shows figure models from the Minton figure-design book which are merely samples, showing some models often mistaken for Coalport.

EARLY COALPORT (COALBROOKDALE) PORCELAIN MENTIONED IN NINETEENTH-CENTURY SALE CATALOGUES

The following items have been gleaned from Messrs Christie's and Messrs Phillips's sale catalogues for the years 1800 to 1820. The contemporary descriptions and components of services are interesting, even if the prices are tantalizing!

The description 'compotier' refers to low side dishes of various forms, not the high-footed stand normally associated with the name 'compotier' today.

PHILLIPS. 11/12/1801.
> *A Catalogue of the Prime part of the stock in trade*
> *of Mr. Joseph Tansley—a bankrupt.*

199. A dessert set of English porcelain, dragon pattern; comprising 1 centre-piece *on feet*, 2 tureens, covers & stands, 12 compotiers, 24 plates.   £2. 9. 0
    (The name of the manufacturer is not given against this lot, but the dragon pattern was a standard early Coalport one—see Plate 24).

CHRISTIES.

8th October, 1802.   *The Elegant Household Furniture . . . of the late*
> *R^{t.} Hon. Lady Jane Ferry.*

Lot. 73. A Coalbrook Dale sandwich set, 4 compotiers (segment dishes), centrepiece and cover, and 7 plates.   £2. 3. 0.

Lot. 85. Five Coalbrook Dale tea cups, 6 coffee cans, 5 saucers and water bowl.

26th March, 1804.   *Household Furniture etc. . . . . the property of*
> *J. L. Greffulke Esq. Portland Place.*

Lot 70. An extensive Table (Dinner) service of the Coalbrook Dale manufacture, painted with tulip border enriched with gold, consisting of 16 dishes in sizes, 4 square dishes with covers (probably vegetable dishes), 1 salad bowl, 2 terrines (tureens) and covers, 4 sauce terrines and stands, 22 soup plates and 66 flat plates, total 119 pieces.   £43. 1. 0.   143

4th February, 1808. *Household Furniture, china, books & prints . . . of a Gentleman.*

Lot 113. A beautiful dessert service of the Colebrook Dale, in imitation of old coloured Japan, comprising 1 centre dish, 12 comports (dishes), 2 sugar and cream terrines, covers and stands, 24 plates and 2 ice pails, covers and liners. £16. 16. 0.

5th May, 1809. *Assemblage of ancient and modern china . . . of the Hon. Aug. Cavendish Bradshaw . . .*

Lot 28. A dessert service of Colebrook Dale china, of gilt vermicelli pattern, with coloured medallions in the centre, the greek (key) border, consisting of a pair of Ice pails, 4 oval dishes, 4 pin cushion ditto, 4 shells, an oval centre dish, sugar and cream terrines and dishes (stands to small tureens) and 32 plates. £21. 0. 0.

17th October, 1809.

Tea and coffee set of Colebrook Dale china, to imitate Japan. £8. 8. 0.

6th April, 1810.

An inkstand of Colebrook Dale china, fashioned as an Etruscan drinking horn.

26th March, 1811. *The neat Household Furniture . . . the property of a Lady deceased.*

Lot. 22. Three vases, and 2 matchpots, Colebrook Dale. £1. 0. 0.

17th June, 1811. *Beautiful French and other Porcelain . . . the Genuine property of Joseph Wyndham Esq. Dec.*

Lot 98. A tea and coffee equipage of Colebrook Dale, old Japan pattern. £3. 18. 0.
Lot 99. A small ditto, Dessert service. £7. 10. 0.

20th June, 1811. *Pictures Drawings, Porcelain, etc. . . . the property of the late Sir Jas. Pulteney, Bart.*

Lot 4. 16 Plates of Colebrook Dale china, green and gold flowered border. £2. 0. 0.

8th February, 1812. *Property of Col. James Brunton.*

Lot 65. A wafer tray and a pair of match pots of Colebrook Dale china. £1. 2. 0.

12th April, 1815. *Household Furniture etc., the property of a Nobleman.*

Lot 97. A dessert set of Colebrook Dale, with flowers and gold edges, centre piece, 2 cream bowls and stands, 12 compotiers, and 24 plates. £2. 18. 0.

12th July, 1815. *The remaining stock of Mr. Jones, chinaman, retiring and having disposed of his long established premises in Ludgate Hill.*

Heading for second day
'COLEBROOK DALE, STAFFORDSHIRE, ETC.'
(The following items have been selected as being in all probability the 'Colebrook Dale' objects, the 'Japan' patterns and especially the Dragon-patterned ware (Lots 1, 2, 15, 16 & 17) matching half finished objects and wasters recently found on the Caughley/Coalport site. It is most unfortunate that the various lots are grouped under this general heading rather than being individually described, for as they are the stock of a retiring chinaman, the true attribution of all lots would probably have been known at the time of cataloguing.)

Lot 1. Part of a breakfast set, consisting of 12 BLUE DRAGON pattern breakfast cups and saucers, a roll tray, 2 slop basins, a bread & butter plate, 19 tea saucers, and a cream jug.   £1. 0. 0.

Lot 2. Part of a ditto consisting of 18 handled breakfast cups and saucers, and a slop basin.   £1. 2. 0.

Lot 4. 13 table plates in imitation of the oriental enamel, in compartments.   £1. 1. 0.

Lot 5. A pair of mazarine blue and gold and flowered essence vases, and a centre white and flowered ditto.

Lot 7. A dessert service consisting of 2 ice pails, covers and liners, a salad bowl, 4 oval, 4 square, 4 shell shaped dishes, a pair of cream and sugar terrines, covers and stands, and 24 plates, painted with Roses.   £9. 15. 0.

Lot 9. A pair of ice pails, covers and liners, mazarine blue, green and gold, with compartments.   £2. 0. 0.

Lot 10. A tea service mazarine blue and gold, 12 tea cups and saucers, 8 coffee cups, a sugar basin and cover, a slop basin, 2 bread and butter plates, a cream jug, a teapot, cover & stand.   £3. 1. 0.

Lot 15. A dinner service of red & green dragon pattern, consisting of 1 large 2 handled tureen and cover, 2 soup ditto & covers, 3 square and 4 oval vegetable dishes and covers, 1 small & 1 larger sallad bowl, 4 sauce tureens, covers & stands, 15 oval dishes in sizes, 1 fish dish, and 2 strainers, 9 baking dishes, 20 soup plates, 35 table plates, 14 pie plates.   £14. 0. 0.

Lot 16. Part of a dessert service same pattern, 2 sugar tureens, covers & stands, 20 dessert dishes.   £1. 19. 0.

Lot 17. 2 large dragon pattern dishes, 2 smaller ditto and 12 table plates.   £1. 1. 0.

June 19th, 1816. *The property of the R^t· Honble· Lord Visc. Gardner, dec.*

Lot 48. A dessert service of Colebrook Dale china of rich pattern, with arms, consisting of centre piece compotiers, and 24 plates.   £5. 5. 0.

Lot 49. A dessert service ditto, consisting of 13 dishes, 2 sauce boats (tureens ?), stands and covers and 24 plates.   £14. 14. 0.

Lot 75. 2 Pair of Colebrook Dale, Ice pails, for flower pots.   £6. 6. 0.

Lot 82. 2 Pair of rich pattern Colebrook Dale Ice pails.   £4. 0. 0.

June 26th, 1816.

Lot 59. A tea service Colebrook Dale china, rich border and gilt edges, consisting of 12 cups and saucers, 8 coffee cups, sugar box, slop basin, cream ewer, and a bread & butter plate.   £1. 17. 0.

December 17th, 1817. *Household Furniture, china & glass . . .
effects of Sir Hugh Monro, Bart.*

A neat Colebrook Dale, china déjeune, consisting of a teapot, sugar basin, milk pot, 2 cups and saucers and an oval stand for the whole.

The collection of Queen Charlotte was sold by Mr Christie in a series of sales held from May 5th, 1819, to the end of the year, the following items of Colebrookdale china being included. It is to be expected that the auctioneers exercised every care in the cataloguing, and it is probable that records were kept showing the origin of the Royal pieces—so these catalogue attributions are likely to be accurate. The various items could, of course, have been purchased at any time prior to the sale.

May 6th, 1819.

Lot. 8 A breakfast service of Colebrook Dale china, consisting of teapot and stand, cream pot, and sugar basin, two large and four small plates, eleven cups and twelve saucers. £5. 15. 6.

Lot 13. One French and two Colebrook Dale two handled cups, covers and saucers, with flowers and richly burnished. £4. 0. 0.

August 26th, 1819.

Lot 27. A Sandwich tray, consisting of a centre bowl of Colebrook Dale china, in imitation of old Japan, in a mahogany tray. £4. 4. 0.

Lot 53. A square plateau, with déjeune of Colebrook Dale china . . . £2. 10. 0.

Lot 55. A sweetmeat plateau of Colebrook Dale china . . . £2. 2. 0.

On December 14th and 15th, 1820, Christies sold a 'portion of the very extensive and valuable stock of Porcelain of Mr Mortlock'. This sale is very important, as Mortlock advertised as the agent for the Coalbrook Dale Company—or rather, as manufacturer of Coalbrook Dale porcelain. The following lots have the name 'Coalbrook Dale' included in the description, while many other lots are probably of Coalport manufacture although this is not stated. It is probable that the stock sold at this sale was of old unsaleable goods.

Lot 27. A pair of Colebrook Dale ice pails, covers & liners, white with gold borders.

Lot 28. A Table (Dinner) service of Colebrook Dale blue bouquets, on white basket ground, consisting of 11 dishes in sizes, 4 round do and covers, tureen, cover & stand (this is crossed through in ink), 4 sauce tureens, covers & stands, 60 plates, 12 soup ditto and a sallad bowl. £5. 12. 6.
with Lot 27 above.

Lot 32. A pair of ice pails, covers & liners, rose pattern, richly gilt of Colebrook Dale china. 17. 0.

Lot 37. A Colebrook Dale breakfast set, green flowers, consisting of 12 breakfast cups and saucers, 12 coffee cups & saucers, 2 slop basins, cream ewer, sugar basin & cover, muffin plate & cover, egg stand, roll tray, 2 meat dishes, 14 plates. £1. 13. 0.

Lot 40. Six deep fruit dishes with medallion centres and arabesque gold borders, and 18 Colebrook Dale dessert plates with figured centres and etruscan borders. £1. 9. 0.

Lot 42. 27 table plates of Colebrook Dale, with roses and small blue sprig. £1. 18. 0.

Lot 53. Twenty Colebrook Dale dessert plates, with figured centres, and black and red etruscan borders. £1. 3. 0.

Lot 99. A dinner service of Colebrook Dale, consisting of 16 dishes in sizes, 2 soup tureens and covers, 4 sauce do, covers and stands, 4 square dishes and covers, 72 table plates, and 18 soups. Passed (not sold)

Lot 17. A Colebrook Dale dinner service, with blue sprig, 114 pieces. £4. 6. 0.
(2nd Day)

COALPORT ARTISTS AND WORKPEOPLE AS RECORDED IN THE 1841 AND 1861 CENSUS RETURNS

The most complete guide to the workpeople employed at the Coalport factory in the early 1840s is contained in the June 1841 census returns housed in the Public Record Office. (The fuller 1861 returns have been tabulated and are given from Page 150 to Page 151). Here the names, employment and ages of the local inhabitants are given, and it is also shown whether they were born in the same county—Shropshire. Regarding the artists, listed as china painters, this latter information is of the utmost interest, and relevant facts are incorporated in the notes on artists given in Chapter VII.

The census returns cover the district around Coalport, including Coalport itself, Jackfield (on the opposite bank of the River Severn), the near-by town of Broseley, and the Madeley district. For the purpose of the census, the county was divided up into small areas, each being the responsibility of different returning officers—a fact which results in some inconsistency in the methods of recording the facts.

The official instructions were that ages should be given fully for persons under fifteen, but for persons over fifteen the age should be recorded as the lowest in each four-year division. That meant that fifteen was given for all ages between fifteen and nineteen, '20' would be written for those aged between twenty and twenty-four, and so on: though, happily, in some instances the census officer chose to record the exact age. The following list of Coalport employees records the ages of these workpeople. Ages given in multiples of five may be regarded as the lowest possible age—which, in fact, could be one, two, three or four years more. As a reminder of this, a plus sign has been added to these. Ages not given in multiples of five may be regarded as the exact age of the person listed.

Names bracketed together indicate that these persons were part of the same household; and when the surname is the same, one may assume that these bracketed names represented the same family.

The following list gives the summary of workpeople employed in the various   147 branches of the factory in 1841. These are minimum numbers in 1841, not maximum, for the employment of some persons is not given fully in the census returns. For example, although several males are listed as 'Potters', they have not been included, as there were several near-by potteries producing utilitarian ware, and there is no evidence that these 'Potters' were employed in the Coalport *china* factory. Only persons clearly indicated as employed in the china industry are here included.

China potters (24)

Male persons listed under this category would probably be employed on the production of ware—turners, moulders, glaze dippers, etc.—or in the preparation of the raw materials, clay or glaze.

A further eighteen should be added to the twenty-four listed as 'China Potters'. These eighteen were listed under the all-embracing term 'china M', indicating that they were employed at the china manufactory, but probably at rather mundane tasks that did not warrant a special description.

China firemen (5)

Five persons were listed under this heading, or as 'Firemen of China'.

China handler (1)

One person chose to give this description, though others must have been employed at this task of affixing the handles on to cups, jugs or teapots, but are probably included under the all-embracing term 'China Potter'.

Engravers (3)

Three persons are listed as engravers: Thomas Radford, William Sneyd, and John Walton. Radford and Walton are described only as 'Engravers', but it may be assumed that they were, in fact, employed at the Coalport factory engraving the copper plates from which the transfer-printed designs were produced. William Sneyd is described in full as a 'China Engraver'. John Walton's age is given as 75 (that is, between 75 and 79) in 1841, and consequently he may have been employed at the factory from its earliest days in the 1790s.

Printers or transferers (3)

Printers, printresses and transferers were responsible for transferring, by means of inked tissue-like paper, the design from the engraved copper plate to the porcelain. Only three persons (one male and two females) gave their employment as printers in the 1841 census returns; but many other females must have been employed on this basic task, and perhaps some of the ten females listed only as working at the 'china m(anufactory)' should be included under this heading. There is the further possibility that others, giving their employment as 'paintresses' were in reality printresses.

Gilders (5)

William Billingsley (aged 44), Abraham Milner (aged 55), Edward Pugh (aged 20), William Street (aged 45) and George Wright (aged 45) were described as gilders. With the exception of Pugh, all were above average age and must have been experienced china gilders. Abraham Milner's age was 55 (meaning between 55 and 59) in 1841 and he could consequently have served the Coalport firm for very many years. It is probable that some gilders gave their employment as 'china painters'.

Burnishers (45)

The task of burnishing the gold ornamentation after it has emerged matt from the firing is traditionally a female occupation. Forty-five persons recorded their occupation as 'burnishers' in the Coalport district during the 1841 census, their ages ranging from forty-five to ten years of age. Very many girl burnishers were in their early teens.

Painters (75)

A surprisingly high number of male 'china painters', seventy-five in all, were recorded in the 1841 census covering the Coalport district. Many of the names link with well-known ceramic artists (see Chapter VII), but many of the younger 'china painters' must have been employed on simple repetitive work, such as colouring over the transfer-printed designs and in general learning the art of ceramic painting. Nine painters were under twenty years of age, two being only fourteen. Some giving their employment as 'china painters' were probably, in fact, china gilders or 'ground layers'.

Paintresses (77)

The female painters numbered seventy-seven, most of whom would have been employed colouring over the transfer-printed designs and painting free-hand the simple repetitive designs which are the standby of all factories.

China colour manufacturer (1)

The 1841 census returns list George Hancock 'china colour M. 25. yes'. A capital 'M' was the official abbreviation for manufacturer; '25' indicates that his age was between twenty-five and twenty-nine; and 'yes' means that he was born in Shropshire. The name Hancock is very well known in the field of ceramic colour manufacturers, members of the family supplying colours to most early nineteenth-century firms. It would seem that George Hancock was attached to, or closely linked with, the Coalport works. No doubt he was responsible for supplying or mixing the fine ground colours that were in use, as well as the normal colours for the enamelled enrichments. John Randall records that George Hancock introduced the 'Rose du Barri' colour at Coalport. A fine service with this ground was shown at the 1851 Exhibition (see Pages 82–3 and Plate 229, A).

The 1841 census returns also record two warehousemen, three juniors, described as 'china apprentices', and one person—Francis Brewer—described as a 149 'china modeller'. Francis Brewer is described as a modeller at the small works at Madeley, near Coalport, which closed in 1840, and 'Brewer vases' and 'Brewer jugs' are drawn in the Coalport traveller's design-book (see Page 73).

While the 1841 census returns give most valuable information on the names and ages of the Coalport artists and gilders, surprising gaps are apparent. No employee chose to indicate that he or she was a 'flowerer', employed in forming and applying the fine-quality raised flowers on the so-called 'Coalbrookdale'-type porcelain (see Plates 177–89). Several of the persons described as 'China Potters', or simply as being employed at the china manufactory, must have been engaged on this important task. Similarly, several of the younger painters or paintresses would have been employed in colouring these applied flowers.

THE COALPORT MANAGEMENT AND STAFF IN 1861
compiled from information incorporated in the official census returns

WILLIAM PUGH, aged 59. China manufacturer employing 154 men, 160 women, 56 boys and 40 girls. Farmer of 176 acres, employing 7 labourers, 2 women and 4 boys.

'CLERK AT CHINA WORKS'	Edwin Jones
'ACCOUNTANTS AT CHINA WORKS'	George Oswell and Richard Harper
'COMMERCIAL TRAVELLER'	William Hedley (see Page 73)
'OVERLOOKER CHINA WORKS'	Joseph Birbeck and Edward Jones
'MODELLER OF CHINA'	Peter Stephen (see Page 127) and Alfred Stephan
'ENGRAVER FOR CHINA'	William Sneyd (aged 45, born at Hanley)
'COLOUR MAKER'	George Hancock (see Page 149)
'MOULD MAKER'	Thomas Cloebury
'ENGINEER AT CHINA FACTORY'	Thomas Curzon
MALE PAINTERS	46
FEMALE PAINTRESSES	59
GILDERS	24
FEMALE BURNISHERS OF GOLD	37
'FIREMEN' or 'BURNERS OF CHINA'	11
'CHINA TURNER'	2+
'LATHE TURNER'	2
'CHINA SLIP MAKER'	2
'CHINA PRESSER'	1
'COLOUR (OR GOLD) GRINDERS'	8
'CHINA PACKER'	2
PRINTERS (MALE)	4
PRINTRESSES	8

GROUND LAYERS	2
CLEANERS (OF CHINA)	3
SAGGER MAKER	1
ENGINE DRIVER	1
WAREHOUSE HANDS (MALE AND FEMALE)	17
'CHINA POTTERS'	44

(It is not known what trades are covered by this general term, it probably embraces glaze dippers, turners, finishers, kilnmen, etc.).

'LABOURERS'	13
'WORKS AT CHINA WORKS'	19 (see note under 'China Potters')
WATCHMAN	1
APPRENTICES	12

The total number of persons included in this list is 340—a very large staff. But for some reason it does not tally with William Pugh's statement to the returning officer that he employed 410 persons (154 men, 160 women, 56 boys, and 40 girls). Nevertheless, this reconstructed list gives a good indication of the staff employed in the various branches of the industry. Further details of the artists and gilders are given in Chapter VII.

BIBLIOGRAPHY

Here are listed earlier books written about the Coalport factory, although recent research has shown many of the views expressed in them to be based on tradition rather than fact. This is not to say that all information given in them is incorrect but that it should be checked before being taken as true. The author will, of course, be pleased to discuss his own views—which are, he feels, amply supported by the available evidence—with collectors or students wishing to question them.

Clay Industries on the Banks of the Severn, John Randall (Printed and published by the Salopian and West-Midland Office), 1877.

The Ceramic Art of Great Britain, L. Jewitt (J. S. Virtue & Co Ltd, London), 1878 (revised edition, 1883).

(The Coalport section is in the main taken from an article by Jewitt published in the *Art Journal* magazine of March 1862.)

History of Madeley, John Randall (Published by The Wrekin Echo Office), 1880.

Caughley and Coalport Porcelain, F. A. Barrett (F. Lewis Ltd), 1951.

The House of Coalport, Sir Compton Mackenzie (Collins, London), 1951.

Apollo Magazine, January 1959; article by T. A. Sprague entitled 'New Light on Polychrome Caughley'.

Victorian Porcelain, G. A. Godden (Herbert Jenkins, London), 1961.

English Porcelain, 1745–1850, edited by R. J. Charleston (Ernest Benn Ltd, London), 1965.

('Caughley and Coalport' chapter by Franklin A. Barrett.)

An Illustrated Encyclopaedia of British Pottery and Porcelain, G. A. Godden (Herbert Jenkins, London), 1966.

INDEX

. Detail of early nineteenth-century map
howing both the 'Coalport China Manu-
actory' and the 'Caughley China Manu-
actory'.

2. Bricks, saggars and factory wasters near the
hedge bordering the Caughley factory site.

3. General view of the site of the Caughley
factory, showing open-cast clay mining. 1965.

4. Winter view of the Caughley site, showing open
countryside, with heap of top soil containing factory
wasters.

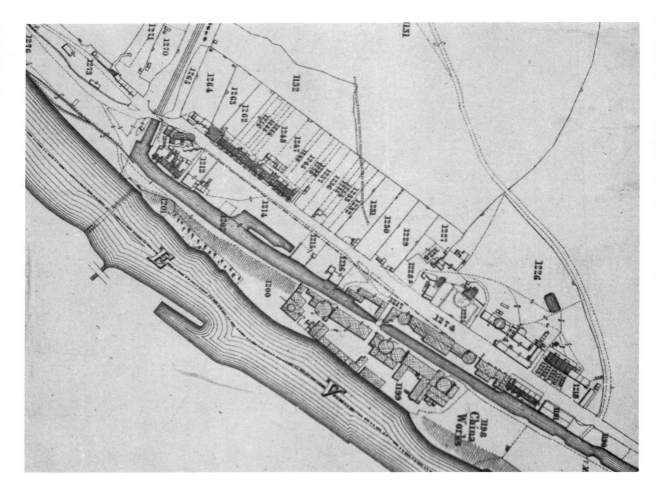

5. Detail of map showing the River Severn and the china factory each side of the canal (see page 51).

THE CANAL THROUGH THE
CENTRE OF THE COAL-
PORT WORKS.

6. Early twentieth-century photograph showing the narrow canal between the two parts of the factory.

7. *Left*. The scene in 1966, with the canal filled in.

8. Cream-coloured earthenware tankard inscribed in the print 'Manufactured at Coalport. 1797' (see page 2). *Sotheby & Co.*

9. Impressed marked 'Bradley & Co. Coalport' basalt ware teapots. Other examples of different shapes have the same lion knobs and form of spout. *c.* 1800. 4¼ ins. high (see page 3). *Victoria & Albert Museum.*

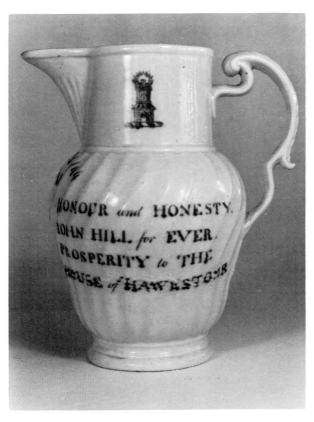

10. John Hill election jug painted in under-glaze-blue and dated 1796 (see page 44). *City Museum & Art Gallery, Stoke-on-Trent.*

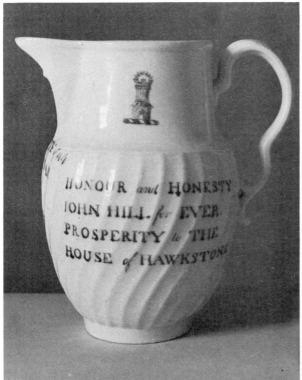

11. A further John Hill election jug recording the majority gained in 1796. Unmarked but almost certainly of Coalport manufactury. 8 ins. high. *Shrewsbury Museum.*

12. *Left*. Chinese blue-painted Nankin-type tureen and cover. *Right*. Coalport 'British Nankin' blue-*printed* tureen of the same shape and pattern, shown with a matching factory waster. Other unglazed portions of similar tureens were found (see page 29). *c*. 1800–5. *Godden of Worthing Ltd*.

13. Part of a fine Coalport dinner service of the 1800–10 period showing typical shapes, lobed-edged plates and dishes, oval tureen, and shaped covered vegetable dish (see also Plates 14–16 and pages 29–30). *Sotheby & Co*.

14. Crested Coalport oval tureen and ice-p[ ]
base (see Plate 25 for complete exampl[ ]
Note end view of unglazed handle shown [ ]
foreground with knob from factory site. U[ ]
marked. *c.* 1805. Tureen 12¾ ins. high. *God[ ]*
of Worthing Ltd.

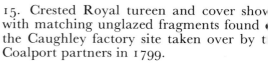

15. Crested Royal tureen and cover show[ ]
with matching unglazed fragments found [ ]
the Caughley factory site taken over by t[ ]
Coalport partners in 1799.

6. Factory wasters of moulded bordered dinner wares; tureen and part salad bowl shown at bottom (see page 12). *c.* 1800–5.

17. Soup and sauce tureen, almost certainly of Coalport origin. *c.* 1805–10. *Godden of Worthing Ltd.*

18. Small sauce tureen decorated with the so-called 'Bishop Sumner' design, popular at most factories of the period. *c.* 1805. *Godden of Worthing Ltd.*

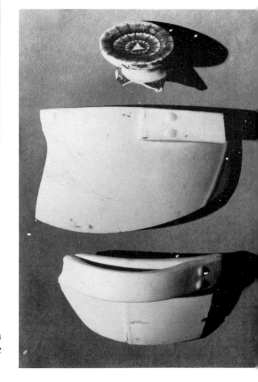

19. Wasters of large soup tureen of the same rare basic shape as the sauce tureen seen in Plate 18.

I. A selection of fine, early Coalport lobed-edged plates with various styles of decoration. The 'Japan' pattern plate, top centre, is marked 'COALBROOKDALE'. Some of the other ornately-decorated plates were probably painted in London by the many talented painters practising their craft there (see also Plates 32–3 & 92 and pages 17 & 29–30).

20. Part of a 'Japan' pattern Coalport dinner service, in the Derby style. The platter has been inverted. *c.* 1805–10. Tureen $9\frac{1}{2}$ ins. high. *Messrs D. Newbon, London.*

21. Coalport tureen and ice-pail of the 'Japan' style flower vase pattern (see also Plates 48, 55, 83 & 85). *c.* 1805. Tureen 12 ins. high. *Sotheby & Co.*

22. Selection of Coalport porcelain bearing tasteful relief-moulded design found on all types of Coalport porcelain of the 1805–20 period. A part mould for this pattern was found on the pre-1815 Caughley site, also unglazed fragments. Impressed numeral '7' on large platter, which measures $18\frac{1}{4} \times 14\frac{1}{4}$ ins. *Godden of Worthing Ltd.*
N.B. Continental porcelain may also bear this moulded design.

23. Moulded-edged dessert ware, the plates with impressed numerals. *c.* 1805–10. Centre-piece $13\frac{1}{4}$ ins. long. *Godden of Worthing Ltd.*

II. John Ròse teaware of Class D (see page 34). The creamer is of a shape normally found with Classes B and C teasets (see Plates 38–40). The shape shown in Plate 44 is that normally found with these prow-type teapots. *c.* 1807–10. Teapot 6½ ins. high. *Godden of Worthing Ltd.*

24. Coalport dessert service shapes decorated with the Broseley Dragon pattern. This and several other Dragon designs are printed and then washed-over with various colours – green, red, blue, etc. It is also found in underglaze-blue. The site fragment of a lobed-edged plate shows basic printed outline design. *c.* 1800–5. Oval shaped-edged dish, bottom $10\frac{3}{4} \times 7\frac{1}{2}$ ins. *Godden of Worthing Ltd*.

25. Rich, dark-blue ground dessert set, showing typical shapes of the 1800–10 period. The same shape of ice-pail occurs in pre-1799 Caughley porcelain. Messrs J. & E. D. Vandekar, London.

26. Superb, yellow-bordered dessert set, painted with specimen flowers which are named on the reverse. Note the lobed-edged plate and other typical early Coalport forms. *c.* 1805–10. *Reproduced by Gracious Permission of Her Majesty The Queen.*

27. A superb Coalport covered sauce tureen and stand, the shape also shown in Plates 24–6. Part of a service painted with different subjects. *c.* 1805. *Paul B. Riley Collection.*

28. Part of a superb Coalport 'Japan' pattern dessert service in the Royal Collection at Buckingham Palace. Note the lobed-edged plate. Many partly finished examples of this rock and tree design were found on the factory site (see Plate 85). *c.* 1805. Ice pail 10½ ins. high. *Reproduced by Gracious Permission of Her Majesty The Queen.*

29 A & B. Part of a fine 'Japan' pattern dessert set. Fragments of the rare sauce tureen form were found on the Caughley site. Note the lobed-edged plate. *c.* 1805–10. Ice pail 12½ ins. high. *Messrs Christie, Manson & Woods.*

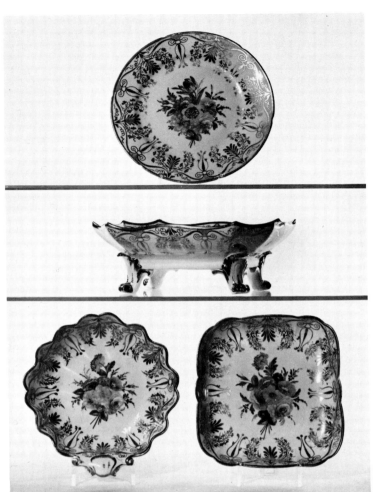

30. Part of a fine, floral painted dessert service. Note the lobed-edged plate, with impressed numeral '2'. *c.* 1805–10. *Godden of Worthing Ltd.*

31. Part of a superb 'Star of the Garter' Coalport service at Buckingham Palace. Note the lobed-edged plate and covered tureen. Fragments of this form were found on the site, perhaps decorated in London in Baxter's or Mortlock's studio, where so much fine Coalport porcelain was painted (see pages 42-4 & 138). *c.* 1805–10. *Reproduced by Gracious Permission of Her Majesty The Queen.*

32. Lobed-edged plate with ver rare painted 'Coalbrook Dale mark. (Two further marked lobed-edged plates are in the author's collection). *c.* 1805–10 9⅛ ins. dia. *Mr & Mrs Pilkington Collection.*

33. Coalport lobed-edged plate with Worcester-type scale-blue ground (see also Plates 114 & 117) *c.* 1805. 9¾ ins. dia. *Victoria & Albert Museum.*

34. Standard early John Rose teaware forms shown with matching factory wasters. These basic forms occur with various moulded fluting (see pages 31–2 and Plates 35). *c.* 1800. *Godden of Worthing Ltd.*

35. Fluted John Rose teaware forms of the 1800 period, with factory wasters. Compare shapes, and especially the knobs, with the Anstice examples shown opposite (see page 32). *Godden of Worthing Ltd.*

36. Fluted Anstice, Horton & Rose Coalport teaware of the 1800 period. Compare the knobs with John Rose examples shown in Plates 34 & 35, also the shape of the jug (see page 58). *Godden of Worthing Ltd.*

37. Anstice, Horton & Rose teapot, with a John Rose version of the same basic shape shown below it. Note the different knobs and the fluting on the spout (see page 32). The wasters are John Rose pieces. *c.* 1800. 9¾ ins. high. *Godden of Worthing Ltd.*

38. Rare John Rose yellow and gold bordered teaware showing typical forms of the 1800–3 period. Note the lobed-edged plate. Several fragments matching the rare shapes were found on the site. *Godden of Worthing Ltd.*

39. Standard Coalport creamers of the 1800–5 period. *Left.* Anstice, Horton & Rose example with a high handle. *Right.* John Rose creamer with the handle low down the body (see page 58). 4 ins. high. *Godden of Worthing Ltd.*

40. Sample John Rose teaware forms of the 1803–7 period, in this case decorated with the 'Japan'-type 'Finger' pattern. A site waster of matching cup is shown on the top shelf (see page 33). Teapot $5\frac{3}{4}$ ins. high. *Godden of Worthing Ltd.*

41. Anstice, Horton & (Thomas) Rose teaware of the same basic forms as the John Rose set shown in Plate 40. Note the squat knobs and the flat handle close to the body of the teapot (see page 59). *c.* 1805. Teapot 5¾ ins. high. *Godden of Worthing Ltd.*

42. View of Thomas Baxter's London decorating studio, drawn by Thomas Baxter, Jnr. in 1810. *Below*. Detail showing Coalport teaware on the work bench (see page 43). *Victoria & Albert Museum.*

43. Selection of John Rose's Coalport porcelain matching in general shapes those shown on Baxter's work bench in 1810 (see opposite and page 43).
N.B. The foremost teapot is an Anstice, Horton & Rose example included with the John Rose pieces in error.

44. John Rose prow-type teapot and related teaware.
Some pieces of this set are dated 1807. Compare the
knobs with the Anstice pieces shown in Plate 45 (see
also pages 60–1). *Sotheby & Co.*

45. Anstice, Horton & Rose Coalport teaset of the same basic forms as the John Rose examples shown in Plate 44. Compare the knobs and see pages 60–1. Pattern number '464'. *c.* 1807. *Godden of Worthing Ltd.*

46. *Left.* Anstice, Horton & Rose prow-type teapot. Note the knob and thumb rest on the handle. *Right.* John Rose teapot. Compare the knob form and thumb rest of the handle with Anstice example on left (see also page 60). *c.* 1807. 6½ ins. high. *Godden of Worthing Ltd.*

47. *Left.* End view of Anstice, Horton & Rose covered sugar bowl. Note the tall, narrow knob and beard of the end handle filling the ring. *Right.* End view of John Rose covered sugar bowl, with fluted umbrella-type knob. Note also 'trimmed' beard filling only a third of the ring (see page 61). *c.* 1807. 5¾ ins. high. *Godden of Worthing Ltd.*

48. John Rose 'Japan' patterned teaset showing a rare form of teapot with a ring twig knob (a mould for which was found on the site) and a rare creamer shape. *c.* 1805–10. $6\frac{1}{4}$ ins. high. *Godden of Worthing Ltd.*

49. Very rare small John Rose Coalport teapot, shown with matching unglazed waster cover, and part of the body showing the unusual hump at the back within the handle (see page 36). *c.* 1805–10. $5\frac{1}{2}$ ins. high. *Godden of Worthing Ltd.*

50. Anstice, Horton & Rose teaware, the covered sugar with rare lion-head end handles and unusual creamer handle. Standard Anstice knobs as seen in Plates 45–7. *c.* 1805–10. Teapot 6¼ ins. high (see page 62). *Godden of Worthing Ltd.*

51. Anstice, Horton & Rose teaware of rare forms. Ring twig handles of different shape from the John Rose handle (see Plate 49). Sugar bowl of the same basic shape as that shown in Plate 50. The teapot has the same handle form as the creamer shown above. *c.* 1805–10. Teapot 6¼ ins. high. *Godden of Worthing Ltd.*

52. John Rose fluted teaware showing rare handle forms – matching several unglazed wasters found on the site. Standard John Rose knobs, but note the continued use of the handleless tea bowl. *c.* 1805–10. *Godden of Worthing Ltd.*

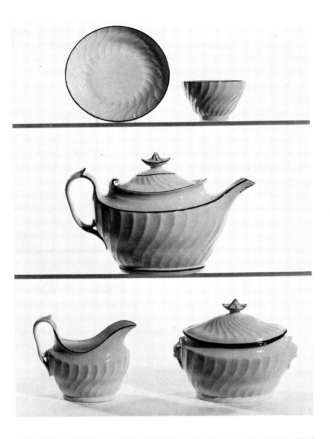

53. John Rose Coalport teaset, similar forms to the set shown above, but with the new teapot handle. Standard John Rose knobs and moulded handles to sugar bowl (see Plate 47). *c.* 1805–10. *Godden of Worthing Ltd.*

54. A superb quality Anstice, Horton & Rose Coalport tea service, bearing painted pattern number '869'. A similar design was used at the Spode factory. Note the new form of applied spout with slight bridge above the main junction, and also the new form of the knobs (still different from the John Rose knobs shown opposite) and the new straight-sided coffee cans. *c.* 1805–10. Teapot 6¾ ins. high. *Godden of Worthing Ltd.*

55. A very colourful John Rose Coalport teaset with a new form of teapot having an applied spout with slight bridge above the main junction and new knob form (see page 34). Note the new straight-sided coffee-can but the old form of covered sugar bowl and creamer. Pattern number '136'. *c.* 1810. Teapot $6\frac{3}{4}$ ins. high. *Godden of Worthing Ltd.*

56. Two John Rose Coalport covered sugar bowls from tea services with rare handle forms. Unmarked. *c.* 1805–10. 5¾ ins. high. *Godden of Worthing Ltd.*

57. John Rose Coalport teapot decorated in the Worcester style, shown with matching unglazed fragments found on the pre-1815 factory site. *c.* 1805–10. 6¾ ins. high. *Godden of Worthing Ltd.*

58. Rare John Rose Coalport teaware with normal covered sugar bowl, but new teapot and creamer shapes and new cup handles. *c.* 1810. Teapot 10½ ins. long. *Godden of Worthing Ltd.*

59. Fine quality John Rose Coalport teapot of very rare form. Painted pattern number '316' which agrees with this design in the original John Rose pattern book, as illustrated with this teapot. *c.* 1810. 6½ ins. high. *Godden of Worthing Ltd.*

60. Rare Anstice, Horton & Rose Coalport teawares, painted pattern '230', with relief-moulded design also employed at the John Rose factory. *c.* 1810. *Godden of Worthing Ltd.*

61. Coalport teaware of Class E form (see page 35). Note the mock-rivets on the teapot handle, seen also on jugs shown in Plate 106. *c*. 1810. *Godden of Worthing Ltd.*

62. Unglazed pieces of a John Rose creamer from the Caughley factory site. Note that the top part of the handle differs from the shown in Plate 61. *D. Holgate Collection.*

63. A colourful Anstice, Horton & Rose Coalport 'Japan' pattern Derby-type teaset. Painted pattern number '1339' (a number not reached at the John Rose factory (see page 56). *c.* 1810–14. Teapot 10¼ ins. long. *Godden of Worthing Ltd.*

64. Colourful John Rose teaware of the same basic shapes as the Anstice set shown in Plate 63. Painted pattern number '315', which agrees with this design in the factory pattern book. *c.* 1810–14. Teapot 6 ins. high. *Godden of Worthing Ltd.*

65. A finely gilt John Rose Coalport teaset of pattern number '385' (see pattern book entry) showing typical shapes [which also occur with various flutings] of the 1810–14 period. Unglazed knob from the pre-1815 factory site shown with the teapot (see page 35). Teapot 6 ins. high. *Godden of Worthing Ltd.*

66. John Rose Coalport teaset of the same basic forms as seen in Plate 64, with different cup shapes and form of creamer. *c.* 1810–14. Teapot 6 ins. high. *Godden of Worthing Ltd.*

67. John Rose blue-printed teapot shown with unglazed fragment of cover and a knob, from the pre-1815 factory site. Compare the basic shape with teapots shown in Plates 64–6. Blue seal-mark with 'C. B. Dale' below (see Plate 70 and page 18). *c.* 1810–14. 9¾ ins. long. *D. B. Roberts Collection.*

68. Very rare Anstice, Horton & Rose teaware shapes. Note the retention of the earlier Coalport creamer form. Similar shaped teapots and covered sugar bowls were made at several other factories. Unmarked. *c.* 1810. Teapot 6¼ ins. high. *Godden of Worthing Ltd.*

69. Colourful John Ros[e] 'Japan' pattern tease[t] showing typical shapes o[f] the 1812–15 period. Pain[t]ed pattern number '597' which agrees with the fac[t]ory pattern book, show[n] *Godden of Worthing Ltd.*

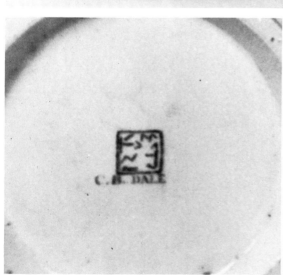

70. Blue-printed Chinese seal-type mark found on John Rose porcelain decorated with willow-type patterns (see Plates 67 & 71). 'C. B. Dale' relates to Coalbrook Dale, a place-name near to the factory.

71. Blue-printed John Rose creamer of the shape that would be found with those shown above in Plate 69. Blue seal-mark as illustrated on the left. *c.* 1812–15. $4\frac{1}{4}$ ins. high. *M. A. Wilson Collection.*

III. Selection of moulded-edged Coalport plates, all with impressed numeral '2'; one also with 1820 'Society of Arts' mark. *Godden of Worthing Ltd.*

72. Anstice, Horton & Rose 'Japan' pattern teaware, pattern number '835'. Drawn as pattern 303 in the John Rose Pattern Book with cross-reference to 835 at the rival works (see page 56). *c.* 1810-14. Teapot $5\frac{3}{4}$ ins. high. *Godden of Worthing Ltd.*

73. Decorative Anstice, Horton & Rose teaware, with painted pattern number '696'. The John Rose pattern book, above the teaware, shows the same yellow and gold pattern as number '319' but also shows the contemporary notation 'No. 696 at Mr. T. Roses' (see page 56). *c.* 1810-14. Teapot $5\frac{3}{4}$ ins. high. *Godden of Worthing Ltd.*

74. John Rose blue ground tea service showing typical shapes of the 1812–15 period. Very similar shapes were made by the rival Anstice, Horton & Rose factory (see Plate 75 *right*, and page 36). Unmarked. Teapot $5\frac{7}{8}$ ins. high. *Godden of Worthing Ltd.*

IV. Part of a fine Coalport dessert service of the early 1830s. Pattern number 2/602 (entry 2/660 is dated March 15th, 1831). Other factories made sets of similar forms, but see page 70. Comport 7½ ins. *Godden of Worthing Ltd*.

75. Anstice, Horton & Rose teaset with painted pattern number '500'. The John Rose Pattern Book shows this design as number '297' with the notation 'or 500 at Mr. Thos. Rose's' (see page 56). These basic shapes were also made at the John Rose factory (see Plate 74, *left*). *c.* 1812–15. Teapot 6 ins. high. *Messrs Trevor-Antiques, Brighton & London.*

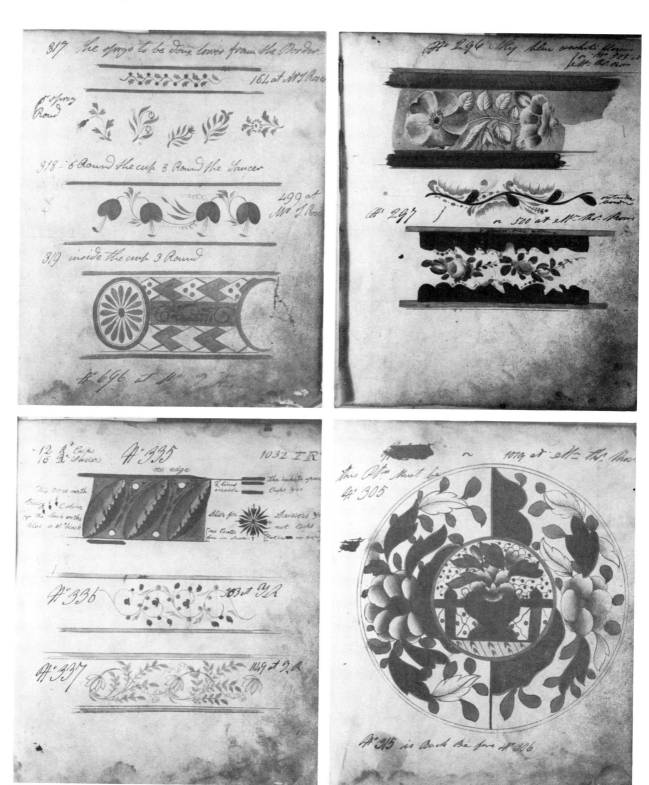

76. Sample pages from the John Rose Pattern Book, with references to the Thomas Rose pattern numbers for the same design (see page 56).

77. A selection of plaster moulds used for press-moulding Coalport porcelain:
    A. Half mould for teapot handle as Plate 40.
    B. Half mould for circular knob.
    C. Half mould for jug handle as Plate 106–7.
    D. Half mould for covered sugar handle as Plates 64–6.
    E. Half mould for ornamental cover with twig knob.
    F. Both parts of a mould for a cup or coffee-can handle.
    G & H. Two half moulds for twig handles to form the top or ring part of handles such as are
       illustrated in Plates 48 & 49, and would complete the handle shown in Mould 'E'.

78. *Top row*. Early John Rose blue-printe[d] Coalport creamer with unglazed facto[ry] waster. *Below*. Pre-1799 Thomas Turn[er] Caughley creamer with factory waste[r]. Note simple John Rose handle and fl[at] base. The Coalport example of *c.* 1800 [is] of a hard-paste body with glassy glaze (se[e] pages 27–8 & 37). 2¾ ins. high. *Godden* [& Worthing Ltd.]

79. Coalport bread tray (?) decorate[d] with blue-printed dahlia design, show[n] against this pattern in the factory 'ra[g] book' with fragments from the facto[ry] site (see page 37). *c.* 1805. 14 ins. long.

80. Two John Rose Coalport jardinières, of two sizes, with separate bases. Shown with fragments from the factory site. A slightly raised band runs under the rim – as shown in fragment applied to large jardinière. The smaller example is finely painted with yellow ground and monochrome panels. Other factories made similar pots but not of these forms (see page 37). *c.* 1805–10. $6\frac{3}{4}$ & $5\frac{1}{4}$ ins. high. *Godden of Worthing Ltd.*

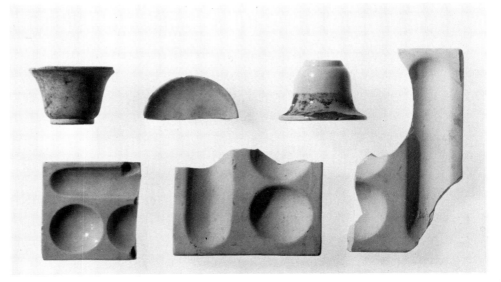

81. Selection of rouge pots and paint-trays found on the Caughley site, of Coalport post-1799 hard-paste. Complete examples are as yet unrecorded. *c.* 1800–10. Right-hand tray $4\frac{3}{4}$ ins. long.

82. Selection of 'Japan' pattern fragments show-ing underglaze-blue por-tions with some overglaze enamel added, proving that some of the rich pat-terns were completed at the Caughley factory. *c.* 1800–10.

83. John Rose Coalport lobed-edged plate decorated with the popular flower vase design; with fragments of a similar plate showing only the underglaze-blue portions of the design without the overglaze enamel colours and gilding. *c.* 1805 (see also Plates 21, 48, 55 & 85).

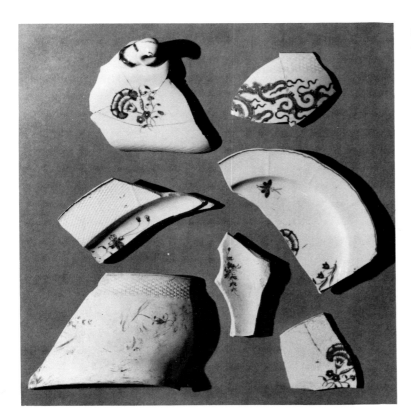

84. Selection of fragments painted or printed in underglaze blue, mainly with moulded basket-work borders, as mentioned in the 1802 advertisement (see page 12).

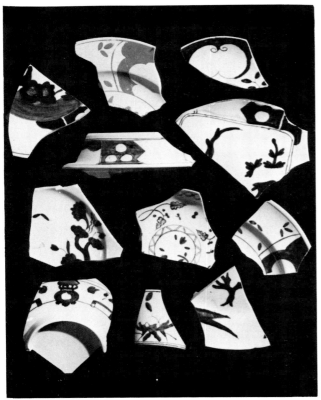

85. Selection of blue painted fragments, being portions of 'Japan' patterns as shown in Plates 21, 28, 48, 55 & 83. The lighter top fragment has not been glazed or the blue fired. *c.* 1800–10.

86. Post-1799 John Rose fragments showi[ng] finely engraved printed floral designs, later [to] be coloured in by hand. Large breakfast c[up] $2\frac{3}{4}$ ins. high.

87. A selection of post-1799 overglaze print[ed] designs, some showing traces of added enam[el] colours washed over the printed outlin[es] *c.* 1805-10.

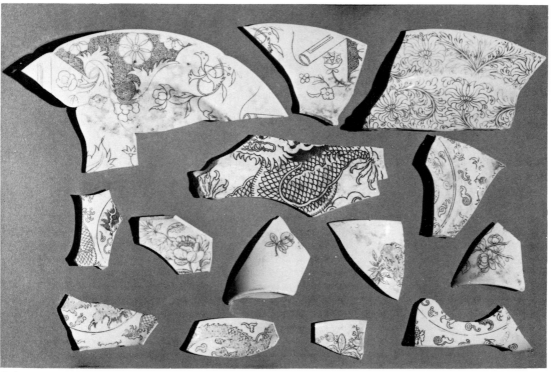

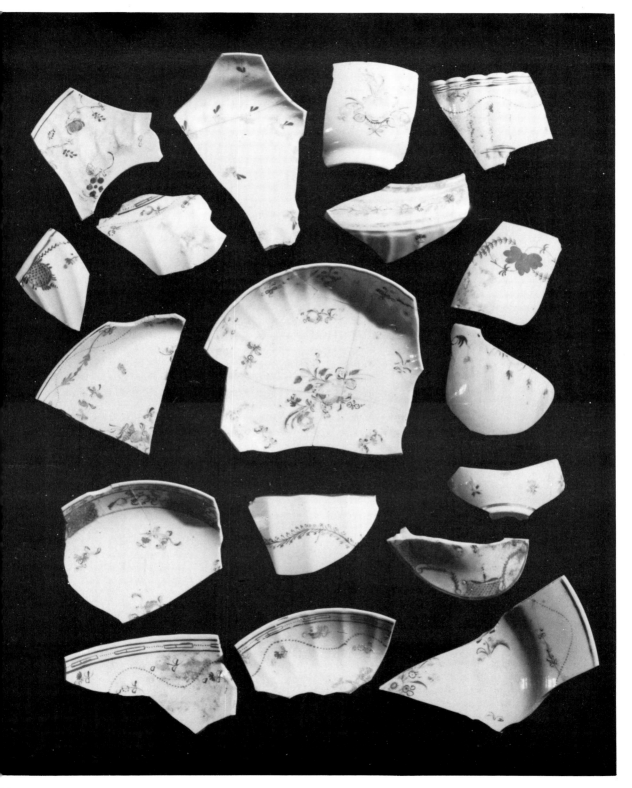

8. Selection of post-1799 John Rose overglaze enamel designs, mainly in the New Hall style.

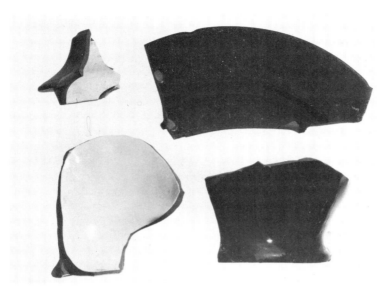

89. Rare John Rose chocolate-brow
earthenware of shapes found also in Coa
port porcelain: lobed-edged plate, sau
tureen cover and fluted jug (as Plate 102
Such earthenware is very rare and w
probably made only for a short perio
Note the white slip applied to the insi
portions to imitate porcelain (see pa
41). *c.* 1805.

90. Earthenware lobed-edged plate dec
rated in gold on copper-lustre ground.
view of wasters found on the factory si
see above, this earthenware lobed-edg
plate could be of Coalport manufactui
The base is washed with white slip a
exactly matches a plate fragment four
on the site (see page 41). *c.* 1805. 9¼ ir
dia. *Victoria & Albert Museum.*

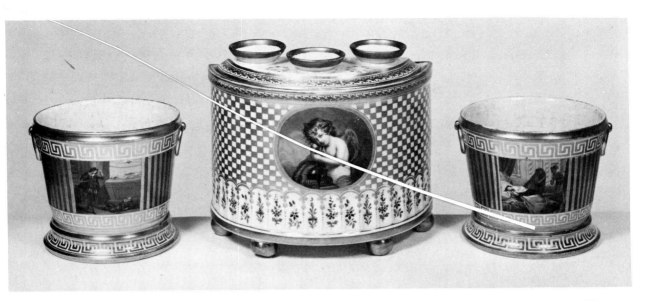

91. A pair of Coalport jardinières (see Plate 80) and a bulb-pot painted and signed by Thomas Baxter in London (see page 43). *c.* 1800–5. 4½ & 7¾ ins. *Christie, Manson & Woods Ltd.*

92. Coalport lobed-edged plates decorated in London by Thomas Baxter. Signed and dated, 1808 and 1809 (see page 43). *Victoria & Albert Museum.*

93. Pair of Coalport-type jardinières and loose bases. Figure panels on yellow ground painted in London by Thomas Baxter. Signed – 'T. Baxter. 1801'. 6¾ ins. high. *Christie, Manson & Woods Ltd.*

94. Superb Coalport-type porcelain teaset, signed 'T. Baxter, 1802. London' and 'T B'. Body of Coalport porcelain. Note the pin-pricks in the body shown in the gilt top section of the teapot. Teapot 4½ ins. high. *Wells Collection, Los Angeles County Museum of Art.*

95. (*Opposite*) John Rose Coalport vase, formerly attributed to the Chamberlain factory at Worcester. Decorated by Thomas Baxter in London, signed and dated 'T Baxter. 1802'. 13½ ins. high. Note pin-pricks in lower part of the body and fault at corner of base, defects not normally found on Worcester specimens. *Victoria & Albert Museum.*

Coalport porcelain, c. 1808–10

96. Three Coalport lobed-edged plates from the Angerstein service showing members of the family in silhouette, early in 1808. All shapes of this fine service link with Coalport factory wasters (see *Connoisseur* magazine, April, 1966). 9¼ ins. dia. *Sotheby & Co.*

97. A rare set of vases with two side 'match-pots' or spill-vases decorated with classical figures in silhouette touched-in with gold details. *c.* 1810. 6 & 4¾ ins. high. *Sotheby & Co.*

98. Selection of Coalport porcelain decorated with figure subjects seemingly scratched through the painted ground of the panel, see detail below. Note double Greek-key border on lobed-edged plates (see also Colour Plate I). Centre bulb-pot $11\frac{1}{2}$ ins. long. *Godden of Worthing Ltd.*

99. Detail from panel on front of large jardinière shown above (see page 44). Size $4\frac{1}{4} \times 3\frac{1}{4}$ ins.

100. Coalport jug printed in underglaze blue and dated 1798, for other jugs of this standard shape see Plate 104. 8¼ ins. high.

101. Coalport jug printed in underglaze blue with Caughley-type Chinese motif but with rare vase of flowers in front and enamelled crest above. *c.* 1800. 6 ins. high.

102. Early John Rose blue-printed jug with printed view of the iron bridge, up stream from the factory. Book in background contains pulls from the Coalport and Caughley copperplates and includes this design. *c.* 1800. 8½ ins. high (see also Plate 103 and page 45).

103. John Rose jug of standard shape decorated with underglaze-blue 'pine-cone' print, as found on much Caughley, Lowestoft and Worcester porcelain (see *Caughley & Worcester Porcelain 1775–1800*, 1968). *c.* 1805. 7 ins. high.

104. Three John Rose Coalport jugs. *c.* 1800–10. Compare with the slightly different Anstice versions shown opposite and note (a) the squat basic form, with low neck; (b) the joint of the handle and body with 'kicks' or returns from the body at the top and bottom junction. Note also the position of the top joint near the rim; (c) nine ribs under the spout. Gilt jug marked 'Coal-port' in red. Top jug 6¾ ins. high (see page 45).

105. Three Anstice, Horton & Rose jugs. Compare with Plate 104, *opposite* and note (a) the high, narrow neck; (b) the joint of the handle and body *without* 'kicks' or returns, and seven ribs under spout; (c) the position of the handle joint, well below the top rim. Large example 6¾ ins. high (see page 65).

106. Two John Rose Coalport jugs turned to show the handle forms and mock rivet heads (see page 46). *Above.* A half mould from which such handles were pressed and two unglazed wasters from the site. Rare covered jug 8¼ ins. high. *Godden of Worthing Ltd.*

107. Two views of a jug with various masonic emblems 'enamelled for the Royal Cornwall Topographical Society' and dated August 1810. Other very similar jugs were decorated in this style. The body and handle links with the wasters and mould found at Caughley, although these particular examples may have been decorated elsewhere. 7½ ins. high. *Grand Lodge Museum, reproduced by permission of the Board of General Purposes.*

108. Two unmarked Anstice, Horton & Rose jugs. Note the lack of mock rivets at the handle junction and the downward return at the top of the handle (see page 65) and compare with Plate 107. $6\frac{1}{4}$ & $5\frac{1}{4}$ ins. high.

109. Coalport tankard of the 1800-5 period decorated with finely engraved shell prints, shown with two similar factory wasters. Note the angled footrim, not straight like pre-1799 Caughley footrims. $4\frac{1}{4}$ ins. high. *Godden of Worthing Ltd.*

110. *Left and centre.* John Rose Coalport mugs with moulded handles (as factory waster shown). Note the handle separated from the body by slight pads. A mug of this form, dated 1809, is recorded. *Right.* Finely decorated Anstice, Horton & Rose mug, with similar moulded handle fitted direct to the body. *c.* 1805-10. Centre mug 4 ins. high. *Godden of Worthing Ltd.*

111. Very rare John Rose Coalport yellow ground bulb-pot (pierced cover and finials missing) shown with unglazed waster from the factory site (see page 47). *c.* 1800-5. 5 ins. high. *Victoria & Albert Museum.*

112. An elaborately moulded bombe-shaped bulb-pot, shown without loose top. General style of decoration similar to specimens illustrated in Colour Plate I. Unmarked, but of Coalport hardpaste porcelain (see page 47). $11\frac{1}{4}$ ins. long. *c.* 1805-10. *Godden of Worthing Ltd.*

113. Blue-printed John Rose, Coalport, footed bowl decorated with portions of former Thomas Turner Caughley engravings. For re-use of wide border see Plates 102–3. Inscribed inside bowl 'Success to Trade Peace & Plenty. Coalport for ever Thos. Groome 1802'. Bright underglaze blue $5\frac{1}{4}$ ins. high.

114. Bee-hive honey pot – on the evidence of the body, of Coalport make. Compare floral painting and blue ground with Plates 33 & 117. *c.* 1805–10. 6 & 4 ins. high. *Godden of Worthing Ltd.*

15 A & B. Front and back view of John Rose Coalport Japan-pattern inkstand. Obviously, on the evidence of the body and potting details, of Coalport make, the Chamberlain-Worcester version differing in several respects. A weatherworn part mould found on the Caughley site would appear to match the fish-head handle. *c.* 1805. 9 ins. long. *Godden of Worthing Ltd.*

116. Coalport déjeuner service. Note the lobed-edged plates. Basic shapes are similar to the 1802 set shown in Plate 94 (see page 29). *c.* 1805. Teapot $4\frac{1}{2}$ ins. high. *Sotheby & Co.*

117. Coalport-style vase with scale-blue ground (see also Plates 33 & 114). A foot for a similar vase was found on the factory site. *c.* 1805. 12½ ins. high. *Messrs Jean Sewell, London.*

118. Gold ground floral painted vase of typical Coalport porcelain. *c.* 1805. 10 ins. high. *Messrs Jean Sewell, London.*

119. Coalport porcelain vase very finely decorated and inscribed: 'The memorable 25th Oct. 1809'. Another George III subject is shown in Plate 80. Note pin-pricks seen on gilt plinth. $6\frac{7}{8}$ ins. high.

120. Coalport relief-moulded tureen and stand. Moulded plates of this type are shown in Colour Plate III. Ware decorated in this style is often attributed to former Swansea or Nantgarw painters. *c.* 1815–20. Tureen 10½ ins. high. *Godden of Worthing Ltd.*

121. Two plates and a dish from a fine Coalport dinner service, of the new softer body with a glaze prone to crazing. Typical bold Coalport flower painting of the 1815–30 period. Impressed numerals of plates and dishes. *c.* 1820. *Sotheby & Co.*

122. Plan-view of Coalport comport ($5\frac{1}{4}$ ins. high) finely painted with fruit within moulded borders – as Colour Plate III and Plate 121. *Messrs Christie, Manson & Woods.*

123. Typical moulded-edged Coalport plate, probably decorated outside the factory. Dated 1819. $9\frac{1}{4}$ ins. dia. *Sotheby & Co.*

124. Coalport moulded-edged plate bearing the normal impressed numeral 2, and also the rare impressed anchor mark (see page 18). *c.* 1825. *Godden of Worthing Ltd.*

125. Typical Coalport tureen of the 1820s found in dinner services containing plates as shown above. $11\frac{1}{4}$ ins. high. *Godden of Worthing Ltd.*

126. Part Coalport dinner service of the early 1830s. Note moulded knob also seen in Plate 125. Tureen 10½ ins. high. *Godden of Worthing Ltd.*

V. Representative shapes from a fine Coalport dessert service of the 1835-40 period. Pattern number 3/993, otherwise unmarked; and like other unmarked Coalport porcelain, this set was sold as Rockingham. Comport $8\frac{1}{4}$ ins. high.

127. Part of a maroon and gold Coalport dinner service showing typical forms of 1840s. Rare printed mark – 'John Rose & Co. Coalbrookdale Shropshire'. Tureen 10½ ins. high. *Godden of Worthing Ltd.*

128. Coalport tureen and vegetable dish, part of a fine dinner service. The shapes were registered' at the Patent Office' in January, 1845, and specimens bear the diamond-shaped registration mark. Tureen 12 ins. high. *Godden of Worthing Ltd.*

129. Part of a Coalport dinner service painted with armorial bearings. Moulded shapes registered in December 1847. Unmarked except for diamond-shaped registration mark. Tureen 11¼ ins. high. *Godden of Worthing Ltd.*

130. A pair of Coalport ice pails from a superb dessert service, with the finest floral painting (see page 69). *c.* 1820. *Godden of Worthing Ltd.*

131. Representative pieces from a fine blue ground dessert set, painted with bird and floral panels with rich gilding. The side-dish shapes appear again in Plates 132 & 135 (see page 69). *c.* 1820. *R. A. F. Johnston Collection.*

VI. A superb Coalport floral-encrusted vase, or hunting trophy, with horse handles and modelled hunting cap and other objects on the cover. 'C D' mark in underglaze blue. *c.* 1820. 23 ins. high. *V. Voselis Collection.*

132. Dessert service showing typical Coalport forms of the 1820s. Note the retention of lobed-edged plates, with impressed numeral '2'. Comport 6 ins. high. *Godden of Worthing Ltd.*

133. Side-dish from a Coalport dessert service with fine floral painting. Printed 'Society of Arts' mark. *c.* 1820. $10\frac{1}{4} \times 8\frac{1}{2}$ ins. *Victoria & Albert Museum.*

134. Representative pieces from a superb Coalport dessert service of the early 1820s. Only the finest sets had this ornate comport form. Rare fruit and flower painting. *Sotheby & Co.*

135. Coalport dessert service painted with rare early landscape and seascape subject. Some pieces, but not all, bear the printed 'Society of Arts' mark or impressed numerals (see pages 17 & 19). Square dish 8 ins. *c.* 1820-5. *Godden of Worthing Ltd.*

136. Coalport dessert service marked with impressed anchor mark but with Coalport pattern number 2/335 (see page 18). *c.* 1825. 8 ins. high. *Godden of Worthing Ltd.*

137. Moulded-edged Coalport dessert service of the 1820s. Printed design coloured over by hand. Comport $7\frac{1}{2}$ ins. high. *Godden of Worthing Ltd.*

138. Coalport dish from a 'Union' dessert service. Note moulded emblems on handle. Dated 1826 (see page 70). *Godden of Worthing Ltd.*

139. Covered sauce tureen from a 'Union' dessert set, national emblems relief-moulded on handles (see page 70). *c.* 1820–30. 8½ ins. long. *Godden of Worthing Ltd.*

140. A fine Coalport dessert plate with relief-moulded bunches of grapes spaced round the edge (see page 70). 'Society of Arts' mark. *c.* 1825. *Godden of Worthing Ltd.*

141. Covered sauce tureen from a Coalport dessert service of the 1830s. The plate and dish shown opposite are of the same type but of different pattern. $8\frac{1}{2}$ ins. long. *Godden of Worthing Ltd.*

142. A plate and handled dish from a fine Coalport service, showing typical pierced shapes of the 1830s. Pattern number 2/893, which agrees with the factory pattern book. This design also has the notation 'Fruit by J Birbeck' (see pages 70 & 103). *P. Newbrook Collection.*

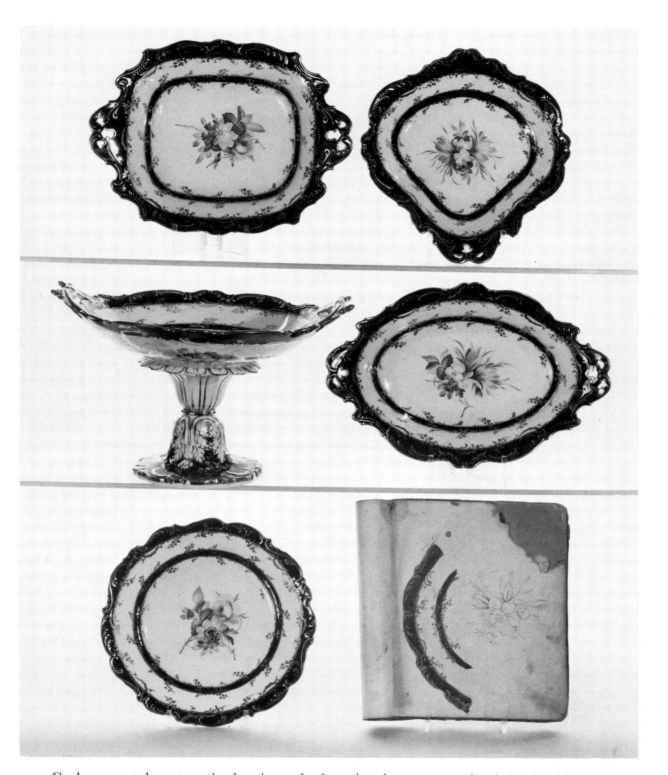

143. Coalport part dessert service bearing only the painted pattern number '4/590', which matches this design in the Coalport Pattern Book, shown bottom right. This has the note 'Flowers by Dixon' (see page 108). *c.* 1840. Comport 8¼ ins. high. *Godden of Worthing Ltd.*

144. Moulded-edged Coalport dessert plate of pattern '3/421', painted with 'Plants painted by J Aston' (see page 101). *c.* 1836–40. *Godden of Worthing Ltd.*

145. Part of a superb Coalport dessert service of the 1839–45 period, showing typical moulded-edged forms which will be found with several different coloured borders and styles of decoration (see page 71). *Messrs Lories Ltd.*

146. Detail of plate from service illustrated below, showing 'Dixon's flowers' (see page 108).

147. Pink bordered Coalport dessert ware, showing relief-moulded plate and related shapes 'registered' in December 1847. Unmarked except for diamond-shaped registration mark and pattern number '5/271'. Flowers painted by Thomas Dixon, see detail above. *c.* 1847–50. Tallest comport 6¼ ins. high. *Godden of Worthing Ltd.*

148. Coalport dessert service showing further moulded-edge shapes, of the 1835–45 period. Unmarked except for pattern number '4/554'. Comport 8 ins. high. *Godden of Worthing Ltd.*

149. Part of a Coalport dessert service, with openwork borders. Basic shapes registered in November 1849, and pieces bear the diamond-shaped registration mark. *Godden of Worthing Ltd.*

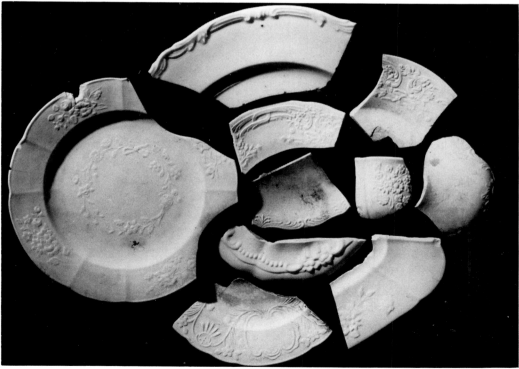

150. A selection of fragments of discarded, unglazed, relief-moulded Coalport tea and dessert ware, found in the River Severn by the factory (see page 71). For matching completed specimens, see Plates 121–3, 133–4, 151, 154, 163, 164 and 165.

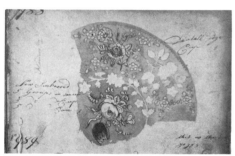

151. Blue ground Coalport teaset showing soft-paste shapes with relief-moulded floral designs – described as 'new embossed' under design 988 in the factory pattern book (see below). The unglazed plate found in the river bed shows the relief-moulding to advantage. *c.* 1815. Plate dia. 6¾ ins. *Godden of Worthing Ltd.*
N.B. The basic embossed design occurs with many different painted ground colours and designs.

152. Coalport teaware of the 1815–25 period, one of several different basic shapes then in favour. Printed 'Society of Arts' mark. *Royal Ontario Museum, University of Toronto.*

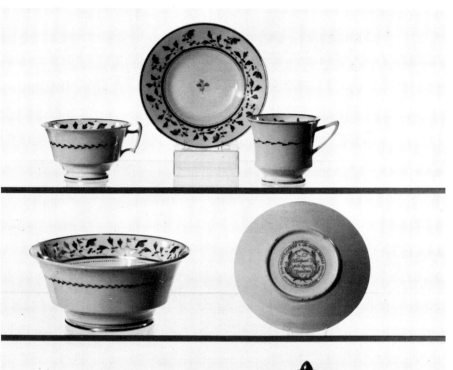

153. Further standard Coalport teaware shapes of the 1820s. One saucer reversed to show the 'Society of Arts' mark. Teapot $5\frac{1}{2}$ ins. high. *Godden of Worthing Ltd.*

154. A rare and finely moulded Coalport teapot. Note the shaped-edge and form of the handle, as other factories made rather similar moulded teaware. This example bears the 'Society of Arts' mark, but other teapots and related ware – creamers, cups, etc. – are unmarked (see page 71). *c.* 1820–5. $5\frac{3}{8}$ ins. high. *D. Rogers Collection.*

255

155. Unmarked teapot bearing only the pattern number '830', which agrees with this design as painted in the first Coalport Pattern Book. *c.* 1820–5. 6¼ ins. high.

156. Unmarked Coalport moulded-edged teaware of the 1820–5 period. Painted pattern number 986, which agrees with the design drawn under this number in the factory pattern book. Teapot 6½ ins. high. *Godden of Worthing Ltd.*

VII. An unmarked Coalport 'Brewer's vase' as shape No. 1 in the Traveller's Design Book (see pages 73-7), but of very large size and early style of decoration. *c.* 1820–25. 15¼ ins. high. *Godden of Worthing Ltd.*

157. Very rare form of Coalport covered sugar basin (cup handle of the same form as that shown in Plates 156 & 160). Unmarked except for painted pattern number '961', the design agrees with that drawn under this number in the factory pattern book. *c.* 1820–5. $5\frac{1}{4}$ ins. high. *Godden of Worthing Ltd.*

158. A rare Coalport covered sugar, with a matching creamer. Printed 1820 'Society of Arts' mark, with pattern number 874. The sugar is similar but not identical to that shown above. *Godden of Worthing Ltd.*

159. Unmarked Coalport teaware of pattern '939', showing a further class of moulded tea service shapes of the 1820s. The pattern agrees with the factory pattern book. Covered sugar $5\frac{1}{2}$ ins. high. *Godden of Worthing Ltd.*

VIII. A fine Coalport porcelain vase of the 1820s, without raised flowers. Note the typical tightly-bunched flowers painted in the centre panel. 15 ins. high. *Godden of Worthing Ltd.*

160. Representative parts of a Coalport service bearing only the pattern number '2/220'. The design agrees with the factory pattern book, here shown open at the correct page. many other painted designs will, of course, be found on the basic shapes – examples will be unmarked. *c.* 1820–5. Teapot 6 ins. high. *Godden of Worthing Ltd.*

161. A further range of Coalport teaware shapes. Unmarked except for painted pattern number '2/316'. *c.* 1836–40. Teapot 6 ins. high. *Godden of Worthing Ltd.*
N.B. Slight variations of the basic shapes occur, with lobed bodies or different knobs or cup handles.

162. A fine Coalport rococo-shaped teapot of a type often attributed to the Rockingham factory. Unmarked except for painted fractional pattern number '2/675', a number not reached at Rockingham. *c.* 1840. 8¾ ins. high.

163. Further pieces matching the fine unmarked teapot shown above. The plate is one of two bread and butter plates originally sold with each set (the tea plate of today was not then in use). The moulded edge to this plate is largely painted over but it matches the unglazed waster shown in Plate 150. The cup handle also matches a waster found in the river by the factory. *c.* 1840. Plate 10¼ × 9 ins.

164. White and gold Coalport teaware, unmarked except for painted pattern number '4/396'. This agrees with the factory pattern book, and some matching forms were found in the river by the factory. The creamer is different from those shown in Plates 163 & 165, although the cup handles are the same. *c.* 1845. Creamer $4\frac{1}{4}$ ins. high. *Godden of Worthing Ltd.*

165. Unmarked Coalport teaware forms of the 1840s. Painted pattern number '4/477', the design agreeing with that drawn under this number in the factory pattern book. Note the moulding faintly showing on the bread and butter plate, which links with wasters found in the river by the factory (see Plate 150). Teapot 8¾ ins. high. *Godden of Worthing Ltd.*

166. Hanging letter or note rack, bearing the 'Society of Arts' mark of the early 1820s. Other styles of decoration were employed on these rare objects, which are often unmarked. 7¼ ins. high. *Sotheby & Co.*

167. Coalport blue-ground letter or note rack – the standing version of the hanging variety shown above. This typical Coalport style of decoration is also seen in Plate 131. *c.* 1820. 6¼ ins. high.

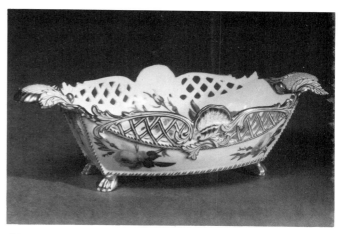

168. *Left*. Rare covered jug or coffee pot decorated with the famous Coalport 'Indian tree' pattern (see page 72). *c.* 1820–5. 9 ins. high. *Godden of Worthing Ltd.*

169. *Above*. A fine quality and rare Coalport basket, bearing the printed 'Society of Arts' mark. *c.* 1820–5. 10½ ins. long. *Godden of Worthing Ltd.*

170. A rare 'chamber candlestick' bearing the printed 'Society of Arts' mark. *c.* 1825. 3⅛ ins. high. *Godden of Worthing Ltd.*

Coalport porcelain, c. 1825–35

171. *Left.* Unmarked Coalport mug bearing printed views of the nearby iron bridge and Buildwas Abbey, showing a standard mug form. *c.* 1825–35. $4\frac{1}{8}$ ins. high. *Godden of Worthing Ltd.*

172. *Below left.* Floral plaque, signed and dated 'S Lawrance. 1826' (see page 116). $10\frac{3}{4} \times 9$ ins. *Godden of Worthing Ltd.*

173. *Below.* Unmarked Coalport 'brewer's' jug as design No. 47 in the Traveller's Design Book (see page 76 and Plate 227D). *c.* 1835. 11 ins. high. *Godden of Worthing Ltd.*

174. Coalport jug made for Queen Victoria soon after her accession in 1837, with the printed Mortlock retailer's mark, with 'Buckingham Palace' (see page 73). Note the typical jug shape of the 1830s. 6½ ins. high.

176. *Below*. Parian-type porcelain group, the only figure or group featured in the Coalport Traveller's Pattern Book (see pages 73 & 76). *c.* 1840–5. 7½ ins. high. *Godden of Worthing Ltd.*

175. *Below*. A pair of rare Coalport figure-candlesticks marked 'Coalport' in underglaze blue. *c.* 1825–35. 9¼ ins. high. *Godden of Worthing Ltd.*

177. Very rare, floral-encrusted covered pot of small size. 'C.D' mark in underglaze blue. *c.* 1820. 6¼ ins. long. *F. Turner Collection.*

178. Floral-encrusted Coalport basket, bearing 'C D' mark in underglaze blue. Most examples of this form are unmarked. *c.* 1820. 10 ins. long. *Sotheby & Co.*

179. Floral-encrusted vase, bearing the 'C D' mark in underglaze blue. *c.* 1830. 8 ins. high. *Shrewsbury Museum.*

180. A fine floral-encrusted teapot, or kettle, on separate stand. 'C Dale' mark (for Coalbrook Dale) in underglaze blue. *c.* 1820–30. 7½ ins. high. *Lories Ltd.*

181. A superb green-ground floral-encrusted Coalbrook Dale style vase, having the 'Coalport' mark in underglaze blue. *c.* 1820. 11¾ ins. high. *Godden of Worthing Ltd.*

182. Rare cottage pastile-burner, with loose cover, and bearing a 'C D' mark in underglaze blue, unmarked examples are known. *c.* 1820. $4\frac{1}{4}$ ins. high. *Godden of Worthing Ltd.*

183. A fine 'Coalbrook Dale' floral-encrusted vase bearing the 'C D' underglaze blue mark. *c.* 1820. $10\frac{1}{2}$ ins. high. *Royal Scottish Museum, Edinburgh (Crown copyright).*

184. A Coalport floral-encrusted eau-de-cologne bottle with the mark 'W T' (see page 77). *c.* 1835–40. 11¼ ins. high. *Sotheby & Co.*

185. Coalbrook Dale-type inkstand and a 'chamber' or hand candlestick. 'C D' marks in underglaze blue. *c.* 1820–30. Inkstand 8½ ins. long. *Christie, Manson & Woods Ltd.*

186. A Coalbrook Dale-type, floral-encrusted urn vase. It bears the 'Coalport' mark in underglaze blue. A very similar vase was made by Minton's, having a deeper plinth than the Coalport example shown. *c.* 1820. 9 ins. high. *Sotheby & Co.*

187. Coalbrook Dale-type floral-encrusted tray. 'Coalport' name mark in underglaze blue. *c.* 1820–30. 13 ins. long. *Sotheby & Co.*

188. Unmarked Coalport vase, as design 35 in the Traveller's Design Book (see page 76 and Plate 225). *c.* 1840. $15\frac{3}{4}$ ins. high. *Godden of Worthing Ltd.*

189. Unmarked floral-encrusted Coalport vase, as design 11 in the Traveller's Design Book (see page 74 and Plate 221). *c.* 1835. $10\frac{1}{2}$ ins. high. *Sotheby & Co.*

IX. A superb pair of Coalport vases and covers, turned to show both panels – birds painted by John Randall (see page 122) and flowers and fruit by Willian Cook (see page 107). Ampersand mark in gold. *c.* 1861–70. 18¾ ins. high. *Godden of Worthing Ltd.*

N.B. This basic shape, like other forms, was made in several different sizes and, of course, is found with various styles of decoration.

190. Unmarked Coalport vase as design 2 in the Traveller's Design Book (see page 74). Originally priced at 21/-. *c.* 1835. 10¼ ins. high. *Godden of Worthing Ltd.*

191. Apple-green ground Coalport vase, as design 37 in the Traveller's Design Book (see page 76). Original price 63/-. *c.* 1835–40. 13¼ ins. high. *Sotheby & Co.*

192. Coalport 'new cornucopia, raised flowers', as design 7 in the Traveller's Design Book. Original price 15/-. *c.* 1830–5. $5\frac{1}{2}$ ins. high. *Godden of Worthing Ltd.*

193. 'Tall-cross-handled round basket and cover', as design 12 in the Coalport Traveller's Design Book. Original price 15/-. *c.* 1830–5. $6\frac{1}{2}$ ins. high. *Christie, Manson & Woods Ltd.*

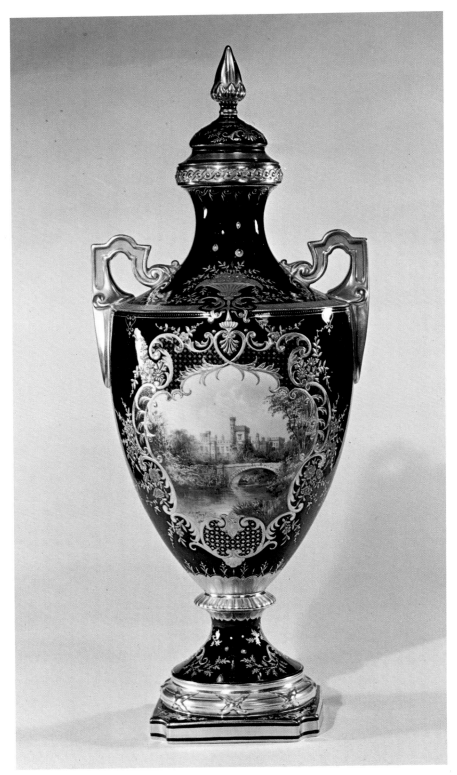

X. A magnificent Coalport vase (one of a pair) richly gilt in typical late style. The panel painted by J. Plant (see page 121). Printed crowned 'Coalport' mark (see page 23). 20 ins. high. *c.* 1900. *Shrewsbury Museum Collection.*

Coalbrookdale-type porcelain, c. 1830–5

194. Unmarked Coalport inkstand, with separate ink containers and taper-stick. Design No. 30 in the Traveller's Design Book (see page 75 and Plate 224). Made in three sizes and sold for 21/–, 25/– or 36/–. *c.* 1830–5. *Godden of Worthing Ltd.*

195. Unmarked Coalport 'new poperee' (entry No. 16 in the Traveller's Design Book, see page 75 and Plate 222). The basic form also occurs without the raised flowers. The inner-cover is shown. Pot pourri vases originally had these inner-covers to preserve the perfume of the contents. Original price £3.3.0. *c.* 1830–5. 11½ ins. high.

281

196. Two fine quality Coalport plates. The moulded border shape was registered in November 1850. They are unmarked except for diamond-shaped registration mark. *c.* 1850–5.

197. Representative parts of an unmarked Coalport dinner service. Shapes registered in December 1850. Printed registration diamond-shaped device only. *c.* 1850–5. Large tureen 11 ins. high. *Godden of Worthing Ltd.*

198. Richly gilt Coalport tea service showing forms registered in April 1850. Many other designs were painted on these basic shapes. *c.* 1850–5. Teapot 8 ins. high. *Godden of Worthing Ltd.*

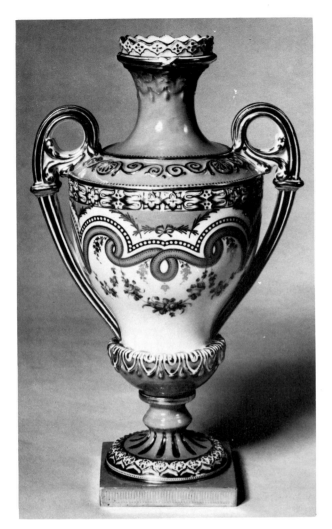

199. Turquoise ground Coalport vase. 'C B D' monogram mark in gold (see page 85). *c.* 1851–61. 11 ins. high. *Godden of Worthing Ltd.*

200. Maroon ground Coalport vase with monochrome figure-subject panels. *c.* 1850–60. 13½ ins. high. *Godden of Worthing Ltd.*

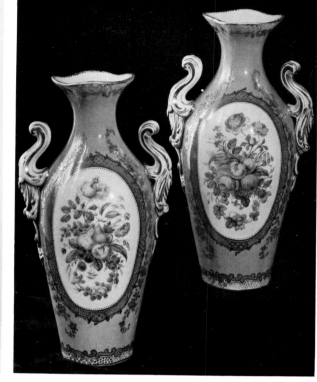

201. One of a fine pair of Coalport vases with figure-subject panels. 'C B D' monogram mark. *c.* 1851–61. 12 ins. high. *Christie, Manson & Woods Ltd.*

202. A pair of Chelsea-shape Coalport vases, but bearing a mock Sévres mark (see page 22). Painted panels by William Cook. *c.* 1850. 11 ins. high.

203. A pair of attractive Coalport vases, showing the front and reverse sides, with figure painting in the style of James Rouse. Unmarked. *c.* 1850–60. 8½ ins. high. *Godden of Worthing Ltd.*

204. A pair of Coalport vases decorated with bird studies by John Randall (see page 122), similar to vases shown at the 1871 Exhibition. The ampersand mark is in gold. *c.* 1871. 17 ins. high. *Godden of Worthing Ltd.*

205. Coalport covered cup and stand shown at Daniell's (the retailers) Stand at the 1862 Exhibition. It bears a 'C B D' initial mark with Daniell name mark. *c.* 1862. Cup 4½ ins. high. *Victoria & Albert Museum (Crown copyright).*

206. An unmarked Coalport jug of a popular shape, with a pink band at the top and printed flower sprays coloured over by hand. *c.* 1860. 7½ ins. high.

207. *Below left.* Coalport vase, shape No. 154, painted by E. Ball (see page 102). *c.* 1910. 13 ins. high. *Right.* Vase, shape 186, painted by F. Howard. *c.* 1910. 10 ins. high. *Godden of Worthing Ltd.*

208. *Below right.* A Coalport blue-ground vase, with scenic painted panel by Percy Simpson. Printed Crown 'Coalport. AD 1750' mark. *c.* 1900. 11½ ins. high. *Godden of Worthing Ltd.*

209. A Coalport goblet-vase commemorating King Edward VII's Coronation in August 1902. Printed mark, pattern V 5145, shape 144. $11\frac{1}{2}$ ins. high.

210. Three decorative cups and saucers of the 1880–1900 period. The gold-ground example on *right* is of a shape registered in January 1883. *Centre*. A raised-gold design on blue ground, pattern 'A 5897'. *Left*. A miniature cup and saucer of moulded design, mark 'Coalport. A.D. 1750' (see page 23). *Godden of Worthing Ltd.*

211. Coalport dessert service of pattern number X 6289, with a blue border painted with birds in landscapes by W. Waterson and H. Hughes. The printed crowned 'Coalport A.D. 1750' mark has impressed date numerals – '2 G 12' for 1912. Many different patterns were applied to the standard dessert ware shapes. Diameter of plate 9$\frac{1}{4}$ ins. *Godden of Worthing Ltd.*

212. Two pages from a Coalport shape book showing some typical shapes of the early 1900s. Factory shape numbers are shown and these will also appear under finished specimens. All basic shapes were made in several different sizes.

213. A fine quality Coalport plate with dark-blue border and tooled gilding, the landscape signed by Percy Simpson, 1909, and bearing the printed crowned 'Coalport' mark (see page 23). *Godden of Worthing Ltd.*

214. Coalport workpeople about to embark on the bus taking them to the new works in the Staffordshire Potteries in 1926. *Front row, left to right:* J. Llewellyn, N. Gainham, S. Small, A. Cleobury, M. Malden, Thomas J. Bott, P. Rogers, H. Richards, M. Jones, V. Morton, E. Roberts, B. Berbeck, G. Langford, A. Langford and W. Rogers.

215. Selection of modern Coalport porcelain cottages in the style of antique examples – not necessarily of Coalport origin (see page 92). *Messrs Coalport China Ltd.*

216. Modern Coalport porcelain in the style of the so-called 'Coalbrookdale' floral-encrusted ware of the 1820–40 period (see page 93). *Messrs Coalport China Ltd.*

217. Modern Coalport yellow and gold-bordered crested service. 1965. *Messrs Coalport China Ltd.*

218. Modern Coalport porcelain of 'Hampton' shape based on an antique form (see Plate 144). Pattern 9231. *Messrs Coalport China Ltd.*

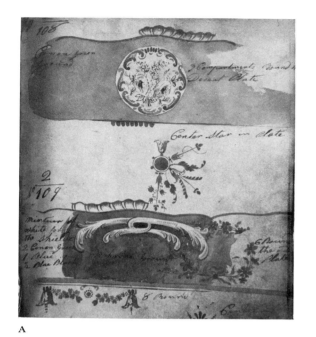

A

B

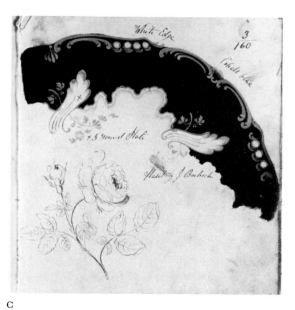

C

D

219 A–D. Sample pages from the
Coalport Pattern Books, with three
pages giving the artists' names:
Kelshall, J. Birbeck and J. Randall.

A

B

C

D

E

F

220 A–F. Pages from William Hedley's Design Book (see page 73).

221 A–F. Pages from William Hedley's Design Book (see page 73).

A

B

C

D

E

222 A–F. Pages from
William Hedley's Design
Book (see page 73).

F

A

B

C

D

E

F

223 A–F. Pages from William Hedley's Design Book (see page 73).

A

B

C

D

E

224 A–F. Pages from William Hedley's Design Book (see page 73).

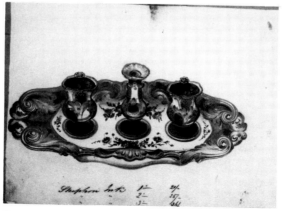

F

A

B

C

D

E

F

225 A–F. Pages from William Hedley's Design Book (see page 73).

A

B

C

D

E

F

226 A–F. Pages from
William Hedley's Design
Book.

Pages from the Traveller's Design Book

A

B

C

D

E

F

227 A–F. Pages from William Hedley's Design Book.

A

B

C

D

228 A–D. Pages from William Hedley's Design Book.

229 A–D. Contemporary engravings of Coalport porcelain shown at the 1851 Exhibition (see page 82). Reproduced from the official catalogue.

A

B

C

D

230 A–C. Coalport porcelain shown at the Dublin Exhibition of 1853. Reproduced from the *Art Journal* magazine.

A

B

C

231. Coalport porcelain shown at the 1862 Exhibition. *Art Journal* engravings.

232. Three Coalport vases shown at the 1862 Exhibition. The centre vase painted by R. F. Abraham (see page 100). Reproduced from Waring's 'Masterpieces . . .' of the 1862 Exhibition.

233. Three Coalport vases shown at the 1871 Exhibition. *Left.* Painted by John Randall (see page 122 and Plate 204). *Centre.* Painted by James Hartshorne (see page 111). *Right.* Painted by William Cook (see page 107). Reproduced from the *Art Journal* magazine.

A

C

D

B

234 A–D. Reproductions of designs in the Minton Pattern Books, showing forms often mistaken for Coalport porcelain. *Messrs Minton's Ltd.*

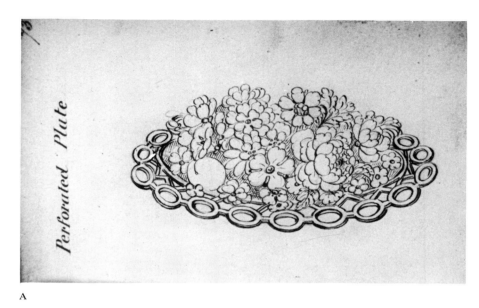

A

B   C   D

235 A–D. Reproductions of designs in the Minton Pattern Books, showing forms often mistaken for Coalport porcelain. *Messrs Minton's Ltd.*

236 A–D. Reproductions of designs in the Minton Pattern Books, showing forms often mistaken for Coalport porcelain. *Messrs Minton's Ltd.*

A

B

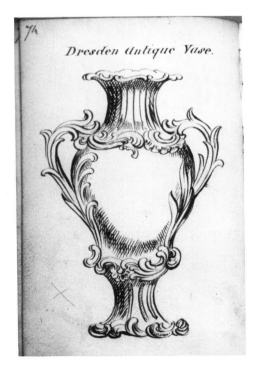

C

D

237 A–D. Reproductions of designs in the Minton Pattern Books, showing forms often mistaken for Coalport porcelain. *Messrs Minton's Ltd.*

A

B

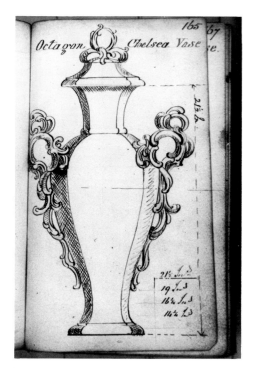

C

D